Unsung Champions of Women

Unsung
Champions
of Women

Edited by MARY COHART, PH.D.

UNIVERSITY OF NEW MEXICO PRESS
Albuquerque

Preface

The purpose of this compilation is to bring to the attention of the general reader the writings of a few perceptive thinkers who as early as the fourth century B.C. transcended the traditional conceptions of their own times in their view of the political, historical, biological, social, intellectual, creative, or emotional condition of woman. Only a few authors are presented here; a large gallery of equally worthy writers lies gathering dust on library shelves. I have omitted John Stuart Mill because he is already represented in other anthologies and in reprints of his work. Although I should have liked to include Sir James Frazer, Robert Briffault, and Havelock Ellis, for their works fit the purpose of this book and inclusion might help to revive interest in their prodigious contributions, my primary concern was to bring to public attention writers and works less likely to be found either in bookstores or in public libraries.

The contributions of Condorcet and Spencer are presented in full inasmuch as they are brief and may be considered classics. Other writings have been abridged and condensed to make possible the inclusion of samples of large volumes in one book. At times I have resorted to condensation to avoid repetitiveness, to eliminate digressions into areas not pertinent to the basic thesis, and occasionally to exclude reference to problems very specific to another time and place. In no case has there been an attempt to alter the material in order to update the language; in fact, the earlier style of phrasing and spelling lends a certain cachet to the discourse. While I have tried in every instance to present an accurate reflection of the author's fundamental thesis about women, in those cases where an excerpt is only a small part of a large work the skeptical reader may legitimately be troubled by selective editing and may wish to seek out the original text. The documentation associated with each selection appears in the Notes following the selection and adheres to the original style and content. Notes added by the editor are identified accordingly. The documentation relating to the editor's contributions appears at the end of the book.

Gratitude for the impetus to compile this book must go to all the many women who in recent years through their writings and their courageous activities have focused attention on the subject of woman's subordinate role in our society. Special thanks go to the members of my consciousness-raising group, who spurred me on to undertake this project and who were supportive critics of the work in progress. Above all, I have been fortunate in having a husband who from the beginning of our relationship fostered my continuing education, valued my mind more than my housekeeping, and saw our family unit as one in which each member shared responsibility —whether for household chores, child care, financial support, or exchange of ideas relative to intellectual productivity. We didn't call it "Women's Lib"; we just thought of it all as pitching in to cope and to make a life together. In the preparation of this work he "pitched in" on all counts.

I would be remiss if I failed to express appreciation for an institution without which this project could never have been executed. I was fortunate in having access to the Yale University Library, housing one of the most comprehensive collections in the world. Roaming the library stacks I discovered the yellowing and frayed volumes on women that captured my interest and prompted me to share these treasures with others.

Contents

INTRODUCTION

After an interregnum of two generations of quiescent submission to the prevailing doctrine that woman is subordinate to man, we are suddenly witnessing a veritable explosion of the assertion of woman's right to equality. We might trace the initiation of this change to Simone de Beauvoir's *The Second Sex*[1] or we might consider the real catalyst to have been Betty Friedan's *The Feminine Mystique.*[2] Many of us, conditioned by the indoctrination of previous decades and bewildered by the startling views now being expressed, think we are seeing a new movement expounding unconventional and disconcerting ideas. But, *mirabile dictu*, there is little in the women's movement today, however radical, that has not been voiced in the past. The latter part of the nineteenth century and the early twentieth century saw a literary outpouring concerned with the emancipation of woman.

It will no doubt astonish most readers to learn that the renowned philosopher Plato, back in the fourth century B.C., was an exponent of equality for women. A plea for the rights of women surfaced at the end of the eighteenth century in an essay by Condorcet, in this respect a solitary voice even among the French libertarians. Some sixty years later John Stuart Mill took up the cudgels for women in his essay, *The Subjection of Women.*[3] He too was a lone pioneer among his fellow economists and philosophers, but by this time the *Zeitgeist* was operating to bring innovative thinkers in diverse fields to address themselves to issues concerned with women. Pursuing varying approaches and arriving at analogous conclusions, these thinkers reflected an increasing awareness of the debased position of woman and expressed the need to rectify the injustices. In 1861, the same year in which Mill's essay appeared, Johann Jakob Bachofen published in German that remarkably imaginative and original work, *Mother Right,*[4] propounding the theory of matriarchy preceding patriarchy as a universal phenomenon.

Although the writers to whom I have referred achieved some measure of recognition in their time, today mention of the name Bachofen draws a blank from all but a select group of scholars, and, while most people have heard of Plato and some few of Condorcet,

1

it is the rare person who is informed of their advocacy of the rights of women. The growing familiarity with Mill's essay is a recent phenomenon, triggered by the women's movement. How empty has been our well of knowledge of those who championed women! Is there not general ignorance that harbingers of equal rights for women are to be found in the writings of Herbert Spencer, Emmanuel Kant, Alfred, Lord Tennyson, George Meredith, and Robert Browning?

Another well, however, is full to overflowing. It is the well of deprecatory statements and acid remarks about women. Who has not heard of Samuel Johnson's analogy between a woman preaching and a dog walking on its hind legs?[5] What knowledgeable person has not become familiar with the insults to women by such protagonists of wisdom as Nietzsche,[6] Rousseau,[7] and Schopenhauer?[8]

One wonders why those ideas that enhance the position of woman in society have been rejected, scorned, or consigned to oblivion. Is it a coincidence that works dealing with woman in a favorable way, many now out of print and unavailable in public libraries, are never included in the curriculum of our schools but are left to yellow in out-of-the-way stacks of university libraries? Hardly. The academic molders of recorded history and arbiters of our cultural inheritance have permitted their own bias to color the body of accumulated knowledge that we transmit from one generation to another. This bias can be expressed passively by ignoring items of history distasteful to those charged with responsibility for the dissemination of knowledge.

It is not my contention that the authors presented here are oracles of truth. My grievance is that they were unknown to me and my world. If their ideas can be questioned or assailed, so too can those of Aristotle, Darwin, Marx, and countless other thinkers who are firmly ensconced in the traditional educational curriculum.

During the nineteenth and early twentieth centuries there was a tenor of sympathy, compassion, and open-mindedness among the social scientists, most of them men, who were eagerly exploring subjects embracing women. There were many besides those included in this book—Lewis Henry Morgan,[9] John F. MacLennan,[10] Edward Carpenter,[11] Robert Briffault,[12] James G. Frazer,[13] and Havelock Ellis,[14] to name a few. Today it is usual in academic circles to dismiss these authors or to put a new interpretation on their assertions. These men, as well as those included in this book, responded not only without fear but almost with relish to the concept that woman might be equal to man. They did not see their world as collapsing if women should attain equal rights with men.

In recent years one notes, with a rare exception such as Ashley Montagu, a diminution of interest in such subject matter among men of science, with the more popular writers impelled to assert the machismo qualities of man, as in *The Territorial Imperative*,[15] *Men in Groups*,[16] *Sexual Suicide*,[17] and *The Inevitability of Patriarchy*.[18] Even in the so-called exact sciences researchers frequently "discover" findings that they were partial to in advance. How much more must this be true in the less exact social sciences. Also, it is hardly debatable that the choice of a subject for investigation has a strong emotional component. It is difficult to avoid the conclusion that the "objective" research of many present-day social scientists is colored by personal needs and anxieties.

One can only speculate on the significance of the change in male attitudes. In the initial stages of a revolutionary movement it is easy and comfortable for those whose way of life is threatened to support a radical change as long as its realization is still far distant. As the concrete effects of a reorganization of values impinge on individuals, anxiety develops. Perhaps the imminence of change augured by the present women's movement kindles a countervailing trend in men. No doubt the abrasive character of some militant feminist writing and action contributes somewhat to a hostile reaction. Nonetheless, it is deplorable that there continues to be a shocking neglect by scholars of matters pertaining to women. My husband was recently asked to give a lecture on women's health in a course being offered for the first time at the Yale Department of Epidemiology and Public Health. After painstaking search he expressed frustration in connection with the task because of the dearth of information. In a recent issue of *Daedalus*, Carl N. Degler wrote of Mary Beard's *Woman as Force in History*, "Most reviewers found it scholarly, while a few went so far as to predict that it would reshape the subsequent writing of history. Yet today scholars rarely refer to it, and its influence on the writing of history is virtually undiscoverable."[19] In other words, the predominantly male historians continue to interpret history as what males do.

The reluctance on the part of male scholars to concern themselves with the study of matters pertaining to women is particularly striking when one considers recent clues that hint at rich fields to be mined. Consider, if you will, what a rush to speculation regarding male primacy would have taken place if it had been discovered that Y-type sperm carried more DNA, the basic archive of genetic formation, than X-type sperm. However, the reverse was found; X-type sperm, which forms the female, carries more DNA. What hypothesizing would we have if it were discovered that all embryos began as male? But again the reverse was found—that all begin as female.

We are well informed of the orthodox Freudian psychoanalytic theory of penis envy propounded from observation of late nineteenth century Viennese middle class society. Why have analysts not drawn reverse conclusions from the implications of such primitive practices as couvade (the male practice of mock childbirth) and mica (carving the male penis to resemble the female vulva), of the practice of priests wearing a feminine type of garb, of the phenomenon that most persons seeking surgical sexual change are males wishing to be females?

What would social scientists be inferring regarding the prehistoric civilization that has come to light in the diggings at Çatal Hüyük in Anatolia if it had been found that funerary honors and reverent burial were reserved for men? In fact, they were reserved for women,[20] as they also were in Etruscan tombs unearthed in Italian Tuscany.[21]

I have chosen the particular contributors to this collection from the standpoint of presenting a variety of approaches to the subject of woman's condition. However, the authors' views are not mutually exclusive, but are frequently complementary and, to some extent, overlapping. While all the writers are sympathetic to women, there are differing opinions among them. Condorcet and Ward are anticlerical while Bachofen is deeply religious, and the attitudes of all three toward religion affect their resultant theories about women. The Vaertings' view that changes in dominance of the sexes are due to pendulum swings contrasts with the theories of other writers that males achieved dominance through superior strength. The Vaertings counter the theory that the acquisition of property contributed to the rise of androcracy with the claim that the ownership of property characterized female-dominated states also. And while Bachofen believes that the male-dominated society represents progress toward peace, happiness, and prosperity, this idea is not to be found in any of the other writers. The Vaertings, by contrast, argue that only equality of the sexes can bring such a boon to humanity.

The issues addressed in this collection are: the evolution of woman and man, and the origin and development of their relationships; comparison of male-dominated and female-dominated societies; differentiation of sexes by work role, dress and adornment, freedom of sexual activity, governing power, deities, and the like; influence of religion on sexual inequality; demeaning of women in literature, art, law, and journalism; deprivation suffered by women in education and opportunity; comparison of relative abilities of males and females; contributions of women to civilization; expectations for both sexes if equality is achieved. A few of the contributors are persons of such intellectual stature and such noble spirit that I consider myself privileged to bring to a wider audience even a small portion of the excitement and uplift that I experienced in discovering them.

PART 1

Evolution of Women—and Men

ELIZA BURT GAMBLE (1841–1920)

The subtitle to Eliza Burt Gamble's book *The Evolution of Woman* is *An Inquiry Into the Dogma of Her Inferiority to Man*. In her preface the author states that as early as 1882 she had reached the conclusion that the female organization was in no way inferior to that of the male. Based on a systematic investigation of the studies of naturalists, particularly Darwin, she propounded the theory that the female represented a higher stage of development than the male. This same theory, following a similar line of reasoning, was enunciated a few years later by Lester Frank Ward, the second author in this anthology. I have found no evidence that either of these writers knew of the work of the other. It is quite remarkable that both should have developed the same theory at approximately the same time. Ward received some acknowledgment, particularly from the feminists at the turn of the century, and references to him still turn up in the literature, but Gamble's contribution appears to be passing into oblivion.

My investigation of Eliza Burt Gamble yielded two fragments of information, one the mere mention in the British Museum General Catalogue of Printed Books of the two major works that will be alluded to in the present volume, and the other a few short paragraphs in the National Cyclopaedia of American Biography.[1]

Eliza Burt Gamble was born in Concord, Michigan, on June 4, 1841. At age nineteen she found herself an orphan, wholly dependent upon her own resources for a livelihood. She taught school, progressing to the position of high school assistant superintendent. At the age of twenty-five she married James Gamble, a lawyer. They had three children, one of whom died in infancy. As a firm believer in human rights and individual liberty, Gamble supported the women's suffrage movement. However, her chief work was with her pen, and her primary interest of study the fields of evolution and primitive religion.

To appreciate Gamble fully one has to remember how daring and unorthodox her statements were in the 1880s. In her writing there is no pussyfooting in regard to the dogmas of established religions or those of a masculinist society. She makes blunt,

9

unapologetic assertions of the superiority of woman's organization to man's and she indicts organized religion for its arrogation to the male of woman's prerogatives. She is more dauntless and forthright than many accomplished women of more recent times. For example, while such outstanding women as Karen Horney, Clara Thompson, and Margaret Mead dared to revolt against some orthodox, patriarchal assumptions, they did not stray very far from the fundamental theses laid down by their male mentors. These women differed from Gamble in that they were members of a learned discipline, an organized hierarchy of power. One can only speculate as to the pressures they were under to fit their rebellious concepts into the orthodox larger framework. Gamble, as a maverick, may have had greater freedom to examine the field of evolution without the preconceptions of the student already conditioned to accept traditional theories, and without concern that she had anything to lose from the established hierarchy. She shares this position with others in this collection, notably Bachofen, Ward, Child, and Morgan. Do we have here a clue to the neglect their work has experienced?

To find resource material Gamble spent a year in Washington, D.C., where she had access to the Library of Congress, with its storehouse of available studies on early races of the world. Her books are the most compelling testament to her comprehensive research, indicating her thorough acquaintance with authorities in the fields of anthropology, religion, natural science, and Greek and Roman history.

In her extensive examination of Darwin she pinpoints the male bias of his conclusions. Following her exposition of woman's superiority to man, Gamble develops the thesis that the eventual degradation of women in the dependent condition of marriage had its origin in the practice of wife capture and the subsequent control of property by males. Her prognosis for the future, no doubt somewhat colored by her female bias, was that by elevating the position of wife and purifying the state of marriage women would eventually civilize man. In words befitting a present-day feminist she affirms: "Before this may be accomplished wives and mothers must be absolutely free and wholly independent of the opposite sex for means of support."[2]

The modern reader may find areas of disagreement among the remarkable insights in Gamble's arguments. Whatever the defects of her work, such pioneer conceptions as Gamble's deserve recognition and careful study by future generations.

The Evolution of Woman

Preface

After a somewhat careful study of written history, and after an investigation extending over several years of all the accessible facts relative to extant tribes representing the various stages of human development, I had reached the conclusion, as early as the year 1882, that the female organization is in no wise inferior to that of the male. . . .

In the year 1885 . . . I began a systematized investigation of the facts which at that time had been established by naturalists relative to the development of mankind from lower orders of life. It was not, however, until the year 1886, after a careful reading of *The Descent of Man*, by Mr. Darwin, that I first became impressed with the belief that the theory of evolution, as enunciated by scientists, furnishes much evidence going to show that the female among all the orders of life, man included, represents a higher stage of development than the male. Although, at the time indicated, the belief that man has descended from lower orders in the scale of being had been accepted by the leading minds both in Europe and America, for reasons which have not been explained, scientists, generally, seemed inclined to ignore certain facts connected with this theory which tend to prove the superiority of the female organization. . . .

. . . it seemed clear to me that the history of life on the earth presents an unbroken chain of evidence going to prove the importance of the female. . . .

When we bear in mind the past experiences of the human race, it is not perhaps surprising that, during an era of physical force and the predominance of the animal instincts in man, the doctrine of male superiority should have become firmly grounded; neither is it

From Eliza Burt Gamble, *The Evolution of Woman* (New York: G. P. Putnam's Sons, 1894).

remarkable that throughout an age of metaphysical speculation and
theological dogmatism, and during the entire absence of exact
knowledge concerning the subject, the male of the human species
should have continued to regard himself as an infinitely superior
creature, and as representing the highest development in nature. It
has been, and to a certain extent still is sufficient for the theologian
and metaphysician that God made man first. Man, according to
their speculations, is the real or direct object of the special
creation, while woman is only an after-thought—a creature brought
forth in response to the needs of man.

These are views which, in the mouths of early speculators, and
perhaps in the mouths of theologians of the present time, need
occasion little surprise; but with the dawn of scientific investigation
it might have been hoped that the prejudices resulting from lower
conditions of human society would disappear, and that in their
stead would be set forth not only facts, but deductions from facts,
better suited to the dawn of an intellectual age. When, however,
we turn to the most advanced scientific writers of the present
century, we find that the prejudices which throughout thousands of
years have been gathering strength are by no means eradicted, and
any discussion of the sex question is still rare in which the effects of
these prejudices may not be traced. Even Mr. Darwin, notwithstanding his great breadth of mental vision, and the important work
which he accomplished in the direction of original inquiry,
whenever he had occasion to touch on the mental capacities of
women, or, more particularly, on the relative capacities of the
sexes, manifested the same spirit which characterizes the efforts of
an earlier age; and, throughout his entire investigation of the
human species, his ability to ignore certain facts which he himself
adduced, and which all along the line of development tend to
prove the superiority of the female organization, is truly remarkable. . . .

Chapter II. The Origin of Sexual Differences

. . . according to naturalists, the earliest forms of life which
appeared on the earth were androgynous or hermaphrodite,—in
other words, . . . the two elements necessary for reproduction
were originally confined within one and the same individual,
within which were carried on all the functions of reproduction.

Later, however, a division of labor arose, and these two original functions became detached, after which time the reproductive processes were carried on only through the commingling of elements prepared by, or developed within, two separate and distinct individuals.

As the belief is entertained by our guides in this matter that greater differentiation, or specialization of parts, denotes higher organization, it is believed that the division of labor by which the germ is prepared by one individual and the sperm by another individual, as is the case at the present time with all the higher orders of life, constitutes an important step in the line of progress. Here this line of argument, as it is generally treated, ceases, and, until very recent times, concerning the course of development followed by each sex little has been heard. This silence on a subject of such vital importance to the student of biology is not perhaps difficult to understand; the conclusion, however, is unavoidable that the individual which must nourish and protect the germ, and by processes carried on within her own body provide nourishment for the young during its pre-natal existence, and sometimes for years after birth, must have the more highly specialized organization, and must, therefore, represent the higher stage of development. Indeed, it is admitted by the scientists that the advance from the egg-layers to the milk-givers indicates one of the most important steps in the entire line of development; and yet the peculiar specialization of structure necessary for its accomplishment was for the most part carried on within the female organization.

. . . according to Mr. Darwin, it is through a long selection by females of the more attractive males that the present structure of the latter has been acquired.[1]

We are informed that the female is sometimes charmed through the power of song; that at other times she is captivated by the diversified means which have been acquired by male insects and birds for producing various sounds resembling those proceeding from certain kinds of musical instruments; and not unfrequently she is won by means of antics or love dances performed on the ground or in the air. On the pairing-ground, combs, wattles, elongated plumes, top-knots, and fancy colored feathers are paraded for the admiration and approval of the females. . . .

Although the immense teeth, tusks, horns, and various other

weapons or appendages which ornament the males of many species of mammals, have all been developed through Sexual Selection for contending with their rivals for the favors of the females, we are assured that the "most pugnacious and best armed males seldom depend for success on their ability to drive away or kill their rivals," but that their special aim is to "charm the female." Mr. Darwin quotes from a "good observer," who believes that the battles of male birds "are all a sham, performed to show themselves to the greatest advantage before the admiring females who assemble around."[2] . . .

We are assured that among nearly all the lower orders of life the female exhibits a marked preference for certain individuals, and that an equal degree of repugnance is manifested towards others, but that the male, whose predominant character is desire, "is ready to pair with any female."[3] . . .

Because of the indifference of the female to the attentions of the male, in order to carry on the processes of reproduction it was necessary among the lower orders that the male become eager in his pursuit of her, and as a result of this eagerness excessive passion was developed in him. . . .

On the subject of the acquirement of secondary sexual characters, Mr. Darwin says: "The great eagerness of the males has thus indirectly led to their much more frequently developing secondary sexual characters."[4] Indeed, by all naturalists, the fact is recognized that the appearance of these characters is closely connected with the reproductive function.

Regarding the power of the female to appreciate the beauty of the males, Mr. Darwin says: "No doubt this implies powers of discrimination and taste on the part of the female which will at first appear extremely improbable; but by the facts to be adduced hereafter, I hope to be able to shew that the females actually have these powers."[5] . . .

Although this power of choice, which we are given to understand is exercised by the female throughout the various departments of the vertebrate kingdom (evidences of it having been observed among creatures even as low in the organic scale as fishes), implies a degree of intelligence far in advance of that manifested by males, it is admitted that the qualities which bespeak this superiority, namely, the power to exercise taste and discrimination, constitute a "law almost as general as the eagerness of the male."[6] . . .

We have been assured by our guides in these matters that in the processes of evolution there is no continuous or unbroken chain of progress; in other words, that growth or change does not necessarily imply development, but, on the contrary, only as a structure becomes better fitted for its conditions, and only as its organs become more highly specialized for the performance of all the duties involved in its environment, may it be said to be in the line of progress. If this be true, particular attention should be directed to the fact that as secondary sexual characters do not assist their possessor in overcoming the unfavorable conditions of his environment, they are not within the line of true development, but, on the contrary, as their growth requires a great expenditure of vital force, and, as is the case among birds, they often hinder the free use of the legs in running and walking, and entirely destroy the use of the wings for flight, they must be detrimental to the entire structure. For the reason that females have managed to do without them, the plea that the great tusks, horns, teeth, etc., of mammals have been acquired for self-defense, is scarcely tenable. . . . in fact, as these excrescences hinder him in the performance of the ordinary functions of life, they may be regarded in the light of actual hindrances to higher development.

Chapter III. The Female Superior to the Male

. . . Secondary sexual characters, being so far as males are concerned, wholly the result of eagerness in courtship, cannot appear before the time for reproduction arrives, and as it is a law of heredity that peculiarities of structure which are developed late in life, when transmitted to offspring, appear only in the sex in which they originated, these variations of structure are confined to males.

According to Mr. Darwin's theory little difference exists between the sexes until the age for reproduction arrives; it is at this particular time, the time when the secondary sexual characters begin to assert themselves, that the preponderating superiority of the male is observed.

Although, according to this writer, variability denotes low organization, and shows that the various organs of the body have not become specialized to perform their legitimate functions, it is owing to pugnacity, or perseverance and courage, characters correlated with and dependent upon these varying parts, that the male has ultimately become superior to the female. As these qualities, which we are given to understand are the special inheritance of males, have been of such great importance in determining men's capacities and power, too much care and pains cannot be expended in analyzing them and in endeavoring to gain a clear understanding of their origin.

Sexual Selection, we are told, resembles artificial selection, save that the female takes the place of the human breeder. In other words, she represents the intelligent factor or cause in the operations involved. If this be true, if it is through her will, or through some agency or tendency latent in her constitution that Sexual Selection comes into play, then she is the primary cause of the very characters through which man's superiority over woman has been gained. As a stream may not rise higher than its source, or as the creature may not surpass its creator in excellence, it is difficult to understand the processes by which man, through Sexual Selection, has become superior to woman. . . .

While the female has been performing the higher functions in the processes of reproduction, through her force of will, or through her power of choice, she has also been the directing and controlling agency in the development of those characters in the male through which, when the human species was reached, he was enabled to attain a limited degree of progress.

Since the origin of secondary sexual characters is so clearly manifest, perhaps it will be well for us at this point to examine also their actual significance, that we may be enabled to note the foundation upon which the dogma of male superiority rests.

Although the gay coloring of male birds and fishes has usually been regarded as an indication of their superiority over their somber-colored mates, later investigations are proving that these pigments represent simply unspecialized material, and an effort of the system to cast out the waste products which have accumulated as a result of excessive ardor in courtship. The same is true of combs, wattles, and other skin excrescences; they show a feverish condition of the skin in the over-excited males, whose temperature is usually much higher than is that of females. We are assured that the skin eruptions of male fishes at the spawning season "seem more pathological than decorative."[7] In the processes of reproduction, the undeveloped atoms given off from each varying part are reproduced only in the male line.

The beautiful coloring of male birds and fishes, and the various appendages acquired by males throughout the various orders below man, and which, so far as they themselves are concerned, serve no other useful purpose than to aid them in securing the favors of the females, have by the latter been turned to account in the processes of reproduction. The female made the male beautiful that she might endure his caresses.

From the facts elaborated by our guides in this matter, it would seem that the female is the primary unit of creation, and that the male functions are simply supplemental or complementary. Parthenogenesis among many of the lower forms of life would seem to favor this view. We are given to understand that under conditions favoring katabolism, the males among rotifera wear themselves out, under which conditions the females become katabolic enough to do without them.

> Among the common rotifera, the males are almost always very different from the females, and much smaller. Sometimes they seem to have dwindled out of existence altogether, for only the females are known. In other cases, though present, they entirely fail to accomplish their proper function of fertilization, and, as parthenogenesis obtains, are not only minute, but useless.[8]

So long as food is plentiful, the females continue to raise parthenogenetic offspring, but with the advent of hard times, when food is scarce or of a poor quality, the parthenogenetic series is interrupted by the appearance of males. Although, unaided by the male, the female of certain species is able to reproduce, he has never been able to propagate without her co-operation. . . .

Among the lower orders of animal life—notably insects, we are assured that an excess of females denotes an excess of formative force, and that an excess of males indicates a deficiency on the part of the parents. In the case of bees, the queen, which is the highest development, is produced only under the highest circumstances of nutrition, while the birth of the drone, which is the lowest result of propagation, is preceded by extremely low conditions.

The working bee which, being an imperfect female, may not be impregnated, will, however, give birth to parthenogenetic off-spring, such offspring always being male. . . . We are assured also that if caterpillars are shut up and starved before entering the chrysalis stage, the butterflies which make their appearance are males, while the highly nourished caterpillars are sure to come out females. In the case of moths innutritious food produces only males. . . .

Recent observations show that among the human species nutrition plays a significant part in determining sex. Statistics prove that in towns and in well-to-do families there is a preponderance of girls, while in the country, and among the poor, more boys are born; also, that immediately following epidemics, wars, and famines, there is an excess of male births. On examination, it was found that in Saxony "the ratio of boy-births rose and fell with the price of food, and that the variation was most marked in the country."[9]

That the female represents a higher development than the male is proved throughout all the various departments of nature. Among plants, staminate flowers open before pistillate, and are much more abundant, and less differentiated from the leaves, showing that they are less developed, and that slighter effort, a less expenditure of force, is necessary to form the male than the female. A male flower represents an intermediate state between a leaf and a perfect, or we might say, a female flower, and the germ which produces the male would, in a higher stage, produce the female.[10]

The most perfect and vigorous specimens of cuniferous trees are of the female kind. We are told that in its highest and most luxurious stage the larch bears only female blossoms, but that so soon as its vigor is lost male flowers appear, after which death soon ensues. . . .

Among the lower orders of animals, there appears an excess of males, and among the higher forms of life, man included, the fact that the male is the result of cruder, less developed germ, has been clearly shown, not alone by the facts brought forward by Mr. Darwin, but by those enunciated by all reliable writers on this subject. As a result of the excessive eagerness in males, and the consequent expenditure of vital force among the lower orders of life to find the female and secure her favors, they are generally smaller in size, with a higher body temperature and shorter life. Among the higher orders, the human species for instance, although man is larger than woman, he is still shorter lived, has less endurance, is more predisposed to organic diseases, and is more given to reversion to former types, facts which show that his greater size is not the result of higher development. We are assured that the liability to assume characters proper to lower orders belongs in a marked degree to males of all the higher species—man included.

Doubtless man's greater size (a modification which has been acquired through Sexual Selection) has been of considerable value to him in the struggle for existence to which he has been subjected, but the indications are already strong that after a certain stage of progress has been reached, even this modification of structure will prove useless, if not an actual hindrance to him. On mechanical principles, every increase of size requires more than a corresponding increase of strength and endurance to balance the activities and carry on the vital processes, yet such have been the conditions of man's development, that his excess of strength does not compensate for his greater size and weight, while his powers of endurance fall below those of women.

We are informed by Mr. Darwin that by a vast number of measurements taken of various parts of the human body in different races, during his Novara Expedition, it was found that the men in almost every case presented a greater range of variations than women, and, as Mr. Wood has carefully attended to the variations of the muscles of man, Mr. Darwin quotes from him that "the greatest number of abnormalities in each subject is found in males."[11] . . . These variations usually consist in a reversion to lower types—a reversion in which muscles proper to lower forms of life make their appearance. . . .

According to the testimony of those who have made a study of the various abnormalities in the human organization, the ears of men present a greater range of variations than do those of women, and the cases in which supernumerary digits appear in males are as two to one, compared with females presenting the same structural defect. . . . Mr. Darwin wishes us to remember, however, that "women would more frequently endeavor to conceal a deformity of this kind than men."[12] . . .

One of the principal characters which distinguishes the human animal from the lower orders is the absence of a natural covering for the skin. That mankind have descended from hair-covered progenitors is the inevitable conclusion of all those who accept the theory of the evolution of species, the straggling hairs which are scattered over the body of man being the rudiments of a uniform hairy coat which enveloped his ancestors.

We are told that a hairy covering for the body, pointed ears which were capable of movement, and a tail provided with the proper muscles, were among the undoubted characters of the antecedents of the human race. In addition to these, among the males, were developed great canine teeth which were used as weapons against their rivals.

As the lack of a hairy coat for the body constitutes one of the principal characteristics which distinguishes man from the lower animals, it would seem that a knowledge of the order of time in which the two sexes became divested of their natural covering would serve as a hint to indicate their relative stages of development. . . . Upon this subject of hairiness, Mr. Darwin says: "As the body in woman is less hairy than in man, and as this character is common to all races, we may conclude that it was our female semi-human ancestors who were first divested of hair, and that this occurred at an extremely remote period before the several races had diverged from a common stock."[13] After our female ancestors had acquired the new character, nudity, they must have transmitted it to their own sex, and by continually selecting their mates from among the least hairy, in process of time males too would become divested of their animal covering. Whether or not our semi-human ancestors were subjected to the scorching heat of the torrid zone, nudity must have been better suited to their improved condition, not wholly, however, because of its greater beauty and comfort, but because it was a condition better suited to cleanliness; and, as the hairy coat had become a useless appendage, or was not necessary to their changed conditions, it disappeared from the body of females, while doubtless for ages it was retained upon the body of males. That hairiness denotes a low stage of development, Mr. Darwin incautiously admits,[14] yet in dealing with this subject he is not disposed to carry his admission to its legitimate conclusion by treating its appearance on the body of man as a test in determining the comparative development of the female and male organizations. . . . Mr. Darwin assures us that around sores of long standing stiff hairs are liable to appear, thus showing that hair on the body is indicative of undeveloped tissues and low constitutional conditions. The same writer, however, does not neglect to inform us that the loss of man's hairy covering was rather an injury to him than otherwise;[15] but whether or not the diminution in the quality of prehension in his toes, the loss of his canines, and the disappearance of his tail have likewise proved detrimental to him, Mr. Darwin fails to state.

The fact that throughout the vertebrate kingdom males possess rudiments of the various parts appertaining to the reproductive system which properly belong to females, is regarded as evidence that some remote progenitor of this kingdom must have been hermaphrodite, or androgynous, especially as it has been ascertained that at a very early embryonic period both sexes possess true male and female glands. As high in the scale of life as the mammalian class, males are said to possess rudiments of a uterus, while at the same time mammary glands are plainly manifest; which fact would seem to show that in the high state of development indicated by this great class, male organs have not through the processes of differentiation become specialized for the performance of their legitimate functions. In reference to the subject of atavism Mr. Darwin cites as a case of reversion to a former type, an instance in which a man was the possessor of two pairs of mammae.

It is true that instances have been observed in which characters peculiar to males have been developed in females. This phenomenon, however, seldom appears among individuals of the higher orders, and among the lower forms of life where it occurs, it is always manifested under low circumstances of nutrition, or in cases of old age, disease, or loss of vitality. Instances are cited in which hens, after they have become old or diseased, have taken on characters peculiar to males.

In all "old-settled" countries women are in excess of men, and this is true, notwithstanding the fact that more boys are born than girls. Regarding the excess of male over female births, Mr. Darwin quotes from Prof. Faye, who says: "A still greater preponderance of males would be met with, if death struck both sexes in equal proportion in the womb and during birth. But the fact is, that for every one hundred still-born females, we have in several countries from 134.6 to 144.9 still-born males."[16] During the first four or five years of life, more male children die than female; for example, in England, during the first year, one hundred and twenty-six boys die for every one hundred girls. In France the population is still more unfavorable to the males.

Although whenever throughout Mr. Darwin's *Descent of Man* he has been pleased to deal with the subject of structural variations, he has given us to understand that they are injurious to the constitution, and although he has shown that their appearance is much more frequent in men than in women, yet he does not seem to realize whither his admissions are leading him. He has proved by seemingly well established facts that the female organism is freer from imperfections than the male, and therefore that it is less liable to derangements; also, that being more highly specialized, it is less susceptible to injury under unfavorable conditions; yet, in attempting to explain the reason why so many more male than female infants succumb to the exigencies of birth, he expresses the opinion that the size of the body and "especially of the head" being greater in males, they would be "more liable to be injured during parturition."[17]

. . . While the dangers to which men are exposed because of their greater physical activity have been many, and the accidents liable to occur from their harder struggle for existence more numerous than those to which women have been subjected, still it would seem that the danger to female life, incident to the artificial relations of the sexes under our present semi-civilized conditions, is more than an offset for that to which men are liable. . . .

That the imperfections of the male organization are already beginning to interpose themselves between man and many of the occupations and activities of advancing civilization, is only too apparent.

Sight, far more than any other sense, is the most intellectual, yet in the development of the visual organs it has been proved that men are especially deficient. . . .

In an examination which was carried on a few years ago under the supervision of Dr. Jeffries, among the pupils of the Boston schools, in which were fourteen thousand four hundred and sixty-nine boys and young men, and thirteen thousand four hundred and fifty-eight girls and young women, it was found that about one male in every twenty-five was color-blind, while the same defect among the girls and young women was extremely rare, only 0.066 per cent. of them being thus affected.[18] . . .

Not only is man's sense of sight less perfectly developed than is woman's, but his sense of touch is less acute. The hand, directed as it is by the brain, is the most completely differentiated member of the human structure. . . . The female hand . . . is capable of delicate distinctions which the male has no means of determining. . . .

Although throughout the ascending scale of life, the female has been expending all her energy in the performance of her legitimate functions—functions which, as we have seen, are of a higher order than those performed by the male, through causes which will be discussed further on in these pages, within the later centuries of human existence, she has been temporarily overcome by the destructive or disruptive forces developed in the opposite sex —forces which are without the line of true development, and which through overstimulation and encouragement have overleaped the bounds of normal activity, and have therefore become disruptive and injurious.

During the past five thousand years, woman's reproductive functions have been turned into means of subsistence, and under the peculiar circumstances of her environment, her "struggle for existence" has involved physical processes far more disastrous to life and health than are those to which man has been subjected. Owing to the peculiar condition of woman's environment, there has been developed within her more delicate and sensitive organism an alarming degree of functional nervousness; yet, with the gradual broadening of her sphere of activity, and the greater exercise of personal rights, this tendency to nervous derangement is gradually becoming lessened. . . .

NOTES

1. *The Descent of Man*, pp. 209–11 [Charles Darwin (New York: D. Appleton and Co., 1892)].
2. Ibid., p. 367.
3. Ibid., p. 226.—Ed.
4. Ibid., p. 223.—Ed.
5. Ibid., p. 211.
6. Ibid., p. 222.
7. Geddes and Thomson, *The Evolution of Sex*, p. 24 [Patrick Geddes and J. Arthur Thomson (The Humboldt Publ. Co., 1890)].
8. Ibid., p. 20.
9. W. K. Brooks, *Popular Science Monthly*, vol. xxvi., p. 326.

10. Thomas Meehan, *Native Flowers and Ferns*, vol. i., p. 47 [Boston, 1878].
11. *The Descent of Man*, p. 223.—Ed.
12. Ibid., p. 224.—Ed.
13. Ibid., p. 601.—Ed.
14. Ibid., pp. 601–2.—Ed.
15. Ibid., p. 600.—Ed.
16. Ibid., p. 243.—Ed.
17. Ibid., p. 244.—Ed.
18. *Pop. Science Monthly*, vol. xix, p. 567.

LESTER FRANK WARD (1841–1913)

Lester Frank Ward, trailblazer in sociology in America, was at once scientist and social philosopher, concerned with the ennobling of human life through the universalization and democratization of knowledge. A brilliant thinker with a vast range of intellectual interests whose writings made a wide variety of original contributions to science, he has been conspicuously overlooked and ignored.

This titan, who was a century ahead of his time, grew up in poverty on the early American frontier, educating himself while working as an unskilled laborer and teaching in country schools. After serving his country for twenty-seven months in the Civil War, he worked as a clerk in the Treasury. By the time he entered college he was twenty-six, married, and a father. Within a few years he received his degrees of Bachelor of Arts and Bachelor of Laws and the diploma in medicine. His linguistic abilities covered French, German, Greek, Latin, Hebrew, Spanish, Italian, Russian, Sanskrit, Chinese, and Japanese.

The disregard of Ward is remarkable because he was highly regarded by European colleagues and hailed as a prophetic genius by some of his contemporaries here in America. As one of those who esteemed Ward, Charles A. Beard stated, "Ward was high among the giants of his time. . . . In both learning and practical knowledge of science and life, he was so superior to Herbert Spencer and most of his contemporaries that they must be placed entirely out of his class."[1] Henry Steele Commager "ranked Ward as a thinker equal to William James, John Dewey, and Oliver Wendell Holmes and superior to Henry Adams, Thorstein Veblen and Louis Sullivan."[2] Ward is in the tradition of Plato, Aristotle, the Abbé de Saint-Pierre, Saint-Simon, and Comte in advocating the idea of government based on wisdom and knowledge.

The contribution of Ward's thought to the status of women can best be epitomized in the words of Charlotte Perkins Gilman, the well-known feminist, who wrote in 1911 in the dedication of her book *The Man-Made World*:

> With reverent love and gratitude to Lester F. Ward, sociologist and humanitarian, one of the world's great men; a creative thinker to whose wide knowledge and power of vision we are indebted for a new grasp of the nature and processes of society, and to whom all women are especially bound in honor and gratitude for his Gynaecocentric Theory of Life, than which nothing so important to humanity has been advanced since the Theory of Evolution, and nothing so important to women has ever been given to the world.[3]

The condition of woman was only one of many problems of humanity to which Ward addressed himself. He founded sociology in America and made inestimable contributions to the fields of evolution, social psychology, government, environment, education, and humanism.

The selection included in this book, excerpted from his massive work *Pure Sociology*, presents his gynaecocentric theory, which purports to prove that the female sex is primary in the organic scheme and which develops an explanation for the factors that have led to male supremacy. He saw in his own time a burgeoning improvement in the status of women and was optimistic that equality between the sexes would eventually be a reality.

Brevity has necessitated omissions and condensation, but it is hoped that Ward's systematic presentation has been preserved. Those readers whose interest is captured by this abridged selection can refer to the original, since this book is still in publication. And for those who would like a further acquaintance with this "man for all seasons," an inspiring portrait of Ward can be found in Samuel Chugerman's beautifully written *Lester F. Ward, The American Aristotle*,[4] which surveys and interprets Ward's thought.

The Gynaecocentric Theory

The gynaecocentric theory is the view that the female sex is primary and the male secondary in the organic scheme, that originally and normally all things center, as it were, about the female, and that the male, though not necessary in carrying out the

---

From Lester F. Ward, *Pure Sociology*, 2d ed. (1907; reprint ed., New York: Augustus M. Kelley, 1970), pp. 296 ff. (First edition, New York: Macmillan Co., 1903.)

scheme, was developed under the operation of the principle of advantage to secure organic progress through the crossing of strains. The theory further claims that the apparent male superiority in the human race and in certain of the higher animals and birds is the result of specialization in extra-normal directions due to adventitious causes which have nothing to do with the general scheme, but which can be explained on biological and psychological principles; that it only applies to certain characters, and to a relatively small number of genera and families. It accounts for the prevalence of the androcentric theory by the superficial character of human knowledge of such subjects, chiefly influenced by the illusion of the near, but largely, in the case of man at least, by tradition, convention, and prejudice. . . .

As the theory, so far as I have ever heard, is wholly my own, no one else having proposed or even defended it, scarcely any one accepting it, and no one certainly coveting it, it would be folly for me to pretend indifference to it. At the same time it must rest on facts that cannot be disputed, and the question of its acceptance or rejection must become one of interpreting the facts. . . .

Of all modern writers the one most free from the androcentric bias, so far as I am aware, is Mr. Havelock Ellis. In his excellent book "Man and Woman," he has pointed out many of the fallacies of that Weltanschauung, and without apparent leaning toward anything but the truth has placed woman in a far more favorable light than it is customary to view her. While usually confining himself to the facts, he occasionally indicates that their deeper meaning has not escaped him. Thus he says: "The female is the mother of the new generation, and has a closer and more permanent connection with the care of the young; she is thus of greater importance than the male from Nature's point of view" (pp. 383–384). To him is also due the complete refutation of the "arrested development" theory, . . . by showing that the child, and the young generally, represent the most advanced type of development, while the adult male represents a reversion to an inferior early type, and this in man is a more bestial type. . . .

. . . In fact statements of the androcentric theory are to be met with everywhere. Not only do philosophers and popular writers never tire of repeating its main propositions, but anthropologists and biologists will go out of their way to defend it while at the same time heaping up facts that really contradict it and strongly support the gynaecocentric theory. This is due entirely to the power of a predominant world view (Weltanschauung). The androcentric theory is such a world view that is deeply stamped upon the popular mind, and the history of human thought has demonstrated many times that scarcely any number of facts opposed to such a world view can shake it. It amounts to a social structure and has the attribute of stability in common with other social structures. Only occasionally will a thinking investigator pause to consider the true import of the facts he is himself bringing to light.

Bachofen, McLennan, Morgan, and the other ethnologists who have contributed to our knowledge of the remarkable institution or historic phase called the matriarchate, all stop short of stating the full significance of these phenomena, and the facts of amazonism that are so often referred to as so many singular anomalies and reversals of the natural order of things, are never looked at philosophically as residual facts that must be explained even if they overthrow many current beliefs. . . . Thus I find in Ratzenhofer's work the following remark:

> It is probable that in the horde there existed a certain individual equality between man and woman; the results of our investigation leave it doubtful whether the man always had a superior position. There is much to indicate that the woman was the uniting element in the community; the mode of development of reproduction in the animal world and the latest investigations into the natural differences between man and woman give rise to the assumption that the woman of to-day is the atavistic product of the race, while the man varies more frequently and more widely. This view agrees perfectly with the nature of the social process, for in the horde, as the social form out of which the human race has developed, there existed an individual equality which has only been removed by social disturbances which chiefly concern the man. . . .[1]

. . . Among botanists, Professor Meehan was the only one in whose writings I have found an adumbration of the gynaecocentric theory. He several times called attention to a certain form of female superiority in plants. . . .

. . . The advancement of truth has always been in the direction of supplanting the superficial and apparent by the fundamental and real, and the gynaecocentric truth may be classed among the "paradoxes of nature."[2] . . .

. . . there can be no more vital or fundamental field of truth than that of reproduction upon which depends the existence not merely of the individual but of the species, race, or ethnic group of men. . . .

. . . Reproduction has for its sole object to perpetuate life. To enable the individual to attain its maximum size, to live out its normal period of existence, to carry itself on into new beings that will do the same, and to produce as large a number as possible of such beings—these are the primary ends of nature in the organic world . . . .

Origin of the Male Sex

Although reproduction and sex are two distinct things, and although a creature that reproduces without sex cannot properly be called either male or female, still, so completely have these conceptions become blended in the popular mind that a creature which actually brings forth offspring out of its own body is instinctively classed as female. The female is the fertile sex, and whatever is fertile is looked upon as female. Assuredly it would be absurd to look upon an organism propagating asexually as male. Biologists have proceeded from this popular standpoint, and regularly speak of "mother-cells" and "daughter-cells." It therefore does no violence to language or to science to say that life begins with the female organism and is carried on a long distance by means of females alone. In all the different forms of asexual reproduction, from fission to parthenogenesis, the female may in this sense be said to exist alone and perform all the functions of life including reproduction. In a word, life begins as female.

The further development of life serves to strengthen this gynaecocentric point of view. It consists, as we might say, exclusively in the history of the subsequent origin and development of the male sex. The female sex, which existed from the beginning, continues unchanged, but the male sex, which did not exist at the beginning, makes its appearance at a certain stage, and has a certain history and development, but never became universal, so that . . . there are probably many more living beings without it than with it, even in the present life of the globe. The female is not only the primary and original sex but continues throughout as the main trunk, while to it a male element is afterward added for the purposes above explained [of fertilization]. The male is therefore, as it were, a mere afterthought of nature. Moreover, the male sex was at first and for a long period, and still throughout many of the lower orders of beings, devoted exclusively to the function for which it was created, viz., that of fertilization. Among millions of humble creatures the male is simply and solely a fertilizer.

The simplest type of sexuality consists in the normal continuance of the original female form with the addition of an insignificant and inconspicuous male fertilizer, incapable of any other function. In sexual cells there is no character in which the differentiation goes so far as in that of size. The female or germ cell is always much larger than the male or sperm cell. In the human species, for example, an ovum is about 3000 times as large as a spermatozoon.[3] . . .

. . . Female superiority . . . of a more or less marked degree still prevails throughout the greater part of the invertebrates. It is perhaps greatest among the Arachnidae or spider family. The courtships of spiders are so often described in popular works that allusion to them almost calls for an apology.[4] They are always regarded as astonishing anomalies in the animal world. While the behavior of the relatively gigantic female in seizing and devouring the tiny male fertilizer when he is only seeking to do the only duty that he exists for, may seem remarkable and even contrary to the interests of nature, the fact of the enormous difference between the female and the male, is, according to the gynaecocentric hypothesis, not anomalous at all, but perfectly natural and normal.[5] . . .

. . . Even in the lower vertebrates there are cases of female superiority. The smallest known vertebrate, *Heterandria formosa* Agassiz, has the females about twenty-five per cent larger than the males.[6] Male fishes are commonly smaller than female. In trout this is well known, and trout fishermen sometimes throw the little males or "studs," as they call them, back into the stream, as not worth taking. Even in birds, which are the mainstay of the androcentric theory, there are some large families, as, for example, the hawks, in which male superiority is rare, and the female is usually the larger and finer bird. There are even some mammals in which the sexes do not differ appreciably in size or strength, and very little, or not at all, in coloration and adornment. Such is the case with nearly all of the great family of rodents. It is also the case with the Erinaceidae, at least with its typical subfamily of hedgehogs. . . .

If we regard stamens and pistils as individuals, it becomes obvious that in the higher plants generally, and to a much greater extent than in animals, the male is simply a fertilizer, while the female goes on and develops and matures the fruit. Stamens always wither as soon as the anthers have shed their pollen. They have no other function. If we take the other and more popular view of individuality, and look upon the whole plant as the vital unit, the only comparisons between the sexes that can be instituted are those of dioecious plants. Here of course we usually find the sexes practically equal. This we should expect, since sexual differentiation has alone brought about this state from a former state of hermaphroditism. If any cases could be found of either male or female superiority they could only be accounted for either by special over-development of the superior or by degeneracy of the inferior sex. In point of fact there are such cases, but only those of female superiority. An examination of them clearly shows that they are due to a loss on the part of the male of the powers once possessed. Again, there are found to be cases in which this decline does not take place until after the function of fertilization has been performed.

The best known example is that of the hemp plant, *Cannabis sativa*. It has long been known that when hemp is sown in a field the sexes cannot at first be distinguished, and this condition of equality persists until the plants of both sexes reach the period of fertility. The male plants then shed their pollen and the female plants are fertilized thereby. Soon thereafter, however, the male plants cease to grow, begin to turn yellow and sere, and in a short time they droop, wither, die, and disappear. The fertilized female plants are then found not to have as yet reached their maximum development. They continue to grow taller and more robust, while at the same time the fruit is forming, swelling, and ripening, which requires the remainder of the season. It is only from these tall, healthy, robust female stalks that the hemp fiber is obtained. . . .

All these facts from both kingdoms, and the number that might be added is unlimited, combine to show that the female constitutes the main trunk, descending unchanged from the asexual, or presexual, condition; that the male element was added at a certain stage for the sole purpose of securing a crossing of ancestral strains, and the consequent variation and higher development; that it began as a simple fertilizer, assuming a variety of forms; that for reasons hereafter to be considered, the male in most organisms gradually assumed more importance, and ultimately came to approach the size and general nature of the female; but that throughout nearly or quite the whole of the invertebrates, and to a considerable extent among the vertebrates, the male has remained an inferior creature, and has continued to devote its existence chiefly to the one function for which it was created. The change, or progress, as it may be called, has been wholly in the male, the female remaining unchanged. This is why it is so often said that the female represents heredity and the male variation. "The ovum is the material medium through which the law of heredity manifests itself, while the male element is the vehicle by which new variations are added. . . . The greater variability of the male is also shown by a comparison of the adult male and female with the immature birds of both sexes."[7]

The last fact is the one usually adduced in support of the theory that in birds and mammals where the male is superior the female is an example of "arrested development." Such is, however, probably not the case, and the female simply represents the normal condition, while the condition of the male is abnormal due to his great powers of variability. That the female should resemble the young is quite natural, but the statement is an inverted one, due to the androcentric bias. The least unbiased consideration would make it clear that the colors of such male birds as Professor Brooks had in mind are not the normal colors of the species, but are due to some abnormal or supra-normal causes. The normal color is that of the young and the female, and the color of the male is the result of his excessive variability. Females cannot thus vary. They represent the center of gravity of the biological system. They are that "stubborn power of permanency" of which Goethe speaks. The female not only typifies the race but, metaphor aside, she *is* the race.

Sexual Selection

The fact that requires to be explained is that, as we have seen, the male, primarily and normally an inconspicuous and insignificant afterthought of nature, has in most existing organisms attained a higher stage of development and somewhat approached the form and stature of the primary trunk form which is now called the female. That which might naturally surprise the philosophical observer is not that the female is usually superior to the male, but that the male should have advanced at all beyond its primitive estate as either a fertilizing organ attached to the female, or at most a minute organism detached from her but devoted exclusively to the same purpose. In other words, while female superiority is a perfectly natural condition, male development requires explanation. . . .

We saw at the outset that in order to fulfill his mission the male must be endowed with an innate interest in performing his work. . . . This attribute was absolutely necessary to the success of the scheme, and throughout all nature we find the male always active and eager seeking the female and exerting his utmost powers to infuse into her the new hereditary *Anlagen* that often make up the greater part of his material substance. This intense interest in his work is the *natura naturans*, the voice of nature speaking through him and commanding him, in season and out of season, always and under all circumstances, to do his duty, and never on any pretext to allow an opportunity to escape to infuse into the old hereditary trunk of his species the new life that is in him. This duty he always performed, not only making extraordinary efforts but incurring enormous risks, often actually sacrificing his life and perishing at his post. . . .

. . . The sacrifice of males was a matter of complete indifference, as much so as is the sacrifice of germs, because the supply was inexhaustible, and in fact, throughout the lower orders an excess of males over females is the normal condition, and often the number of males greatly exceeds that of the females. That a hundred males should live and die without once exercising their normal faculty is of less consequence than that one female should go unfecundated. Biologic economy consists in unlimited resources coupled with the multiplication of chances.[8] Success in accomplishing the main purpose is the paramount consideration. The cost in effort, sacrifice, and life is a comparatively unimportant element.

But it is obvious that the interest of the male is wholly unlike the interest of the female. That the female has an interest there is no doubt. She also has to a limited extent the appetent interest of the male, but this is not usually strong enough to cause her even to move from her place, much less to seek the male. From this point of view she is comparatively indifferent, and is, as is so commonly said, the passive sex. But the female has another and wholly different interest and one which is wanting in the male. Through her nature secures another end which is second only to the two great ends thus far considered, viz., reproduction and fertilization. The male element is in a high degree centrifugal. Unlimited variation would be dangerous if not destructive. Mere difference is not all that is required by evolution. Quality is an element as important as degree. The female is the guardian of hereditary qualities. Variation may be retrogressive as well as progressive. It may be excessive and lead to abnormalities. It requires regulation. The female is the balance wheel of the whole machinery. As the primary, ancestral trunk she stands unmoved amid the heated strife of rivals and holds the scales that decide their relative worth to the race. While the voice of nature speaking to the male in the form of an intense appetitive interest, says to him: fecundate! it gives to the female a different command, and says: discriminate! The order to the male is: cross the strains! that to the female is: choose the best! Here the value of a plurality of males is apparent. In such a plurality there are always differences. The female recognizes these differences, and instinctively selects the one that has the highest value for the race. This quality must of course coincide with a subjective feeling of preference, a coincidence which is brought about by the action of the well-known laws of organic adaptation.

This subjective feeling it is which constitutes the distinctive interest of the female. It is clearly quite other than the interest of the male. It is wanting in the plant and in the lowest animals, but nevertheless makes its appearance at a very early stage in the history of sentient beings. In considering it we have to do with a psychic attribute a grade higher than that of pure appetency. In fact it represents the dawn of the esthetic faculty. . . .

The foundation of the whole process is the fundamental law of heredity, that offspring inherit the qualities of both their parents. The qualities of the mother, being those of the species in general, are of course inherited and do not concern the transformation. This comes through the qualities of the male. The incipient esthetic tastes of the female cause her to select the qualities from among her suitors that she prefers, and to reject all males that do not come up to her standard. The qualities selected are transmitted to the offspring and the new generation again selects and again transmits. As all females may be supposed to have substantially the same preferences the effect is cumulative, and however slowly the transformation may go on, it is only necessary to multiply the repetitions a sufficient number of times to secure any required result. The particular characters thus selected are called secondary sexual characters; they are chiefly seen in the male because the female already has the normal development. There can be no doubt that in cases, like spiders, where the males are so exceedingly small, one of the preferred qualities is a respectable stature and bulk, and that throughout the lower orders the chief selecting has been that of larger and larger males, until the observed present state of partial sex equality was attained. This is exactly the kind of facts that would be overlooked by the average investigator, attention being concentrated on certain more striking and apparently abnormal facts, such as brilliant coloration, peculiar markings, special ornamental organs, weapons of destruction, etc. These latter, under the joint action of the principle of selection and the law of parsimony are often not only confined to the male, but do not appear until the age of maturity, at which time they can alone serve the purpose for which they were selected and created, viz., to attract the female and lead to the continued selection of those males in which they are best developed. It is upon these that biological writers chiefly dwell. They point to a certain degree of development in the tastes of the females which lies beyond the simply useful.

To use the language of figure based on fact, it is small wonder that the female should be ashamed of her puny and diminutive suitors and should always choose the largest and finest specimen among them. If her selection were mainly confined to this quality during all the early history of every species the naturalist without the gynaecocentric theory to guide his observations would never discover it. He would simply notice that the difference in the size of the sexes differs widely in different species and families and set it down as a somewhat remarkable fact but without significance. He would be specially attracted by the superficial differences, particularly in the matter of ornamentation in the male. These are certainly remarkable, and a vast array of examples has been marshaled by Darwin and his coadjutors and successors. . . .

. . . Darwin takes up each class and group of animals in the ascending order of development all the way to man, and makes out an unanswerable case in favor of his principle of sexual selection. Later writers have multiplied facts in its support until it is to-day as firmly established as that of natural selection. . . .

Jealousy, the "green-eyed monster which doth mock the meat it feeds on," here showed its usefulness, for it coöperated with the esthetic faculty of the female and led to all those intense activities of the rival males that developed the characters that the females preferred. Success in these struggles for favor, due in turn to the qualities that insured success, was the sure passport to favor, and female favor meant parenthood of the race. Size and strength, even more than the accompanying organic weapons, were the elements of success, and in this way the respectable stature and compact build of the males of developed species gradually replaced the diminutiveness and structural frailty of the primitive males. All these influences have been at work in all the types of animal life since the dawn of the psychic faculty, and the effects, as we should naturally expect, have been roughly proportioned to the length of the phylum. There are of course exceptions to this rule, due to other collateral and partially neutralizing influences, often of a very obscure and complex nature, but upon the whole this has been the result, and consequently, we find that it is in the birds and mammals, the two latest classes, and the two that possess the longest phylogenetic ancestry, that the effects of sexual selection are the most marked. Here the struggle for size, strength, courage, and beauty reaches its maximum intensity, and begins in a sort of geometrical progression to augment and multiply all the secondary sexual characters of the male and to threaten the overthrow, at least for a time, of the long prevailing gynaecarchy of the animal world.

Male Efflorescence

We have presided at the birth of the male being, long subsequent to that of the true organism, in the form of a minute sperm-plasm to supplement the much older germ-plasm, not as an aid to reproduction, but simply as a medium of variation and a condition to higher development. We have watched the progress of this accessory element subjected to the esthetic choice of the organism or real animal, until, through the inheritance of the qualities thus chosen it slowly rose in form and volume into somewhat the image of its creator and became a true animal organism resembling the original organism, on account of which naturalists call it the male and the other the female of the same species. Seeing these two somewhat similar forms habitually together, the one still performing the office of fertilizer and the other the work of reproduction, they class them alike, and until recently regarded fertilization as an essential part of reproduction. But the deeper meaning of it all has generally escaped observation.

The esthetic sense of the females has produced many beautiful objects in the form of male decoration in the invertebrate and lower vertebrate classes, but with the advent of bird life this sense became more acute, and having such decorative materials as feathers to work with, it soon surpassed all its previous achievements and wrought gorgeous products on the most ornamental patterns. . . .

. . . As was remarked of the tastes of insects in virtually creating the world of flowers,[9] so we may now say of birds, the similarity of their tastes to those of men, even of the men of the highest culture, is proved by the universal admiration of mankind for the objects of their esthetic selection and creation. From a certain point of view, therefore the standard of taste is universal among sentient and psychic beings, and the beautiful colors, markings, and forms of butterflies, moths, and beetles, of ostrich feathers and peacocks' tails, speak for an esthetic unity throughout all the grades and orders of life. It is the same standard of taste, too, that again comes out in the highest class of animals, the mammals, and that produces such universally admired objects as the antlers of the stag, which are the type of a true secondary sexual character. It is through such influences that the males of so many birds and mammals have attained their extraordinary development in the direction of size, strength, activity, courage, beauty, and brilliancy.

The faculty exercised by the female in sexual selection may in a broad sense be called esthetic, but many other qualities than those that are popularly classed as beauty are preferred and created. Some of these may be called moral qualities, such as courage. This is a special element of success, and its development leads to the universal rivalry in the animal world for mates. It is not that the rivals decimate and destroy one another leaving only the final victor. As has been remarked,[10] the battles of the males, however fierce, rarely result fatally, and they often take the form of quasi mock battles in which some do, indeed, "get hurt," but it rarely happens that any get killed. Still less is it true that the strongest and ablest males use their powers to coerce the female into submission. The female, even when greatly surpassed in size and strength by the male, still asserts her supremacy and exercises her prerogative of discrimination as sternly and pitilessly as when she far surpassed the male in these qualities. This is why I reject the usual expression "male superiority" for those relatively few cases in which the male has acquired superior size and strength along with the various ornaments with which the female has decked him out. And nothing is more false than the oft-repeated statement inspired by the andocentric world view, that the so-called "superior" males devote that new-gained strength to the work of protecting and feeding the female and the young. Those birds and mammals in which the process of male differentiation has gone farthest, such as peacocks, pheasants, turkeys, and barnyard fowls, among birds, and lions, buffaloes, stags, and sheep, among mammals, do practically nothing for their families. It is the mother and she alone that cares for the young, feeds them, defends them, and if necessary fights for them. It is she that has the real courage—courage to attack the enemies of the species. Many wild animals will flee from man, the only exception being the female with her young. She alone is dangerous. Even the male lion is really somewhat of a coward, but the hunter learns to beware of the lioness. The doe goes off into a lonely spot to bring forth and nurse her fawn. It is the same with the female buffalo and the domestic cow. How much does the bull or the cock care for its mate or its offspring? Approach the brood with hostile intent and it is the old hen that ruffles up her feathers so as to look formidable and dares to attack you. The cock is never with her. His business is with other hens that have no chickens to distract their attention from him.

The formidable weapons of the males of many animals acquired through sexual selection are employed exclusively in fighting other males, and never in the serious work of fighting enemies. The female simply looks on and admires the victorious rival, and selects him to continue the species, thus at each selection emphasizing the qualities selected and causing these qualities to tower up into greater and greater prominence. The whole phenomenon of so-called male superiority bears a certain stamp of spuriousness and sham. It is to natural history what chivalry was to human history. It is pretentious, meretricious, quixotic; a sort of make-believe, play, or sport of nature of an airy unsubstantial character. The male side of nature shot up and blossomed out in an unnatural, fantastic way, cutting loose from the real business of life and attracting a share of attention wholly disproportionate to its real importance. I call it *male efflorescence*. It certainly is not male supremacy, for throughout the animal world below man, in all the serious and essential affairs of life, the female is still supreme. There is no male hegemony or andrarchy. Nevertheless it represents organic evolution of which both sexes have partaken. Its chief value lies in the fact that in lifting the male from nothing to his present estate it has elevated all species and all life and placed the organic world on a higher plane. The apparent male superiority in some birds and mammals instead of indicating arrested development in the female indicates over-development in the male. Male efflorescence is an epiphenomenon. But in all this surplus life infused into the male a certain quantity has found its way into the stock and caused an advance. . . .

Primitive Woman

To the intelligent and sympathetic reader no apology is needed for having dwelt so long on the prehuman stage in the exposition of so unfamiliar a subject as the gynaecocentric theory. . . . Long before we reach the human stage we find all the alleged evidence of the androcentric theory, and without such a study of origins as we have been making there would be no counter-evidence, and in fact no data for understanding the real meaning of this alleged evidence. . . . But it so happens that while the facts depended upon to support the androcentric theory are patent to all, those that support the gynaecocentric theory are latent and known to very few. But in this it does not differ at all from any of the great truths of science. The facts supposed to prove the apparent are on the surface while those that prove the real, which is usually the reverse of the apparent, lie hidden and only come forth after prolonged investigation and reflection. The androcentric world view will probably be as slow to give way as was the geocentric, or as is still the anthropocentric. . . .

On the evolution theory we are obliged to assume that the transition from the truly animal ancestor of man to the truly human being was by a series of imperceptible steps, and therefore the exact line between animal and man cannot of course be drawn and could not be if all the steps were represented in the paleontological and archaeological record. But it is of the greatest interest to discover and trace out in both these sciences as many steps as possible in the series leading up to existing man. From now on we are to deal with man as we actually know him, and to consider the relations between man and woman, physically and socially. In all known human races man is found to be larger and stronger than woman, and to have certain of the typical secondary sexual characters, but these latter differ in different races and have no special value for our subject.

A survey of this field soon shows that we are on a new plane of existence. We have reached another of those turns in the lane of evolution at which a new era begins. It is one of those cosmical crises . . . in which a new and at first unperceived and unimportant element suddenly assumes vast proportions and causes a complete change of front in the march of events. We have encountered several such. The rise of the esthetic faculty which led to sexual selection, evolved the male sex, and carried it up to such giddy heights, should have been set down as one of these differential attributes producing unintended effects, which in this sense are, if not abnormal, at least extra-normal, ultra-normal, and supra-normal. On the human plane we encounter another such an element, not indeed one that has been overlooked, but one that produced a large number of deviations from the norm, some of which have been considered, others of which will be considered later on, and one of which now confronts us in our attempts to explain the relations of the sexes. This new element is none other than the presence in man of a rational faculty. . . . this faculty alone gave man the dominion of the earth. We may now see how the same faculty gave to man in the narrower sense the dominion of woman. We have seen that notwithstanding all the shining qualities with which female taste endowed the males of certain of the higher types of animals, including the immediate ancestors of man, there is not and never can be in any of these types any true male hegemony, and that everywhere and always, regardless of relative size, strength, beauty, or courage, the mothers of the race have held the rein and held the male aspirants to a strict accountability. In a non-rational world there could be no other economy, since to place affairs in the hands of the "fickle and changeable" sex[11] would bring speedy and certain ruin to any animal species.

. . . It is instinct which, throughout the animal kingdom below man, maintains female supremacy and prevents the destruction of animal races. But with man reason begins to gain the ascendant over instinct. This means that it is strong enough to break over the restraints of instinct and still avert danger. . . .

Increased brain mass became a secondary sexual character. . . . Because brain is common to both sexes its increase as the result of female preference is not noticed. Yet there can be no doubt that success in rivalry for female favor became more and more dependent upon sagacity, and that this led to brain development. . . .

Now this male brain development it is that has brought about the great change, and has constituted man a being apart from the rest of creation, enabling him with increasing safety to violate the restraints of instinct and inaugurate a regime wholly different from that of the animal world out of which he has developed. Having become larger and physically stronger than woman, his egoistic reason, unfettered by any such sentiment as sympathy, and therefore wholly devoid of moral conceptions of any kind, naturally led him to employ his superior strength in exacting from woman whatever satisfaction she could yield him. The first blow that he struck in this direction wrought the whole transformation. The aegis and palladium of the female sex had been from the beginning her power of choice. This rational man early set about wresting from woman, and although, as we shall see, this was not accomplished all at once, still it was accomplished very early, and for the mother of mankind all was lost.

Gynaecocracy

In a broad general sense the relations of the sexes throughout the animal kingdom, as above described, might be characterized as a gynaecocracy, or female rule, for which the form *gynaecarchy,* already employed, is perhaps to be preferred. But I propose to restrict the term, as did Bachofen,[12] to the human race, and to a phase of the early history of man, which, though almost unknown prior to the astonishingly erudite and exhaustive researches of Bachofen, is now known always to have existed and still to exist at the proper status of culture or stage of man's history. Making all due allowance for the unreliability of the accounts of travelers, and the disposition to exaggerate everything that is opposed to civilized customs, there still remains far too large a volume of facts bearing on this state to be passed over as meaningless or worthless. In fact this tendency to exaggerate them is doubtless more than counterbalanced by the influence of the androcentric world view in causing them to be overlooked. Ethnographers constantly lean toward their rejection or the minimizing of their significance. They are in their way in working out a complete androcentric system of ethnology.

It must not be forgotten that the true beginnings of man are not known in the sense that races exist representing such beginnings. The lowest races known are relatively far advanced and belong to old stocks. It is natural to suppose that, at much lower stages than any of these represent, woman, almost to the same extent as among the female anthropoids, possessed absolute power of choice and rejection, and in this most vital respect, was the ruling sex. Sexual selection may have been still in action, still further modifying the attributes of men. . . . There are many indications that woman was slow to surrender her scepter, and that the gradual loss of her power of rejection and selection took place with all the irregularity that characterizes all natural phenomena. Circumstances of every kind impeded or favored it, and the scattered hordes exerted no influence on one another to produce uniformity in this respect. Nothing is more varied than the relations of the sexes among existing races of men. Almost every conceivable form of marriage, or union, has been found. While most persons suppose that nothing is so certainly fixed by nature, and even by divine decree, as the particular form of marriage that happens to prevail in their own country, ethnologists know that nothing is so purely conventional as just this fact of the ways in which men and women arrange or agree to carry on the work of continuing the race.

About the time that the transformation from apehood to manhood took place it is probable that the males were considerably larger and stronger than the females, but that the females compelled the males to conform to their choice, thus keeping up the action of selection and its legitimate effects. With the advent of incipient rationality it could scarcely be otherwise than that this long fixed condition should be somewhat disturbed. As rationality was acquired by both sexes, though perhaps in somewhat unequal degrees, if it was to cause one sex to dominate the other, circumstances must decide, at least at first, which should be the dominant sex. As the female sex had thus far always exercised supremacy in the most vital matters, it might be supposed that woman would prove the dominant sex in primitive hordes. That this was the original tendency and logic of events is abundantly shown by the survivals of it that we find, and by the real condition of the lowest existing races.

The first and most striking form of evidence pointing this way consists in a class of facts that may be roughly grouped under the general head of *amazonism*, although they show not only widely different degrees of this state, but also a great variety of forms of it. These are all described in the numerous standard works in which the facts have been laboriously compiled, and space does not permit me to attempt their enumeration. It is enough to note that phenomena of this class, sufficient to show a greater or less degree of female supremacy, have been observed in at least a score of races. Some of those most frequently referred to are the following: Natives of the Khasi Hills in Assam; Naïars of the Malabar coast; Dyaks of Borneo; Batta people in Sumatra; Dahomans, West Africa; Mombuttus, Central Africa; natives of Madagascar; inhabitats of Imôhagh in the desert of Sahara; natives of New Britain (Neu-Pommern), Australasia; Fuegians; Botocudos of Eastern Brazil; Nicaraguans; Indians of the province of Cueva, Central America. This list covers a large part of the world. That it should consist chiefly of somewhat remote, outlying regions is of course what we should expect. That it was once far more general, however, is proved by records of it even in Europe, notably among the ancient Bretons and Scots. It was probably well-nigh universal, in the sense that each race has passed through that stage, although different races doubtless passed out of it not only at different times, but at different relative points in their history or development.

The other principal group of facts that support the claim for a primitive stage of gynaecocracy is that relating to what is variously called matriarchy, motherright, the matriarchate, and the metronymic family. Bachofen greatly disturbed the smooth androcentric current that had thus far been flowing, when in 1861 he announced that the ancient laws and records, both written and hieroglyphic, indicated a widespread system of descent and inheritance in the female line among both Aryan and Semitic peoples, and from data in his possession he worked out an entirely new theory of the early relations of the sexes. . . .

While the animal origin of man is now almost universally admitted by anthropologists and by well-informed persons generally, there is manifest a very tardy recognition of its full meaning. No blame ever attaches to the sexual relations of animals. They are usually or always such as best subserve the needs of different species. . . . A common error tacitly entertained is that animals carry on the process of reproduction and rearing of the young by a conscious attention to this important business. They are supposed to woo and mate for this purpose, and to care for their offspring with an eye to the interests of the species. The fact is that these functional results are the consequences of the law of adaptation, and the agents are wholly unconscious of them as anything to be attained by their actions. They only seek their interests in the form of feelings, which are so regulated by instinct as to secure the results. For example, as has already been said, animals can have no knowledge of the connection between mating and propagating. All they know is that they like to mate. The female brings forth her young with no conception of the part the male has had in it. She cares for her young because she is impelled to do so by an innate interest, in short, because she likes to do so. All this is true of all animal species, and it is not at all probable that the degree of reasoning power that enabled primitive man to perceive that the fertilization of the male was a necessary condition to reproduction was attained until long after the full human estate had been reached and man had advanced far into the protosocial stage. The fact that races still exist incapable of performing such an act of ratiocination proves that the inability to perform it must have once been general.

In such a state it was natural and necessary that everything should be traced to the mother. The father was unknown and unthought of. The idea of paternity did not exist. Maternity was everything. . . . That under such circumstances mother-rule and mother-right should prevail is among the necessities of existence.

Amazonism, matriarchy, and all the forms of gynaecocracy that are found among primitive peoples, instead of being anomalies or curiosities, are simply survivals of this early and probably very long stage in the history of man and society of which no other evidence now exists, but which is the logical and inevitable conclusion that must follow the admission of the animal origin of man.

Androcracy

At some point quite early in the protosocial stage it began slowly to dawn upon the growing intellect of man that a causal connection existed between these couplings of men and women and the birth of children. It was this simple act of ratiocination that literally reversed the whole social system. For the first time the man began to perceive that he, too, had a part in the continuance of the race, that the children were in part his, and not wholly the woman's. The idea, however, was very slow to take root. The only absolutely certain antecedent to the existence of a child was the parturition of the mother. That the child came from her was something about which there could be no doubt. . . . Certain it was that the latter [father right and the patriarchate] could never have been attained so long as children were believed to be the exclusive creation of woman. So long as that view obtained gynaecocracy was the only condition possible.

But the idea once firmly established that the family was a joint product of the woman and the man, it is easy to see the important results that would naturally follow. The same strengthening of the reasoning powers that made the discovery of paternity possible worked in all other directions. Paternity implied power over the child, which was now exercised by the father as well as by the mother. But it went much farther. Equal authority with the mother soon lead to a comparison of physical strength between the sexes, which had never been made before for precisely the same reason that the lion never compares strength with the lioness, the hart with the hind, the bull with the cow, or the cock with the hen. Physical strength never comes in question in the gynaecocratic state. The female dispenses her favors according to her choice, and the males acquiesce after venting their jealousy on one another. The idea of coercing the female or extorting her favor never so much as occurs to the male mind. The virtue of the female animal is absolute, for virtue does not consist, as many suppose, in refusal, but in selection. It is refusal of the unfit and of all at improper times and places. This definition of virtue applies to human beings, even the most civilized, as well as to animals. The female animal or the human female in the gynaecocratic state would perish before she would surrender her virtue.

The passage from the gynaecocratic to the androcratic state was characterized on the part of man by the loss of his normal chivalry and respect for the preferences of woman, and on the part of woman by the loss of her virtue. Both the time-honored assertion of authority by woman and submission to it by man were abrogated. In discovering his paternity and accompanying authority man also discovered his power, which at that stage meant simply physical strength. He began to learn the economic value of woman and to exert his superior power in the direction of exacting not only favors but service from her. The gynaecocratic régime once broken over the steps were short and rapid to complete androcracy. The patriarchate or patriarchal system, in which the man assumed complete supremacy, was the natural sequel to the process that had begun. It was all the product of the strengthening intellect which refused longer to be bound by the bonds of animal instinct and broke away from the functional restraints that adaptation had imposed upon the sexes. The man saw that he was the master creature, that woman was smaller, weaker, less shrewd and cunning than he, and at the same time could be made to contribute to his pleasure and his wants, and he proceeded to appropriate her accordingly.

The Subjection of Woman

When John Stuart Mill used this expression as the title for his book he had only the philosopher's penetration into a great truth. He had comparatively little light from anthropology and scarcely any from biology. Its true meaning, therefore, as a phase of the history of man, as something impossible to the so-called "brute creation," and as a pure product of human reason untempered by altruistic sentiments, was for the most part lost to him. The most unfortunate fact in the history of human development is the fact that the rational faculty so far outstripped the moral sentiments. This is really because moral sentiments require such a high degree of reasoning power. The intuitive reason, which is purely egoistic, is almost the earliest manifestation of the directive agent and requires only a low degree of the faculty of reasoning. But sympathy requires a power of putting one's self in the place of another, of representing to self the pains of others. When this power is acquired it causes a reflex of the represented pain to self, and this reflected pain felt by the person representing it becomes more and more acute and unendurable as the representation becomes more vivid and as the general organization becomes more delicate and refined. This high degree was far from being attained by man at the early stage with which we are now dealing. Vast ages must elapse before it is reached even in its simplest form. And yet the men of that time knew their own wants and possessed much intelligence of ways of satisfying them. . . . Civilization may, indeed, be measured by the capacity of men for suffering representative pain and their efforts to relieve it.

In our long and somewhat dreary journey down the stream of time we have now reached the darkest spot, and fain would I omit its description were this not to leave a blank in the story and to drop out an essential link in the chain of evidence for the gynaecocentric theory. But in recording this history I prefer in the main to let others speak. And first let us hear Herbert Spencer. This is what he says:—

In the history of humanity as written, the saddest part concerns the treatment of women; and had we before us its unwritten history we should find this part still sadder. I say the saddest part because, though there have been many things more conspicuously dreadful—cannabalism, the torturings of prisoners, the sacrificings of victims to ghosts and gods—these have been but occasional; whereas the brutal treatment of woman has been universal and constant. If, looking first at their state of subjection among the semi-civilized, we pass to the uncivilized, and observe the lives of hardship borne by nearly all of them—if we then think what must have gone on among those still ruder peoples who, for so many thousands of years, roamed over the uncultivated Earth; we shall infer that the amount of suffering which has been, and is, borne by women, is utterly beyond imagination. . . . Utter absence of sympathy made it inevitable that women should suffer from the egoism of men, without any limit save their ability to bear the entailed hardships. . . .[13]

. . . I will . . . offer only a few of the briefer accounts, which may be taken as illustrating the subjection of woman in the stage of androcracy. . . .

Du Chaillu describes two distressing cases of the apparently wanton torture of women in Central Africa,[14] one of which he succeeded in relieving. He intimates that this practice of torturing women was connected with some detestable superstition among the natives by which women were suspected of sorcery and witchcraft. But how much better were the people of Europe, and even of America, in this respect, down to the end of the seventeenth century?

"Among the Kaffirs," says Spencer, quoting Shooter, "besides her domestic duties, the woman has to perform all the hard work; she is her husband's ox, as a Kaffir once said to me,—she had been bought, he argued, and must therefore labor."[15]

The complete slavery of woman to man is shown by the following: "Of a Malagasy chief Drury says—'he had scarcely seated himself at his door, when his wife came out crawling on her hands and knees till she came to him, and then licked his feet . . . all the women in the town saluted their husbands in the same manner.'"[16] "Almost everywhere in Africa," says Letourneau, "woman is the property (chose) of her husband, who has the right to use her as a beast of burden, and almost always makes her work as he does his oxen."[17] "In certain Himalayan regions near the sources of the Djemnah in Nepaul, etc., the Aryan Hindoos have adopted Tibetan polyandry. The women are for them a veritable merchandise which they buy and sell. At the time of which Fraser writes a woman among the peasants cost from 10 to 12 rupees, a sum which it was pleasant to receive but painful to expend. They also freely sold their daughters, and the brothers of each family bought a common wife, whom they rented without hesitation to strangers."[18]

That the subjection of woman was due entirely to her physical inferiority to man, or rather to that superior size and strength which men had acquired in common with most of the other higher animals through female selection, seems beyond controversy, the tendency to deny and escape it being inspired wholly by shame at admitting it. I find the following noble sentiment in the fragments of Condorcet:

> Among the advances of the human mind most important for the general welfare, we should number the entire destruction of the prejudices which have produced between the sexes an inequality of rights injurious even to the favored sex. In vain is it sought to justify it by differences in their physical organization, in the strength of their intellects, in their moral sensibilities. This inequality has had no other origin than the abuse of power, and it is in vain that men have since sought to excuse it by sophisms.[19]

Darwin says: "Man is more powerful in body and mind than woman, and in the savage state he keeps her in a far more abject state of bondage than does the male of any other animal;"[20] . . . In New Zealand, according to Moerenhaut, a father or brother, in giving his daughter or his sister to her future husband, would say, "If you are not satisfied with her, sell her, kill her, eat her, you are absolute master of her."[21] "Almost at the origin of human society woman was subjugated by her companion; we have seen her become in succession, beast of burden, slave, minor, subject, held aloof from a free and active life, often maltreated, oppressed, punished with fury for acts that her male owner would commit with impunity before her eyes."[22]

The whole difficulty in understanding these abuses lies in the fact that civilized men cannot conceive of a state in which no moral sentiments exist, no sympathy for pain, no sense of justice. And yet every day, in every civilized country of the world, the public press informs us of wife beatings that are scarcely less horrid than those of savages, and these would of course be far more common and shocking but for the restraints of law and police regulation. At the stage of history of any race at which the transition from gynaecocracy to androcracy took place, and for a long period afterward, all men were morally below the level of the basest wife-beater of modern society, at a state in which the first spark of sympathy for suffering in others had not yet been kindled. It was this manner of man, just coming to consciousness through the dawn of a purely egoistic intellect, who, suddenly as it were, discovered that the physically inferior being who had, without his knowledge, endowed him with his superiority, was in his power and could be made to serve him. Hence the subjection of woman.

The Family

It is customary to speak of the family with the most unreserved respect. Comte, who knew scarce anything of primitive man, and whose own family affairs were wretched in the extreme, made it the unit and the bulwark of society. In this he has been followed by many sociologists, and most of those who prefer some other social unit still hold the family to be an essential if not a sacred institution. . . .

The important thing is to gain something like a just conception of what the primitive family was. . . . With the beginning of the régime of androcracy the women were enslaved and both women and children became the chattels of the men. The men still continued to fight for the women, but instead of thereby seeking to secure their favor and to become the chosen ones, they fought for their possession and seized each as many women as possible. The weaker men were, as before, condemned to celibacy, and the women were subject to a monopoly of the strong. This polygamous life made paternity practically certain, and led direct to the patriarchate or patriarchal family. . . . All women were abject slaves, and the children were compelled to do any service of which they were capable. The patriarchs had absolute power over the persons of all within their families. . . .

It thus appears that, whatever the family may be to-day in civilized lands, in its origin it was simply an institution for the more complete subjugation and enslavement of women and children, for the subversion of nature's method in which the mother is the queen, dictates who shall be fathers, and guards her offspring by the instinct of maternal affection planted in her for that express purpose. The primitive family was an unnatural androcratic excrescence upon society.

Marriage

We have now to invade another "sanctuary" only to find it, like the last, a "whited sepulcher." It may look like a strange inversion of the natural order of things to place marriage after the family, but if the promiscuous intercourse of the sexes that characterized the gynaecocratic stage cannot be properly called marriage, scarcely more can that stage be so called in which the men forcibly seize the women and make them their slaves and concubines without ceremony or pretence of consulting their will. The original patriarchal family implies marriage only in the sense that it is implied in a harem of seals on a rookery under the dominion of an old bull. Less so, in fact, for, although we are told that the bull does sometimes gently bite his refractory cows, he never abuses or injures them, much less kills and eats them. That function is reserved for the "lord of creation," the only being endowed with a "moral sense," made "in the image of his Creator," and often after his death erected by his descendants into a god. Indeed, most gods are themselves accredited with these sublime attributes! . . .

. . . The patriarch who owned all the women disposed of them as he saw fit. They were looked upon by him as so much value, and if the oxen, spears, boats, or other merchandise offered for a woman were worth more to him than the woman, he sold her for a price, and marriage consisted in nothing more than the ratification, by whatever ceremony might prevail, of the bargain thus made. In selling a woman to a man her owner is said to marry her to him, and such was primitive marriage. In later stages and in different tribes of course variations arose in the nature of the ceremonies, and a great variety of so-called forms of marriage has been described, but all of them wholly ignore the wishes of the woman and constitute so many different ways of transferring and holding property in women.

When the protosocial stage was passed and wars, conquests, and social assimilation had begun, the women of the conquered races became the slaves of the conquerors, and ultimately the warriors also and many of the other men. Then commenced the period of universal slavery. . . . The system of caste was no doubt favorable to woman, since those of the noble classes, whatever their relations to the men of those classes, were on a higher plane than those of the lower classes. The patriarchal system was strengthened rather than weakened by social assimilation, and the principal effect it had upon marriage was to diversify forms and, along with its other socializing influences, somewhat to mitigate the rigor of woman slavery. Polygamy prevailed, and with the establishment of a leisure class it was greatly strengthened, the nobility and ruling class being secured in the possession of as many wives as they desired. The enslavement of men was some relief to women from drudgery, and harems were established in which the handsomest women were kept without labor and always fresh for breeding purposes and to satisfy men's lusts.

Among the lower classes, and especially in the large middle class that were neither slaves nor nobles, which carried on the principal industrial operations of the now developing state and people, marriage took more rational forms, becoming, from considerations of enforced justice, more frequently monogamic, and, as was shown, resulting in the complete mixture of the blood of the two races. With the origin of the state and the establishment of more and more complete codes of law, marriage was legalized and regulated and became more and more a human institution. But when we see how little advanced marriage was in Greece and Rome during what we call "antiquity," we may easily imagine what it must have been at an earlier date and among more backward races. . . .

It would be hopeless to attempt to enumerate all the multitudinous forms of marriage, but down to comparatively modern times they all have one thing in common, viz., the proprietorship of the husband in the wife. So slow has the idea of the wife being a slave of her husband been in disappearing that the word "obey" still remains in the marriage ceremony of all countries, and is only stricken out by a few emancipated people or liberal sects.

. . . among men forming themselves into kinship groups, the tendency to interbreed too closely was strong, and required to be checked. . . . In many tribes marriage within the clan is severely punished, often with death. . . . But one of the principal consequences that followed was the introduction of a system of marriage by rape, in which whole races engaged, and women were sought in war as trophies, and were captured for wives, thus effectively crossing the different stocks, and greatly strengthening the physical and mental constitution of the races involved. . . .

Male Sexual Selection

With the earliest forms of social assimilation through conquest the lowest point seems to have been reached in the moral degradation of man. . . .

But with the advent of the metasocial stage due to conquest and subjugation, inaugurating the system of caste and establishing a leisure class, brain development was greatly accelerated by cross fertilization, and for the higher classes the primary sexual wants were more than satisfied by universal polygamy in those classes. It is a sociological law that as the lower, more physical wants are satisfied the higher spiritual wants arise. With an unlimited supply of women men began to compare them, and their esthetic sense was sharpened to stimulate their sated physical sense. Female sexual selection, which for the sake of brevity and precision may be called *gyneclexis*, had long ceased. The advent of androcracy and the subjection of woman had terminated its long and fruitful reign, and throughout the entire protosocial stage of man physical passion was supreme. But now there comes a calm in the long stormy career of man, and a small number are placed in a position to allow the spiritual forces free play. In this way male sexual selection, which may be called *andreclexis*, arose, and this has since played a considerable role in the history of the human race. . . .

Although this effect is chiefly confined to the leisure class, the nobility, and the priesthood where this last is not celibate, and in more advanced and somewhat industrial societies, to the wealthy classes generally, still in polygamous countries it must be very great. . . .

. . . there is some resemblance between the effects of male and of female sexual selection, as the former was described a few pages back. There is a certain unreality, artificiality, and spuriousness about female as well as about male secondary sexual characters. The two processes differ, however, in many respects. Man, for example, does not desire women to be larger and stronger, but prefers frailty and a certain diminutiveness. He does not want cunning nor courage, nor any sterling mental or moral qualities, and therefore woman does not advance in these directions. Even fecundity and the physical development necessary to render it successful are not specially selected, and under this influence woman grows more sterile rather than more fertile. In short, almost the only quality selected is bodily symmetry with the color and complexion that best conform to it. The result is that if this were to go on a sufficient length of time without the neutralizing and compensating effect of other more normal influences, woman might ultimately be reduced to a helpless parasite upon society, comparable to the condition of the primitive male element. . . .

Woman in History

The series of influences which we have been describing had the effect to fasten upon the human mind the habit of thought which I call the androcentric world view, and this has persistently clung to the race until it forms to-day the substratum of all thought and action. So universal is this attitude that a presentation of the real and fundamental relation of the sexes is something new to those who are able to see it, and something preposterous to those who are not. The idea that the female is naturally and really the superior sex seems incredible, and only the most liberal and emancipated minds, possessed of a large store of biological information, are capable of realizing it. At the beginning of the historical period woman was under complete subjection to man. She had so long been a mere slave and drudge that she had lost all the higher attributes that she originally possessed, and in order to furnish an excuse for degrading and abusing her men had imputed to her a great array of false evil qualities that tended to make her despise herself. All Oriental literature, all the ancient sacred books and books of law, all the traditional epics, all the literature of Greek and Roman antiquity, and in fact all that was written during the middle ages, and much of the literature of the fifteenth, sixteenth, and seventeenth centuries, teem with epithets, slurs, flings, and open condemnations of women as beings in some manner vile and hateful, often malicious and evil disposed, and usually endowed with some superstitious power for evil. The horrors of witchcraft were nothing but the normal fruit of this prevailing spirit in the hands of superstitious priests of a miracle-based cult. Near the end of the fifteenth century a certain book appeared entitled, "The Witch Hammer," which received the sanction of Pope Innocent

VIII, and formed the companion to a bull against witches issued by him. The following is a sample passage from this book:—

> The holy fathers have often said that there are three things that have no moderation in good or evil—the *tongue*, a *priest*, and a *woman*. Concerning woman this is evident. All ages have made complaints against her. The wise Solomon, who was himself tempted to idolatry by woman, has often in his writings given the feminine sex a sad but true testimonial; and the holy Chrysostom says: "What is woman but an enemy of friendship, an unavoidable punishment, a necessary evil, a natural temptation, a desirable affliction, a constantly flowing source of tears, a wicked work of nature covered with a shining varnish?" Already had the first woman entered into a sort of compact with the devil; should not, then, her daughters do it also? The very word *femina* (woman) means *one wanting in faith;* for *fe* means "faith" and *minus* "less." Since she was formed of a crooked rib her entire spiritual nature has been distorted and inclined more toward sin than virtue. If we here compare the words of Seneca, "Woman either loves or hates; there is no third possibility," it is easy to see that when she does not love God she must resort to the opposite extreme and hate him. It is thus clear why women especially are addicted to the practice of sorcery. The crime of witches exceeds all others. They are worse than the devil, for he has fallen once for all, and Christ has not suffered for him. The devil sins, therefore, only against the Creator, but the witch both against the Creator and Redeemer.[23]

The Hebrew myth of the rib has been made a potent instrument for the subjection of woman. . . .

The literature and thought of India is thoroughly hostile to woman. A large number of proverbs attest this widespread misogyny. "Woman is like a slipper made to order; wear it if it fits you, throw it away if it does not." "You can never be safe from the cunning artifices of woman." "Woman is like a snake, charming as well as venomous." Hebrew literature breathes the same spirit, and the reading of the Bible often brings the color to the cheeks of a liberal-minded person of either sex. Arabian magic is even worse in this respect, and is so erotic that it is next to impossible to obtain an unexpurgated text of the Arabian Nights Entertainments, about 75 per cent of the matter being expunged from all current editions. The androcentric world view may almost be said to have its headquarters in India. The "Code of Manu" reflects it throughout. According to it "Woman depends during her childhood upon her father; during her youth upon her husband; in her widowhood upon her sons or her male relatives; in default of these, upon the sovereign." "She should always be in good humor and revere her husband, even though unfaithful, as a god." "If a widow she must not even pronounce the name of another man than her deceased husband."[24] The husband always addressed his wife as servant or slave, while she must address him as master or lord. The same code declares that "it is in the nature of the feminine sex to seek to corrupt men," and forbids any man to remain in any place alone with his sister, his mother, or his daughter. Even at the present day in India free choice, especially of the woman, has nothing to do with marriage, and parents and families arbitrarily dispose of the girls, often at a very tender age.

Modern countries differ somewhat in the prevailing ideas about women. No statement is more frequently repeated than that in any country the treatment of women is a true measure of the degree of civilization. It may now be added to this that the treatment of women is a true measure of the intensity of the androcentric sentiment prevailing in any country. It might be invidious to attempt to classify modern nations on this basis, especially as individuals in any country differ so widely in this respect. It is a measure of civilization or civility in individuals as well as in nations, and in every nation there are thoroughly liberal and fully civilized individuals. Neither can the nineteenth and twentieth centuries claim them all, as we have seen in the noble sayings of Condorcet, who was probably the most civilized man of his time, far more so than Comte who made him his spiritual father but did not share his liberality. . . . The German attitude toward women was perhaps typified by the father of Frederick the Great, of whom it is related as among his sterling qualities, that when he met a woman in the street he would walk up to her with his cane raised, saying: "Go back into the house! an honest woman should keep indoors." . . .

Germans as a rule detest American women for their initiative and boldness, daring to act and think independently of their husbands and of men generally, and they apply to them the strongest term of contempt that they have in their language in characterizing them as *emancipirt*. Woman is much more respected in France, but under Napoleon and his code there was a recoil toward barbarism. Napoleon said to the Council of State that "a husband should have absolute power over the actions of his wife." In the "Mémorial de Sainte-Hélène" he is quoted to the following effect:—

> Woman is given to man to bring forth children. Woman is our property; we are not hers; for she gives us children and man does not give any to her. She is therefore his property, as the tree is that of the gardener. . . . A single woman cannot suffice for a man for that purpose. She cannot be his wife when she is sick. She ceases to be his wife when she can no longer give him children. Man, whom nature does not arrest either by age or by any of these inconveniences, should therefore have several wives.[25]

Only a part of the oppressive laws of the code Napoleon have been repealed, but public opinion in France is far in advance of the laws, and judging from outward indications, I should be inclined to place that country, next to the United States, as the most highly civilized nation of the globe. . . .

Throughout the historic period woman has suffered from a consistent, systematic, and universal discrimination in the laws of all countries. In all the early codes she was herself a hereditament, and when she ceased to be a chattel she was not allowed to inherit property, or was cut down to a very small share in the estate. In this and many other ways her economic dependence has been made more or less complete. Letourneau[26] has enumerated many of these discriminating laws, and we have only to turn the pages of the law books to find them everywhere. When a student of law I scheduled scores of them, and could fill a dozen pages with a bare enumeration of such as still form part of the common law of England as taught to law classes even in the United States. All this is simply the embodiment in the jurisprudence of nations of the universal androcentric world view, and it has been unquestioningly acquiesced in by all mankind, including the women themselves.

The Anglo-Saxon word *woman* reflects this world view, showing that it is older than the stock of languages from which this word is derived. For although it is no longer believed by philologists that the first syllable of this word has anything to do with *womb*, still it is certain that the last syllable is the same as the German *Mann*, not *Mensch*, and that the rest signifies wife or female, as though man were the original and woman only a secondary creation. As regards the Latin *femina*, while of course it has no connection with *faith* or *minus*, as stated in the "Witch Hammer," still the syllable *fe* is the hypothetical root from which *fecundity* comes, and the word signifies the fertile sex. Primarily no such conceptions as beauty, grace, delicacy, and attractiveness are associated with woman, and all notions of dignity, honor, and worth are equally wanting from the conception of the female sex. On the contrary, we find many terms of reproach, such as *wench, hag,* etc., for which there are no corresponding ones applicable to man.

Notwithstanding all this vast network of bonds that have been contrived for holding woman down, it is peculiar and significant that everywhere and always she has been tacitly credited with a certain mysterious power in which the world has, as it were, stood in awe and fear. While perpetually proclaiming her inferiority, insignificance, and weakness, it has by its precautions virtually recognized her potential importance and real strength. She is the cause of wars and race hostilities. There are always powerful female deities. Minerva is even made the goddess of wisdom. Ever and anon a great female personage, real or fictitious, appears, a Semiramis, a Cleopatra, a Joan of Arc, a Queen Elizabeth, or a Queen Victoria; Scheherazade with her thousand and one tales, Sibyls with their divinations and oracles, Furies, and Gorgons; and finally the witches with all their powers for evil. Although woman is usually pictured as bad, still there is no uncertainty about the supposed possession by her of some occult power, and the impression is constantly conveyed that she must be strenuously kept down, lest should she by any accident or remissness chance to "get loose," she would certainly do something dreadful. . . .

Throughout all human history woman has been powerfully discriminated against and held down by custom, law, literature, and public opinion. All opportunity has been denied her to make any trial of her powers in any direction. In savagery she was underfed, overworked, unduly exposed, and mercilessly abused, so that in so far as these influences could be confined to one sex, they tended to stunt her physical and mental powers. During later ages her social ostracism has been so universal and complete that, whatever powers she may have had, it was impossible for her to make any use of them, and they have naturally atrophied and shriveled. Only during the last two centuries and in the most advanced nations, under the growing power of the sociogenetic energies of society, has some slight relief from her long thraldom been grudgingly and reluctantly vouchsafed. What a continued and increasing tendency in this direction will accomplish it is difficult to presage, but all signs are at present hopeful.

NOTES

1. "Die Sociologische Erkenntnis," von Gustav Ratzenhofer, Leipzig, 1898, p. 127.
2. "Dynamic Sociology," Vol. I, pp. 47–53 [Lester Frank Ward].
3. John A. Ryder in *Science*, N.S., Vol. I, May 31, 1895, p. 603.
4. Cf. Darwin, "Descent of Man," Vol. I, p. 329.
5. Professors Geddes and Thompson [*sic*] in their useful work on the Evolution of Sex have brought together a large number of examples in various departments of the animal kingdom, many of which have been recorded since Darwin's time. See the edition of 1901, pp. 17 ff. 82. . . .
6. *Science*, N.S., Vol. XV, Jan. 3, 1902, p. 30.
7. W. K. Brooks in *Popular Science Monthly*, Vol. XV, June, 1879, pp. 150, 152.
8. "Psychic Factors of Civilization," Boston, 1893, p. 250.
9. *Supra*, p. 234—But for the possibility of cross fertilization by insects there would have been no flowers in the popular sense, and as I have often pointed out, showy and fragrant flowers came into existence simultaneously with nectar-seeking insects.
10. Espinas, "Sociétés Animales," 2e éd., Paris, 1878, pp. 324, 327.
11. The "varium et mutabile semper femina" of Virgil (Book IV, lines 569–570) is a typical androcentric sentiment, and the precise reverse of the truth.
12. "Das Mutterrecht. Eine Untersuchung über die Gynaikokratie der alten Welt nach ihrer religiösen und rechtlichen Natur," von J. J. Bachofen, Stuttgart, 1861; Zweite unveränderte Auflage, Basel, 1897, 4^0, pp. XL, 440.
13. "Principles of Ethics," New York, 1893, Vol. II, pp. 335, 335 (§428) [Herbert Spencer].
14. "Adventures in the Great Forest of Equatorial Africa and the Country of the Dwarfs," by Paul Du Chaillu, London, 1861, Chapter X, p. 122; Chapter XII, pp. 157–158.
15. "Principles of Sociology," Vol. I, p. 687 (§305) [Herbert Spencer].
16. Op. cit. Vol. II, pp. 124–125 (§386).
17. "La Sociologie d'après l'Ethnographie," p. 336 [Charles J. Letourneau (Paris: C. Reinwald, 1880)].
18. Op. cit., p. 366.
19. "Tableau Historique des Progrès de l'Esprit Humain," Bibliothèque Positiviste, Paris, 1900, pp. 180–181 [Condorcet].
20. "Descent of Man," Vol. II, p. 355 [Charles Darwin].
21. "Voyages aux Îsles du Grand Océan," par J. A. Moerenhaut, Paris, 1837, Vol. II, p. 69. These are the closing words of a set speech delivering the woman to the man, which may not be varied, and which corresponds to that of a modern marriage ceremony.
22. Letourneau, *Rev. Ecole d'Anthrop. de Paris*, Vol. IX, p. 288.

23. The only copy of this work that I have seen is as old as 1487, and although it has no title page, place or date of publication, it bears the name "Malleus Maleficarum" on the back of the cover. . . . This is preceded by the text of the bull of Pope Innocent VIII, "adversus heresim." . . . The authorship of the work is ascribed to Heinrich Institor and Jacob Sprenger.

24. "Code of Manu," Book V, Ordinances, Nos. 148, 154, 157.

25. "Mémorial de Sainte-Hélène," Journal de la vie privée et les conversations de l'Empereur Napoléon à Sainte-Hélène, par le Comte de Las Cases, Londres, 1823, Tome II, Quatrième partie, juin, 1816, pp. 117–118.

26. "La Sociologie d'après l'Ethnographie," pp. 180 ff. [Charles Letourneau].

PART 2

Early Patterns in Regard to Sexual Primacy

JOHANN JAKOB BACHOFEN (1815–1887)

Bachofen was a jurist and historian of Roman law, who deduced through the study of myths, legends, literature, language, Roman legal texts, and archaeological evidence the theory that humanity passed from a period of hetaerism to matriarchy and finally to patriarchy.

Bachofen's interpretations have been viewed skeptically. So hostile was the *Zeitgeist* of the 1950s to a sympathetic view of woman that in the preface to Ralph Manheim's English translation of *Mother Right* George Boas writes: "The name of Johann Jakob Bachofen, if mentioned at all in books of reference, is attached to a theory of social development which maintains that the first period of human history was matriarchal. If any discussion of the theory is added, it will be to the effect that it is almost universally discredited." Is this cavalier dismissal warranted? In contrast, in the introduction to the same translation, Joseph Campbell writes that Bachofen's conception is being "increasingly corroborated as archeologists throughout the world lift forth from the earth, for all to see, the tangible forms that his intangible mytho-analytic method of invisible excavation (pursued at home in his library) had anticipated. One has to keep reminding oneself, when reading this perceptive scholar, that in his day the sites of Helen's Troy and Pasiphaë's Crete had not yet been excavated—nor any of those early neolithic villages that have yielded the multitudes of ceramic naked-goddess figurines now filling museum cabinets."

Bachofen anticipated the rejection that his unconventional ideas and original method of investigation would encounter, as witness the closing sentences of his own introduction to his work: "The present book makes no other claim than to provide the scholarly world with a new and well-nigh inexhaustible material for thought. If it has the power to stimulate, it will gladly content itself with the modest position of a preparatory work, and cheerfully accept the common fate of all first attempts, namely, to be disparaged by posterity and judged only on the basis of its shortcomings." As has frequently happened with unorthodox visionaries, the academic world mercilessly disparaged Bachofen. It is remarkable that, in an age that can accept the unverifiable speculations of Freud or the idea of the inheritance of "male bonding,"[1] Bachofen's inferences from a comparison of historical clues and mythological symbols are given short shrift. In spite of apparent corroboration of some of Bachofen's intuitions in the works of Sir James Frazer,[2] in Jane Harrison's studies,[3] in Sir Arthur Evans's excavations of the ruins of Cretan Knossos,[4] in the deciphering by Michael Ventris[5] of some of the writings discovered there, and in the recent excavations at Çatal Hüyük[6] and surrounding areas in Anatolia, "the scholarly world" is not rushing to investigate the "well-nigh inexhaustible material for thought." Consider too that only about half of Bachofen's original work has been available in English translation.

The excerpt presented here has been taken from Bachofen's introduction to *Mother Right*. The introduction was selected rather than the body of the work because it gives a systematic presentation of his thesis, with occasional illustrative allusions. The material has been considerably abridged and condensed in the interest of brevity and of relevance to the purposes of this book. The English translation is now available in paperback.

An Investigation of the Religious and Juridical Character of Matriarchy in the Ancient World

The present work deals with a historical phenomenon which few have observed and no one has investigated in its full scope. Up until now archaeologists have had nothing to say of mother right. The term is new and the family situation it designates unknown. The subject is extremely attractive, but it also raises great difficulties. The most elementary spadework remains to be done, for the culture period to which mother right pertains has never been seriously studied. Thus we are entering upon virgin territory.

We find ourselves carried back to times antedating classical antiquity, to an older world of ideas totally different from those with which we are familiar. Leaving the nations we commonly

From *Myth, Religion, and Mother Right*, by J. J. Bachofen, translated by Ralph Manheim, Bollingen Series LXXXIV (copyright © 1967 by Bollingen Foundation), reprinted by permission of Princeton University Press: selections from pp. 69–120.

associate with the glory of the ancient world, we find ourselves among peoples who never achieved the level of classical culture. An unknown world opens before our eyes, and the more we learn of it, the stranger it seems. Everything contrasts with the idea of a highly developed culture; everywhere we find older conceptions, an independent way of life that can only be judged according to its own fundamental law. The matriarchal organization of the family seems strange in the light not only of modern but also of classical ideas. And the more primitive way of life to which it pertains, from which it arose, and through which alone it can be explained, seems very strange beside the Hellenic. The main purpose of the following pages is to set forth the moving principle of the matriarchal age, and to give its proper place in relationship both to the lower stages of development and to the higher levels of culture. Thus the scope of this work is far broader than its title indicates. I propose to investigate all aspects of matriarchal culture, to disclose its diverse traits and the fundamental idea which unites them. In this way I hope to restore the picture of a cultural stage which was overlaid or totally destroyed by the later development of the ancient world. This is an ambitious undertaking. But it is only by broadening our horizon that we can achieve true understanding and carry scientific thinking to that clarity and completeness which are the very essence of knowledge.

And now I shall attempt a general survey of my ideas, which, I believe, will facilitate the study of the work itself.

Of all records relating and pertaining to mother right, those concerning the Lycian people are the clearest and most valuable. The Lycians, Herodotus[1] reports, did not name their children after their fathers like the Hellenes, but exclusively after their mothers; in their genealogical records they dealt entirely with the maternal line, and the status of children was defined solely in accordance with that of the mother. Nicolaus of Damascus[2] completes this testimony by telling us that only the daughters possessed the right of inheritance, and traces this institution back to the Lycian common law, the unwritten law which, as defined by Socrates, was handed down by the godhead itself. All these customs are manifestations of one and the same basic conception. Although Herodotus regards them merely as an odd deviation from Hellenic customs, closer observation must lead to a deeper view. We find not disorder but system, not fancy but necessity. And since it is

expressly denied that these customs were influenced by any
positive body of legislation, the hypothesis of a meaningless
anomaly loses its last shred of justification. We find, then, side by
side with the Hellenic-Roman father principle, a family organization which differs diametrically both in its foundation and in its
development, as a comparison of the two clearly shows. This
opinion is confirmed by the discovery of related conceptions among
other peoples. The limitation of the right of inheritance to the
daughters among the Lycians finds a parallel in the obligation
(recorded by Diodorus for Egypt) of the daughters alone to provide
for aged parents. And in line with the same basic conception
Strabo[3] reports that among the Cantabri the sisters provided their
brothers with dowries.

All these traits join to form a single picture and lead to the
conclusion that mother right is not confined to any particular
people but marks a cultural stage. In view of the universal qualities
of human nature, this cultural stage cannot be restricted to any
particular ethnic family. And consequently what must concern us is
not so much the similarities between isolated phenomena as the
unity of the basic conception. Polybius'[4] passage about the
matriarchal genealogy of the hundred noble families among the
Epizephyrian Locrians suggests two further observations which
have been confirmed in the course of our investigation: (1) mother
right belongs to a cultural period preceding that of the patriarchal
system; (2) it began to decline only with the victorious development of the paternal system. The matriarchal forms are observed
chiefly among the pre-Hellenic peoples and are an essential
component of this archaic culture, upon which they set their
imprint as much as do patriarchal forms upon Greek culture.

The principles which we have here deduced from a few
observations are confirmed in the course of our investigation by an
abundance of data. The Locrians lead us to the Leleges, Carians,
Aetolians, Pelasgians, Caucones, Arcadians, Epeians, Minyae, and
Teleboeans, who furnish a diversified picture of mother right and
the culture based on it. The prestige of womanhood among these
peoples was a source of astonishment to the ancients, and gives
them all, regardless of individual coloration, a character of archaic
sublimity that stands in striking contrast to Hellenic culture. Here
we discern the basic idea from which sprang the genealogical

system set forth in the Hesiodic *Eoiai* and "Catalogues,"[5] the unions of immortal mothers wedded to mortal fathers, the emphasis on maternal property and the name of the maternal line, the closeness of maternal kinship, which gave rise to the term "mother country," the appellation "motherland," the greater sanctity of female sacrifices, and the inexpiability of matricide.

In these prefatory remarks, concerned not with individual data but with general perspectives, we must stress the importance of the mythical tradition for our investigation. In view of the central position of mother right among the earliest Greek peoples, we may expect this system to be reflected in myth. And accordingly this oldest form of tradition becomes an important source for our knowledge of matriarchal institutions. The question therefore arises: What importance may we impute to this primordial form of human tradition, and what use are we justified in making of its testimony? The answer to this question is provided by a single example drawn from Lycian mythology.

The maternal transmission of inheritance is attested for this sphere not only by the purely historical account of Herodotus but also by the mythical history of the Lycian kings. Not the sons of Sarpedon, but Laodamia, his daughter, is entitled to his heritage, and she passes the kingdom on to her son, to the exclusion of his uncles. A story recorded by Eustathius[6] gives this system of inheritance a symbolic expression, disclosing the basic idea of mother right in all its sensuous sexuality. If the reports of Herodotus and of Nicolaus had been lost, those who hold the prevailing view would have attempted to discredit Eustathius' story on the ground that its authenticity could not be supported by any older, not to mention contemporaneous sources; they would have argued that its cryptic character indicated invention by some foolish mythographer. They would have said, not that the myth had formed around the fact like a shell, but on the contrary, that the fact had been abstracted from the myth. They would have set it down as worthless rubbish and relegated it to the discard pile whose steady growth marks the destructive progress of the so-called "critical" approach to mythology. But comparison of the myth and the historical account shows the fallacy of this entire method. Tested by historically established truths, the mythical tradition is seen to be an authentic, independent record of the primordial age, a record in which invention plays no part. The preference of Laodamia over her brothers must then be taken as adequate proof that mother right prevailed in Lycia.

There is scarcely a feature of the matriarchal system that cannot be documented in this way, although the parallels cannot always be taken from one and the same people. In fact, we have such parallels even for the general picture of matriarchal culture; and the reason is that mother right was preserved at least partially down to relatively recent times. Both the mythical and the strictly historical traditions present very similar pictures of the system. Products of archaic and of much later periods show such an astonishing accord that we almost forget the long interval between the times when they originated. This parallelism proves the value of the mythical tradition and shows that the attitude of present-day scholarship toward it is untenable. Precisely in regard to the most important aspect of history, namely, the knowledge of ancient ideas and institutions, the already shaky distinction between historic and prehistoric times loses its last shred of justification.

Our question has been answered: the mythical tradition may be taken as a faithful reflection of the life of those times in which historical antiquity is rooted. It is a manifestation of primordial thinking, an immediate historical revelation, and consequently a highly reliable historical source. . . .

There is still another reason why myth demonstrates the authenticity of mother right. The contrast between mythical conceptions and those of subsequent days is so marked that where more recent ideas prevailed, it would not have been possible to invent the phenomena of matriarchy. The older system represented an utter puzzle to the patriarchal mind, which consequently could not have conceived any part of it. Hellenic thought could not possibly have fabricated Laodamia's priority, for it is in diametric opposition to such a conception. The same is true of the innumerable vestiges of matriarchal form woven into the prehistory of all ancient peoples—not excluding Athens and Rome, two most resolute advocates of paternity. The thinking and literature of any period unconsciously follow the laws of its life form. So great is the power of such laws that the natural tendency is always to set the new imprint on the divergent features of former times.

The matriarchal traditions did not escape this fate. We shall encounter some very surprising phenomena produced by the impact of late conceptions on the vestiges of older views and by the weakness which led some writers to replace the incomprehensible by what was comprehensible from the standpoint of their own culture. Old features are overlaid by new ones, the venerable figures of the matriarchal past are introduced to contemporaries in forms consonant with the spirit of the new period, harsh features are presented in a softened light; institutions, attitudes, motives, passions are reappraised from a contemporary point of view. Not infrequently new and old occur together; or the same fact, the same person, may appear in two versions, one prescribed by the earlier, one by the later world; one innocent, one criminal; one full of nobility and dignity, one an object of horror and the subject of a palinode. In other cases the mother gives way to the father, the sister to the brother, who now takes her place in the legend or alternates with her, while the feminine name is replaced by a masculine one. In a word, maternal conceptions cede to the requirements of patriarchal theory.

Thus, far from writing in the spirit of a surpassed, vanished culture, the later age will endeavor to extend the rule of its own ideas to ideas and facts that are alien to it. And this circumstance frequently guarantees the authenticity of the mythical vestiges of the matriarchal age, lending them the force of reliable proof. But where it has succumbed to later influence, myth becomes still more instructive. Since the changes usually result from the unconscious action of the new ideas, and only in exceptional cases from conscious hostility to the old, the legend becomes in its transformations a living expression of the stages in a people's development, and for the skillful observer, a faithful reflection of all the periods in the life of that people. . . .

Since the beginning of all development lies in myth, myth must form the starting point for any serious investigation of ancient history. Myth contains the origins, and myth alone can reveal them. It is the origins which determine the subsequent development, which define its character and direction. Without knowledge of the origins, the science of history can come to no conclusion. . . . The forms of family organization prevailing in the times known to us are not original forms, but the consequences of earlier stages. . . . The strictness of the Roman patriarchal system points to an earlier system that had to be combatted and suppressed. And the same applies to the paternal system of Athens, the city of Athene, motherless daughter of Zeus. With all its Apollonian purity, it too represents the peak of a development, the first stages of which must have belonged to a world characterized by entirely different ideas and institutions. . . .

In the matriarchal culture the homogeneity of a dominant idea is particularly apparent. All its manifestations are of one mold, disclosing a self-contained stage in the development of the human spirit. The primacy of motherhood in the family cannot be regarded as an isolated phenomenon. It is utterly incompatible with a culture such as that of the Greek classical period. The opposition between the paternal and maternal systems is bound to permeate the entire life form surrounding them.

This homogeneity of matriarchal ideas is confirmed by the favoring of the left over the right side. The left side belongs to the passive feminine principle, the right to the active masculine principle. The role played by the left hand of Isis in matriarchal Egypt suffices to make the connection clear. But a multitude of additional data prove its importance, universality, primordiality, and freedom from the influence of philosophical speculation. Customs and practices of civil and religious life, peculiarities of clothing and headdress, and certain linguistic usages reveal the same idea, the *major honos laevarum partium* (greater honor of the left side) and its close connection with mother right. Another no less significant manifestation of the same basic law is the primacy of the night over the day which issued from its womb. The opposite relation would be in direct contradiction to matriarchal ideas. Already the ancients identified the primacy of the night with that of the left, and both of these with the primacy of the mother. And here, too, age-old customs, the reckoning of time according to nights, the choice of the night as a time for battle, for taking counsel, for meting out justice, and for practicing the cult rites, show that we are not dealing with abstract philosophical ideas of later origin, but with the reality of an original mode of life. Extension of the same idea permits us to recognize the religious preference given to the moon over the sun, of the conceiving earth over the fecundating sea, of the dark aspect of death over the luminous aspect of growth, of the dead over the living, of mourning over rejoicing, as necessary characteristics of the predominantly matriarchal age. In the course of our investigation all these traits will appear many times over and take on an increasingly profound meaning.

. . . A gentle hint from the ancients often suffices to open up new insights. An example may be found in the favored position of the sister and of the youngest child. Both notions are aspects of the matriarchal principle and both demonstrate new ramfications of the basic idea. The significance of sisterhood among the Germanic people is disclosed by an observation of Tacitus,[7] and a corresponding statement from Plutarch[8] about Roman customs proves that this is no accidental local notion, but a consistent and fundamental idea. . . . The favoring of the sister over the brother merely lends new expression to the favoring of the daughter over the son, and the preference given to the youngest child identifies the survival of the clan with the youngest scion of the maternal line, who, because he is last born, will also be last to die.

. . . The greater love for the sister leads us into one of the noblest aspects of matriarchal culture. Hitherto we have stressed the juridical aspect of mother right, but now we perceive its ethical significance. . . . At the lowest, darkest stages of human existence the love between the mother and her offspring is the bright spot in life, the only light in the moral darkness, the only joy amid profound misery. . . . The close relation between child and father, the son's self-sacrifice for his begetter, require a far higher degree of moral development than mother love, that mysterious power which equally permeates all earthly creatures. Paternal love appears later. The relationship which stands at the origin of all culture, of every virtue, of every nobler aspect of existence, is that between mother and child; it operates in a world of violence as the divine principle of love, of union, of peace. Raising her young, the woman learns earlier than the man to extend her loving care beyond the limits of the ego to another creature, and to direct whatever gift of invention she possesses to the preservation and improvement of this other's existence. Woman at this stage is the repository of all culture, of all benevolence, of all devotion, of all concern for the living and grief for the dead.

Myth and history express this idea in any number of ways. The Cretan expressed his love for the land of his birth by the term "mother country"; origin in a common womb is regarded as the closest bond, as the true and originally the only relation of kinship;

to help, to protect, and to avenge the mother is seen as the highest duty, while to threaten her life is looked upon as a crime beyond all expiation, even if it is done in the service of offended fatherhood.

. . . Whereas the paternal principle is inherently restrictive, the maternal principle is universal; the paternal principle implies limitation to definite groups, but the maternal principle, like the life of nature, knows no barriers. The idea of motherhood produces a sense of universal fraternity among all men, which dies with the development of paternity. The family based on father right is a closed individual organism, whereas the matriarchal family bears the typically universal character that stands at the beginning of all development and distinguishes material life from higher spiritual life. Every woman's womb, the mortal image of the earth mother Demeter, will give brothers and sisters to the children of every other woman; the homeland will know only brothers and sisters until the day when the development of the paternal system dissolves the undifferentiated unity of the mass and introduces a principle of articulation.

The matriarchal cultures present many expressions and even juridical formulations of this aspect of the maternal principle. It is the basis of the universal freedom and equality so frequent among matriarchal peoples, of their hospitality, and of their aversion to restrictions of all sorts. . . . And in it is rooted the admirable sense of kinship and συμπάθεια (fellow feeling) which knows no barriers or dividing lines and embraces all members of a nation alike. Matriarchal states were particularly famed for their freedom from intestine strife and conflict. The great festivals where all sections of a nation delighted in a sense of brotherhood and common nationality were first introduced among these peoples, and here achieved their finest expression. The matriarchal peoples—and this is no less characteristic—assigned special culpability to the physical injury of one's fellow men or even of animals. The Roman women entreated the Great Mother to provide a husband not for their own but for their sisters' children; the Persians never prayed to the godhead except for the whole nation; the Carians saw the supreme virtue in συμπάθεια [sympathy] for one's kin: in all these traits we find the maternal principle translated into the reality of life. An air of tender humanity, discernible even in the facial expression of Egyptian statuary, permeates the culture of the matriarchal world. And now an aura of Saturnian innocence seems to surround that older race of men who, subordinating their whole existence to the law of motherhood, provided later generations with the main features of their picture of the silver age. How natural we now find Hesiod's world, with its dominant mother lavishing eternal loving care on an ever dependent son who, growing more physically than spiritually, lives beside his mother to a ripe old age, enjoying the peace and abundance of an agricultural life; how close it is to the pictures of a lost happiness which always center round the dominance of motherhood, and to those ἀρχαῖα φῦλα γυναικῶν (primordial race of women) with whom all peace vanished from the earth. Here the historicity of myth finds a surprising confirmation. All the free fancy and poetic ornament in which memory always shrouds itself has been powerless to eradicate the historic core of the tradition, to efface the salient feature and meaning of this earlier life. . . .

From the standpoint of the Roman patriarchate the appearance of the Sabine women in the midst of the battle line was as inexplicable as the genuinely matriarchal form of the Sabine treaty, which Plutarch[9] unquestionably took from Varro. But if we consider them in conjunction with similar phenomena as recorded both in the ancient world and among still living peoples of a lower cultural stage, and in relation to the basic idea of mother right, they cease to puzzle us. They emerge from the realm of poetic invention to which modern opinion has relegated them and take their place as historical reality, as a perfectly natural consequence of the nobility, inviolability, and religious consecration of motherhood. Hannibal's pact with the Gauls stipulated that all disputes were to be settled by the Gallic matrons; and there are innumerable mythical traditions concerning women who either singly or in groups, alone or in collaboration with the men, mete out justice, participate in popular assemblies, and arbitrate peace treaties; who sacrifice their children and lay down their own lives to save their country. . . .

The religious foundation of matriarchy discloses this system in its noblest form, links it with the highest aspects of life, and gives a profound insight into the dignity of that primordial era which Hellenism excelled only in outward radiance, not in depth and loftiness of conception. . . .

. . . There is only one mighty lever of all civilization, and that is religion. Every rise and every decline of human existence springs from a movement that originates in this supreme sphere. Without it no aspect of ancient life is intelligible, and earliest times in particular remain an impenetrable riddle. Wholly dominated by its faith, mankind in this stage links every form of existence, every historical tradition, to the basic religious idea, sees every event in a religious light, and identifies itself completely with its gods. If especially matriarchate must bear this hieratic imprint, it is because of the essential feminine nature, that profound sense of the divine presence which, merging with the feeling of love, lends woman, and particularly the mother, a religious devotion that is most active in the most barbarous times. The elevation of woman over man arouses our amazement most especially by its contradiction to the relation of physical strength. The law of nature confers the scepter of power on the stronger. If it is torn away from him by feebler hands, other aspects of human nature must have been at work, deeper powers must have made their influence felt.

We scarcely need the help of ancient witnesses to realize what power had most to do with this victory. At all times woman has exerted a great influence on men and on the education and culture of nations through her inclination toward the supernatural and divine, the irrational and miraculous. . . . In innumerable cases woman was the repository of the first revelation, and women played the most active part in the propagation of most religions, sometimes engaging in active warfare and often employing their physical charms. Prophecy began with women; woman is more steadfast than man as a keeper of religion, she is "stiffer in the faith"; though physically weaker, woman is capable at times of rising far above man. . . . Endowed with such powers, the weaker sex can take up the struggle with the stronger and emerge triumphant. To man's superior physical strength woman opposes the mighty influence of her religious consecration; she counters violence with peace, enmity with conciliation, hate with love; and thus she guides the wild, lawless existence of the earliest period toward a milder, friendlier culture, in whose center she sits enthroned as the embodiment of the higher principle, as the manifestation of the divine commandment. Herein lies the magic power of the feminine figure, which disarms the wildest passions and parts battle lines, which makes woman the sacrosanct prophetess and judge, and in all things gives her will the prestige of supreme law. The almost divine veneration of Arete, queen of the

Phaeacians, the sanctity in which her word was held, are regarded by so early a writer as Eustathius[10] as poetic touches in a wholly invented fairy tale; and yet they are no isolated manifestation, but rather the perfect expression of a matriarchy resting wholly on a religious foundation, with all the blessings and beauty it could confer upon a nation's existence.

We have numerous indications of the intimate connection between matriarchy and woman's religious character. Among the Locrians only a maiden could enact the rite of the φιαληφορία (bearing of the sacrificial bowl). In citing this custom as the proof that mother right prevailed among the Epizephyrians, Polybius[11] recognized its connection with the basic matriarchal idea. Moreover, the Locrians sacrificed a maiden in expiation of Ajax's sacrilege. This confirms the same relation and indicates the basis of the widespread belief that female sacrifices are more pleasing to the godhead. And this line of thought carries us to the deepest foundation and meaning of the matriarchal idea. Traced back to the prototype of Demeter, the earthly mother becomes the mortal representative of the primordial tellurian mother, her priestess and hierophant, entrusted with the administration of her mystery. This religious primacy of motherhood leads to a primacy of the mortal woman. . . .

These considerations bring new insight into the cultural stage characterized by matriarchy. We are faced with the essential greatness of the pre-Hellenic culture: in the Demetrian mystery and the religious and civil primacy of womanhood it possessed the seed of noble achievement which was suppressed and often destroyed by later developments. The barbarity of the Pelasgian world, the incompatibility of matriarchy with a noble way of life, the late origin of the mysterious element in religion—such traditional opinions are dethroned once and for all. . . .

Hellenism is hostile to such a world. The primacy of motherhood vanishes, and its consequences with it. The patriarchal development stresses a completely different aspect of human nature, which is reflected in entirely different social forms and ideas. In Egypt Herodotus finds the direct antithesis to Greek, and particularly Attic, civilization. Compared to his Hellenic surroundings, Egypt struck him as a world upside down. . . . For Egypt is the land of stereotyped matriarchy, its whole culture is built essentially on the mother cult, on the primacy of Isis over Osiris. . . .

. . . We began by showing matriarchy to be a universal phenomenon, independent of any special dogma or legislation. . . .

. . . Matriarchy is followed by patriarchy and preceded by unregulated hetaerism. . . .

. . . The exclusivity of the marriage bond seems so essential to the nobility and higher calling of human nature that most writers accept it as an original state of affairs, and regard the theory that it was preceded by lower, unregulated sexual relations as an absurd fallacy arising from useless speculation about the beginnings of human existence. . . . But the testimony of history forbids us to heed the voices of pride and self-love. It cannot be doubted that the institution of marriage was the outgrowth of a very slow progress. . . . The observations of the ancients join with those of later generations, and even in our own times contact with peoples of lower cultural levels lends empirical confirmation to this tradition. . . . There is no doubt that matriarchy everywhere grew out of woman's conscious, continued resistance to the debasing state of hetaerism. Defenseless against abuse by men, and according to an Arabian tradition preserved by Strabo, exhausted by their lusts, woman was first to feel the need for regulated conditions and a purer ethic, while men, conscious of their superior physical strength, accepted the new constraint only unwillingly. . . .

. . . A bitter surprise is in store for those who look on marriage as a necessary and primordial state. The ancients held exactly the reverse, they regarded the Demetrian principle as an infringement on an older principle and marriage as an offense against a religious commandment. . . . How else shall we explain the idea that marriage demanded propitiation of the godhead whose law it transgressed by its exclusivity? Woman is not endowed with all her charms in order to grow old in the arms of one man: the law of matter rejects all restrictions, abhors all fetters, and regards exclusivity as an offense against its divinity. This accounts for the hetaeric practices surrounding marriage. Diverse in form, they are perfectly homogeneous in idea. Marriage as a deviation from the natural law of matter must be expiated, the good will of the godhead regained through a period of hetaerism. Hetaerism and strict conjugal law—these two principles that would seem forever to exclude one another—now enter into the closest connection:

prostitution itself becomes a pledge of marital chastity, which exacts a previous fulfillment of woman's natural vocation. . . .

. . . The sacrifice which was first performed annually is later enacted but once; originally practiced by matrons, hetaerism is now restricted to young girls; it is practiced no longer during but only before marriage, and even then it is no longer promiscuous but narrowed down to certain selected persons. . . . All these phases of development have left numerous traces, not only in myth but also in the history of widely divergent nations. . . .

. . . All great nature goddesses, in whom the generative power of matter has assumed a name and a personal form, combine the two levels of maternity, the lower, purely natural stage, and the higher, conjugally regulated stage. . . .

. . . The first great encounter between the Asiatic and Greek worlds is represented as a struggle between the hetaerism of Aphrodite and the conjugal principle of Hera; we shall find the cause of the Trojan War in a violation of the marriage bed; and by an extension of the same idea, we shall date the ultimate defeat of Aphrodite, mother of the Aeneads, by the matronly Juno at the time of the Second Punic War, when the Roman nation was at the height of its inner greatness.

[Bachofen postulates a backtracking to hetaerism in the Dionysian cults, countered by a period of Amazonism, which represents a fierce female struggle against Dionysian manifestations.]

In my exposition of the various stages of the maternal principle and the conflicts between them I have repeatedly mentioned the Amazonian extreme of matriarchy and hinted at the important role played by this phenomenon in the history of the relation between the sexes. . . .

In speaking of the Amazon Omphale, Clearchus[12] remarks that wherever such an intensification of feminine power occurs, it presupposes a previous degradation of woman and must be explained by the necessary succession of extremes. This idea is confirmed by several of the most celebrated myths, the deeds of the women of Lemnos,[13] of the Danaids, even Clytaemnestra's murder. Everywhere it is an assault on woman's rights which provokes her resistance, which inspires self-defense followed by bloody vengeance. In accordance with this law grounded in human and particularly in feminine nature, hetaerism must necessarily lead to

Amazonism. Degraded by man's abuse, it is woman who first yearns for a more secure position and a purer life. The sense of degradation and fury of despair spur her on to armed resistance, exalting her to that warlike grandeur which, though it seems to exceed the bounds of womanhood, is rooted simply in her need for a higher life.

Two conclusions follow from this conception, and both are confirmed by history. First, Amazonism is a universal phenomenon. It is not based on the special physical or historical circumstances of any particular people, but on conditions that are characteristic of all human existence. And it shares this character of universality with hetaerism. The same cause everywhere calls forth the same result. Amazonian phenomena are interwoven with the origins of all peoples. They may be found from Central Asia to the Occident, from the Scythian north to West Africa; beyond the ocean they are no less numerous and no less certain; and even in times very close to our own Amazonism has been observed, accompanied by the same acts of bloody vengeance against the male sex. In accordance with the law of human nature, it is precisely the earliest phases of human development that disclose the most typical and universal character.

The second conclusion is that Amazonism, despite its savage degeneration, signifies an appreciable rise in human culture. A regression and perversion at later cultural stages, it is, in its first appearance, a step forward toward a purer form of life, and not only a necessary stage of human development, but one that is beneficial in its consequences. . . . the Amazonian form of life is an earlier manifestation than conjugal matriarchy, and is in fact a preparation for it. This is made clear in the Lycian myth which represents Bellerophon both as the conqueror of the Amazons and as the founder of matriarchy, and by virtue of these two deeds as the founder of his country's whole civilization. . . .

The destinies of the states growing out of these conquests confirm our interpretation and lend coherence to the history of the matriarchal world. Mythical and historical traditions complement and support one another, permitting us to discern a succession of interrelated stages. After war and warlike undertakings the victorious warriors settle down, build cities, and engage in agriculture. From the banks of the Nile to the shores of the Black Sea, from Central Asia to Italy, Amazonian names and deeds are interwoven with the history of the founding of cities which later became famous. To be sure, this transition from nomadism to domestic settlement is a necessary part of human development, but it is particularly in keeping with the feminine nature and occurs most quickly where the influence of women is paramount. The observation of still living peoples has shown that human societies are impelled toward agriculture chiefly by the efforts of women, while the men tend to resist this change. Countless ancient traditions support this same historical fact: women put an end to the nomadic life by burning the ships; women gave most cities their names, and, as in Rome or in Elis, women inaugurated the first apportionment of the land. In bringing about fixed settlement, womanhood fulfills its natural vocation.

All civilization and culture are essentially grounded in the establishment and adornment of the hearth. By a perfectly consistent continuation of the same development, life takes more peaceful forms and warfare ceases to be the principal occupation of the group. The exercise of arms was never wholly relinquished by the women of matriarchal states, who could not but regard it as indispensable for the defense of their position at the head of warlike peoples, and their preoccupation with horses is reflected even in relatively late religious iconography. Soon, however, where warfare did not become the exclusive business of men, they came at least to share it. Sometimes the male armies marched along with the equestrian women; and sometimes, as in the case of the Mysian Hiera,[14] the order was reversed.

Yet despite this gradual change in forms, woman's domination of state and family long remained undiminished. But even here a progressive shift was inevitable. Step by step the matriarchy was restricted. This development took divergent forms. Sometimes it is woman's political power that was first lost, and sometimes her rule over the family. In Lycia we are informed only of her family position; no record of her political power has come down to us, although we know that it was also inherited according to mother right. Elsewhere, conversely, the political power remained either wholly or partly in the hands of the women, whereas the family ceased to be governed by mother right. Those elements of the old system that were indissolubly bound up with religion were longest to resist the spirit of the times, protected by the higher sanction that attached to everything connected with the cult. But other factors played a part. The geographical isolation of the Lycians and Epizephyrians; the topography and climate of Egypt and of Africa in general, helped to preserve the matriarchy. Elsewhere the political matriarchy was protected by its very weakness, or bolstered by artificial forms, such as are indicated by imputing the origin of letter writing to Asiatic queens confined to the interior of their palaces.[15]

In conjunction with these fragments of what was once an all-embracing system, the reports of Chinese writers on the women's state in Central Asia, which preserved both political and social matriarchy down to the eighth century of our era, take on a very special interest. They accord in all characteristic features with the ancient reports on the Amazonian states, and their praise of the general εὐνομία [order] and tranquility supports my own findings. It was not violence such as early destroyed most of the Amazonian settlements, including the Italic settlement of the Cleitae, that put an end to this existence. It was the quiet workings of time and contact with the powerful neighbor states that here effaced a social condition which for European man represents one of the oldest and obscurest of memories, and even today must be regarded as a forgotten aspect of history. . . .

The progress from the maternal to the paternal conception of man forms the most important turning point in the history of the relations between the sexes. The Demetrian and the Aphroditean-hetaeric stages both hold to the primacy of generative motherhood, and it is only the greater or lesser purity of its interpretation that distinguishes the two forms of existence. But with the transition to the paternal system occurs a change in fundamental principle; the older conception is wholly surpassed. An entirely new attitude makes itself felt. The mother's connection with the child is based on a material relationship, it is accessible to sense perception and remains always a natural truth. But the father as begetter presents an entirely different aspect. Standing in no visible relation to the child, he can never, even in the marital relation, cast off a certain fictive character. Belonging to the offspring only through the mediation of the mother, he always appears as the remoter potency. . . .

All these attributes of fatherhood lead to one conclusion: the triumph of paternity brings with it the liberation of the spirit from the manifestations of nature, a sublimation of human existence over the laws of material life. . . . Maternity pertains to the physical side of man, the only thing he shares with the animals: the paternal-spiritual principle belongs to him alone. Here he breaks through the bonds of tellurism and lifts his eyes to the higher regions of the cosmos. Triumphant paternity partakes of the heavenly light, while childbearing motherhood is bound up with the earth that bears all things. . . .

Myth takes this view of the conflict between the old and the new principle in the matricide of Orestes and Alcmaeon. . . . In the adventures of Orestes we find a reflection of the upheavals and struggles leading to the triumph of paternity over the chthonian-maternal principle. Whatever influence we may impute to poetic fancy, there is historical truth in the struggle between the two principles as set forth by Aeschylus and Euripides. The old law is that of the Erinyes, according to which Orestes is guilty and his mother's blood inexpiable; but Apollo and Athene usher in the victory as a new law; that of the higher paternity and of the heavenly light. This is no dialectical opposition but a historical struggle, and the gods themselves decide its outcome. The old era dies, and another, the Apollonian age, rises on its ruins. A new ethos is in preparation, diametrically opposed to the old one. The divinity of the mother gives way to that of the father, the night cedes its primacy to the day, the left side to the right, and it is only in their contrast that the character of the two stages stands out sharply. The Pelasgian culture derives its stamp from its emphasis on maternity, Hellenism is inseparable from the patriarchal view. . . . the old limits of existence are burst, the striving and suffering Promethean life takes the place of perpetual rest, peaceful enjoyment, and eternal childhood in an aging body. . . . the source of immortality is no longer the child-bearing woman but the male-creative principle, which he endows with the divinity that the earlier world imputed only to the mother.

It is assuredly the Attic race that carried the Zeus character of paternity to its highest development. Though Athens itself has its roots in the Pelasgian culture, it wholly subordinated the Demetrian to the Apollonian principle in the course of its development. The Athenians revered Theseus as a second woman-hating Hercules; in the person of Athene they set motherless paternity in the place of fatherless maternity; and even in their legislation they endowed the universal principle of paternity with a character of inviolability which the old law of the Erinyes imputed only to motherhood. The virgin goddess is well disposed to the masculine, helpful to the heroes of the paternal solar law; in her, the warlike Amazonism of the old day reappears in spiritual form. Her city is hostile to the women who moor their ships on the coasts of Attica in search of help in defending the rights of their sex. Here the opposition between the Apollonian and the Demetrian principle stands out sharply. This city, whose earliest history discloses traces of matriarchal conditions, carried paternity to its highest development; and in one-sided exaggeration it condemned woman to a status of inferiority particularly surprising in its contrast to the foundations of the Eleusinian mysteries.

[Bachofen sets forth his conception of the struggle between the Greek Apollonian striving for male domination and the Oriental adherence to the feminine principle, culminating in the ultimate usurpation of power by the paternal principle.]

. . . Mankind owes the enduring victory of paternity to the Roman political idea, which gave it a strict juridical form and consequently enabled it to develop in all spheres of existence; it made this principle the foundation of all life and safeguarded it against the decadence of religion, the corruption of manners, and a popular return to matriarchal views. Roman law maintained its traditional principle against all the assaults and threats of the Orient, against the spreading mother cult of Isis and Cybele, and even against the Dionysian mystery; it withstood the principle of feminine fertility, first introduced into legislation by Augustus; it withstood the influence of the imperial wives and mothers who, scorning the old Roman spirit, sought, not without success, to seize the *fasces* (rods, the juridical power) and the *signa* (insignia, military power); it held firm against Justinian's inclination toward the wholly natural view of the sexual relation, toward equal rights for women, and toward the veneration of childbearing motherhood. Even in the Orient it was able to combat with success the never fully extinguished resistance to the Roman deprecation of the feminine principle. . . .

. . . A historical investigation which must be the first to gather, verify, and collate all its material, must everywhere stress the particular and only gradually progress to comprehensive ideas. . . . The entire material is arranged according to nations;

these supply our supreme principle of classification. Each section opens with a consideration of the most significant records. . . . Each nation that enters the sphere of our investigation provides the over-all picture and history of gynocracy with new facets and sheds new light on aspects formerly neglected. . . . The present book makes no other claim than to provide the scholarly world with a new and well-nigh inexhaustible material for thought. If it has the power to stimulate, it will gladly content itself with the modest position of a preparatory work, and cheerfully accept the common fate of all first attempts, namely, to be disparaged by posterity and judged only on the basis of its shortcomings.

[The body of the English translation of Bachofen's work addresses itself to presenting his evidence in detail of mother right in ancient Lycia, Athens, Lemnos, Egypt, India, and Lesbos.]

NOTES

1. Herodotus. *The Histories*. Ed. and tr. A. D. Godley. LCL,° 1921–24, 4 vols., 1. 173.

2. Müller, Carl and Theodor (ed.). *Fragmenta Historicorum Graecorum*. Paris, 1841–84, Vol. 3, p. 461.

3. Strabo. *Geography*. Ed. and tr. H. L. Jones, LCL, 1917–32, 34. 18.

4. Polybius. *History*. Ed. and tr. W. R. Paton. LCL, 1922–27, 12. 5. 4.

5. Poems of Hesiod, now lost except for some fragments, which dealt with the mythical and legendary genealogy of the Greek peoples.

6. Eustathius. *Commentarii ad Homeri Iliadem et Odysseam*. Leipzig, 1825–28. 12. 1. 101, 894 (Vol. 3, p. 100).

7. Tacitus, Cornelius. *Germania*. Ed. and tr. William Peterson and Maurice Hutton. LCL, 1914, 20.

8. Plutarch. *Moralia*. Ed. and tr. F. C. Babbitt and others, LCL, 1927, Vol. 4: *Quaestiones Romanae*. 17. 267.

9. Ibid., 85. 284.

10. Eustathius. *Commentarii ad Homeri Iliadem et Odysseam*. Leipzig, 1825–28. 7. 11. 50, 148 ff., 1567, 1575 (Vol. 5, pp. 259, 270).

11. Polybius. *History*. Ed. and tr. W. R. Paton. LCL, 1922–27, 12. 5. 9–11.

12. Müller, Carl and Theodor (ed.). *Fragmenta Historicorum Graecorum*. Paris, 1841–84, Vol. 2, p. 305; Athenaeus, *The Deipnosophists*. Ed. and tr. Charles Burton Gulick. LCL, 1927–41, 12. 515e–516.

13. Here Bachofen refers to a later passage in his book which relates how the Lemnian women, enraged because their men preferred captive maidens, murdered their fathers and husbands. Of the Lemnian matriarchy Bachofen writes: "Warfare removes the men for long periods from home and family, so that the domination of the women becomes a necessity. The mother cares for the children, tills the field, rules over the house and servants, and when necessary takes up arms to defend her hearth and home. The exercise of this domination,

° Loeb Classical Library, London and Cambridge, Mass. (or New York.)

combined with her skill in handling weapons, increases the woman's sense of dignity and power. She towers high above the man, and the physical beauty which distinguishes the women of the matriarchal states, and particularly of Lemnos, reflects the prestige of her position."—Ed.

14. Hiera, according to Philostratus, *Heroicus* (Kayser, 299.30f.) was wife of Telephus, king of Mysia, and fought at Troy as leader of the Mysian women troops; Homer, he says, does not mention her because she was the greatest and fairest of all women, and would have outshone his heroine Helen.

15. Bachofen here refers to Atossa, the mother of Xerxes, who is credited by some late authors with the invention of letter writing. See *Mutterrecht* (in Gesammelte Werke, Vol. 3, p. 976).—Ed.

ELIZA BURT GAMBLE (1841–1920)

While preparing *The Evolution of Woman* (excerpted in Part 1), Gamble amassed a wealth of information relative to the foundations of religious belief and worship. She concluded that sex was the fundamental fact in the construction of a god, which was originally conceived of as female and which assumed male attributes as man gained ascendancy. Gamble maintains that the male priesthood usurped the position of the earlier universal female Deity, even appropriating female titles in transforming the Deity into a male. She also presents evidence of the concealment through the ages of information regarding the female principle in the Deity.

The God-Idea of the Ancients presents the provocative thesis that all religions derive from the same early conception of a Deity, with many similarities retained and many variations developed. With a wealth of illustrative detail she gathers together common elements in religions all over the globe, such as the triune Deity, the coming of a Saviour with the winter solstice, the Virgin Mother and Child, the rebirth of the beneficent Saviour and renewer of life in the springtime, the Tree of Life, and the doctrine of a cyclical catastrophe like a flood or a conflagration, followed by a rebirth and renewal of the world.

In her recognition of the striking similarities of beliefs and practices in religions all over the world and throughout history, Gamble anticipated many of the conclusions of later investigators, such as Robert Briffault,[1] Erich Neumann,[2] and Raphael Patai.[3]

The excerpts printed here are but a fragment of the whole work, and they hardly do justice to her presentation of a mass of source material from commentators on ancient writings from all parts of the world. In my search for her references I found very few works available. Most are out of print. A few of the titles can be found in old Library of Congress catalogs and in the British Museum Catalog of Printed Books. Recent investigators in the field of antiquities do not refer to most of her sources. Here, as elsewhere, one is tempted to wonder why these particular authorities are disappearing from our ken.

The God-Idea of the Ancients, or Sex in Religion

Introduction

Through a study of the primitive god-idea as manifested in monumental records in various parts of the world; through scientific investigation into the early religious conceptions of mankind as expressed by symbols which appear in the architecture and decorations of sacred edifices and shrines; by means of a careful examination of ancient holy objects and places still extant in every quarter of the globe, and through the study of antique art, it is not unlikely that a line of investigation has been marked out whereby a tolerably correct knowledge of the processes involved in our present religious systems may be obtained. The numberless figures and sacred emblems which appear carved in imperishable stone in the earliest cave temples; the huge towers, monoliths, and rocking stones found in nearly every country of the globe, and which are known to be closely connected with primitive belief and worship, and the records found on tablets which are being unearthed in various parts of the world, are, with the unravelling of extinct tongues, proving an almost inexhaustible source for obtaining information bearing upon the early history of the human race, and, together, furnish indisputable evidence of the origin, development, and unity of religious faiths. . . .

The question as to whether the identity of conception and the similarity in detail observed in religious rites, ceremonies, and symbols in the various countries of the globe are due to the universal law of unity which governs human development, or whether, through the dispersion of one original people, the early conceptions of a Deity were spread broadcast over the entire earth, is perhaps not settled; yet, from the facts which have been brought forward during the last century, the latter theory seems altogether probable, such divergence in religious ideas as is observed among the various peoples of the earth being attributable to variations in temperament caused by changed conditions of life. . . .

In an attempt to understand the history of the growth of the god-idea, the fact should be borne in mind that, from the earliest

From Eliza Burt Gamble, *The God-Idea of the Ancients* (New York: G. P. Putnam's Sons, 1897).

conception of a creative force in the animal and vegetable world to the latest development in theological speculation, there has never been what might consistently be termed a new religion. On the contrary, religion like everything else is subject to the law of growth; therefore the faiths of to-day are the legitimate result, or outcome, of the primary idea of a Deity developed in accordance with the laws governing the peculiar instincts which have been in the ascendency during the life of mankind on the earth. . . .

As written history records only those events in human experience which belong to a comparatively recent period of man's existence, and as the primitive conceptions of a Deity lie buried beneath ages of corruption, glimpses of the earlier faiths of mankind, as has already been stated, must be looked for in the traditions, monuments, and languages of extinct races. . . .

If we would unravel the mysteries involved in present religious faiths, we should begin not by attempting to analyze or explain any existing system or systems of belief and worship. If we are really desirous of obtaining information regarding present religious phenomena, it is plain that we should adopt the scientific method and turn our attention to the remote past, where, by careful and systematic investigation, we are enabled to perceive the earliest conception of a creative force and the fundamental basis of all religious systems, from which may be traced the gradual development of the god-idea.

Chapter I.   Sex the Foundation of the God-Idea

In the study of primitive religion, the analogy existing between the growth of the god-idea and the development of the human race, and especially of the two sex-principles, is everywhere clearly apparent.

"Religion is to be found alone with its justification and explanation in the relations of the sexes. There and therein only."[1]

As the conception of a deity originated in sex, or in the creative agencies female and male which animate Nature, we may reasonably expect to find, in the history of the development of the two sex-principles and in the notions entertained concerning them throughout past ages, a tolerably correct account of the growth of the god-idea. We shall perceive that during an earlier age of human existence, not only were the reproductive powers throughout Nature, and especially in human beings and in animals, venerated as the Creator, but we shall find also that the prevailing ideas relative to the importance of either sex in the office of reproduction decided the sex of this universal creative force. We shall observe also that the ideas of a god have always corresponded with the current opinions regarding the importance of either sex in human society. In other words, so long as female power and influence were in the ascendency, the creative force was regarded as embodying the principles of the female nature; later, however, when woman's power waned, and the supremacy of man was gained, the god-idea began gradually to assume the male characters and attributes.

Through scientific research the fact has been observed that, for ages after life appeared on the earth, the male had no separate existence; that the two sex-principles, the sperm and the germ, were contained within one and the same individual. Through the processes of differentiation, however, these elements became detached, and with the separation of the male from the female, the reproductive functions were henceforth confided to two separate individuals.

As originally, throughout Nature, the female was the visible organic unit within whom was contained the exclusive creative power, and as throughout the earlier ages of life on the earth she comprehended the male, it is not perhaps singular that, even after the appearance of mankind on the earth, the greater importance of the mother element in human society should have been recognized; nor, as the power to bring forth coupled with perceptive wisdom originally constituted the Creator, that the god-idea should have been female instead of male.

From the facts to be observed in relation to this subject, it is altogether probable that for ages the generating principle throughout Nature was venerated as female; but with that increase of knowledge which was the result of observation and experience, juster or more correct ideas came to prevail, and subsequently the great fructifying energy throughout the universe came to be regarded as a dual indivisible force—female and male. This force, or agency, constituted one God, which, as woman's functions in those ages were accounted of more importance than those of man, was oftener worshipped under the form of a female figure.

Neith, Minerva, Athene, and Cybele, the most important deities of their respective countries, were adored as Perceptive Wisdom, or Light, while Ceres and others represented Fertility. With the incoming of male dominion and supremacy, however, we observe the desire to annul the importance of the female and to enthrone one all-powerful male god whose chief attributes were power and might.

Notwithstanding the efforts which during the historic period have been put forward to magnify the importance of the male both in human affairs and in the god-idea, still, no one, I think, can study the mythologies and traditions of the nations of antiquity without being impressed with the prominence given to the female element, and the deeper the study the stronger will this impression grow.

During a certain stage of human development, religion was but a recognition of and a reliance upon the vivifying or fructifying forces throughout Nature, and in the earlier ages of man's career, worship consisted for the most part in the celebration of festivals at stated seasons of the year, notably during seed-time and harvest, to commemorate the benefits derived from the grain-field and vine-yard.

Doubtless the first deified object was Gaia, the Earth. As within the bosom of the earth was supposed to reside the fructifying, life-giving power, and as from it were received all the bounties of life, it was female. It was the Universal Mother, and to her as to no other divinity worshipped by mankind, was offered a spontaneity of devotion and a willing acknowledgement of dependence. Thus far in the history of mankind no temples dedicated to an undefined and undefinable God had been raised. The children of Mother Earth met in the open air, without the precincts of any man-made shrine, and under the aërial canopy of heaven, acknowledged the bounties of the great Deity and their dependence upon her gifts. She was a beneficent and all-wise God, a tender and loving parent—a mother, who demanded no bleeding sacrifice to reconcile her to her children. The ceremonies observed at these festive seasons con-sisted for the most part in merry-making and in general thanksgiv-ing, in which the gratitude of the worshippers found expression in song and dance, and in invocations to their Deity for a return or continuance of her gifts.

Subsequently, through the awe and reverence inspired by the mysteries involved in birth and life, the adoration of the creative principles in vegetable existence became supplemented by the worship of the creative functions in human beings and in animals. The earth, including the power inherent in it by which the continuity of existence is maintained, and by which new forms are continuously called into life, embodied the idea of God; and, as this inner force was regarded as inherent in matter, or as a manifestation of it, in process of time earth and the heavens, body and spirit, came to be worshipped under the form of a mother and her child, this figure being the highest expression of a Creator which the human mind was able to conceive. Not only did this emblem represent fertility, or the fecundating energies of Nature, but with the power to create were combined or correlated all the mental qualities and attributes of the two sexes. In fact the whole universe was contained in the Mother idea—the child, which was sometimes female, sometimes male, being a scion or offshoot from the eternal or universal unit.

Underlying all ancient mythologies may be observed the idea that the earth, from which all things proceed, is female. Even in the mythology of the Finns, Lapps, and Esths, Mother Earth is the divinity adored. Tylor calls attention to the same idea in the mythology of England,

> from the days when the Anglo-Saxon called upon the Earth, "Hal wes thu folde fira modor" (Hail, thou Earth, men's mother), to the time when mediaeval Englishmen, made a riddle of her asking "Who is Adam's mother?" and poetry continued what mythology was letting fall, when Milton's Archangel promised Adam a life to last
> ". . . till like a ripe fruit thou drop
> Into thy Mother's lap."[2]

In the old religion the sky was the husband of the earth and the earth was mother of all the gods.[3] In the traditions of past ages the fact is clearly perceived that there was a time when the mother was not only the one recognized parent on earth, but that the female principle was worshipped as the more important creative force throughout Nature.

Doubtless the worship of the female energy prevailed under the matriarchal system, and was practised at a time when women were the recognized heads of families and when they were regarded as the more important factors in human society. The fact has been shown in a previous work[4] that after women began to leave their homes at marriage, and after property, especially land, had fallen under the supervision and control of men, the latter, as they manipulated all the necessaries of life and the means of supplying them, began to regard themselves as superior beings, and later, to claim that as a factor in reproduction, or creation, the male was the more important. With this change the ideas of a Deity also began to undergo a modification. The dual principle necessary to creation, and which had hitherto been worshipped as an indivisible unity, began gradually to separate into its individual elements, the male representing spirit, the moving or forming force in the generative processes, the female being matter—the instrument through which spirit works. Spirit which is eternal had produced matter which is destructible. The fact will be observed that this doctrine prevails to a greater or less extent in the theologies of the present time.

A little observation and reflection will show us that during this change in the ideas relative to a creative principle, or God, descent and the rights of succession which had hitherto been reckoned through the mother were changed from the female to the male line, the father having in the meantime become the only recognized parent. In the *Eumenides* of Aeschylus, the plea of Orestes in extenuation of his crime is that he is not of kin to his mother. Euripides, also, puts into the mouth of Apollo the same physiological notion, that she who bears the child is only its nurse. The Hindoo Code of Menu [sic] which, however, since its earliest conception, has undergone numberless mutilations to suit the purposes of the priests, declares that "the mother is but the field which brings forth the plant according to whatsoever seed is sown."

Although, through the accumulation of property in masses and the capture of women for wives, men had succeeded in gaining the ascendency, and although the doctrine had been propounded that the father is the only parent, thereby reversing the established manner of reckoning descent, still, as we shall hereafter observe, thousands of years were required to eliminate the female element from the god-idea.

We must not lose sight of the fact that human society was first organized and held together by means of the gens, at the head of which was a woman. The several members of this organization were but parts of one body cemented together by the pure principle of maternity, the chief duty of these members being to

defend and protect eact other if needs be with their life-blood. The
fact has been observed, in an earlier work, that only through the
gens was the organization of society possible. Without it mankind
could have accomplished nothing toward its own advancement. . . .

As the human race constructs its own gods, and as by the
conceptions involved in the deities worshipped at any given time in
the history of mankind we are able to form a correct estimate of the
character, temperament, and aspirations of the worshippers, so the
history of the gods of the race, as revealed to us through the means
of symbols, monumental records, and the investigation of extinct
tongues, proves that from a stage of Nature-worship and a pure and
rational conception of the creative forces in the universe, mankind,
in course of time, degenerated into mere devotees of sensual
pleasure. With the corruption of human nature and the decline of
mental power which followed the supremacy of the animal
instincts, the earlier abstract idea of God was gradually lost sight
of, and man himself in the form of a potentate or ruler, together
with the various emblems of virility, came to be worshipped as the
Creator. From adorers of an abstract creative principle, mankind
lapsed into worshippers of the symbols under which this principle
had been veiled.

Although at certain stages in the history of the human race the
evils, which as a result of the supremacy of the ruder elements
developed in mankind had befallen the race were lamented and
bewailed, they could not be suppressed. Man had become a lost
and ruined creature. The golden age had passed away.

Chapter II. Tree, Plant, and Fruit Worship

When mankind first began to perceive the fact of an all-
pervading agency throughout Nature, by or through which everything is produced, and when they began to speculate on the origin
of life and the final cause and destiny of things, it is not in the least
remarkable that various objects and elements, such as fire, air,
water, trees, etc., should in their turn have been venerated as in
some special manner embodying the divine essence. . . . Hence,
in addition to the homage paid to the earth, in due course of time

would be added the worship of trees, upon which the early race was directly dependent for food. . . .

Among the traditions and monuments of nearly every country of the globe are to be found traces of a sacred tree—a Tree of Life. . . .

In the museum of Egyptian antiquities in Berlin is a sepulchral tablet representing the Tree of Life. This emblem figures the trunk of a tree, from the top of which emerges the bust of a woman —Netpe. She is the goddess of heavenly existence, and is administering to the deceased the water and the bread of life, the latter of which is represented by a substance in the form of cakes or rolls. . . .

There is also in the Berlin museum another representation of the Egyptian Tree of Life, in which the trunk has given place to the entire body of a woman. This, also, is Netpe, who is still spiritual wisdom or the maternal principle. We are informed by Forlong[5] that Diana was worshipped by the Amazons under a sacred tree. From this symbol, the tree, which grew first into the figure of a divine woman, and later assumed the form of a divine man, arose the emblem of the cross. . . .

In Dr. Inman's *Ancient Faiths*,[6] is a drawing from the original, by Colonel Coombs, of the "Temptation," or of the ancient tree-and-serpent myth in Genesis. This drawing, in which it is observed that the Jewish idea of woman as tempter is reversed, was copied from the inner walls of a cave in Southern India. The picture is said to be a faithful representation of the version of the story as accepted in the East. . . .

Among the most sacred plants or flowers were the lotus and the *fleur de lis*, both of which were venerated because of some real or fancied organic sexual peculiarity. The lotus is adored as the female principle throughout Nature, or as the "womb of all creation," and is sacred throughout oriental countries. It is said to be androgynous or hermaphrodite—hence its peculiarly sacred character.

It has long been thought that this lily is produced without the aid of the male pollen, hence it would seem to be an appropriate emblem for that ancient sect which worshipped the female as the more important creative energy.

Of the lotus, Inman remarks: "Amongst fourteen kinds of food and flowers presented to the Sanskrit God Anata, the lotus only is indispensable." This emblem, as we have seen, was the symbol of the Great Mother, and we are assured that it was "little less sacred than the Queen of Heaven herself." . . .

The lotus is the most sacred and the most significant symbol connected with the sacred mysteries of the East. . . . It was the consecrated symbol of the Great Mother who had brought forth the fecundative energies, female and male. Not only throughout the Northern hemisphere was it everywhere held in profound venera-tion, but among the modern Egyptians it is still worshipped as symbolical of the Great First Cause. The lotus was the emblem venerated in the solemn celebration of the Mysteries of Eleusis in Greece and the Phiditia in Carthage.

In referring to the degree of homage paid to the lotus by the ancients, Higgins says: "And we shall find in the sequel that it still continues to receive the respect, if not the adoration, of a great part of the Christian world, unconscious, perhaps, of the original reason of their conduct."[7] It is a significant fact that in nearly all the sacred paintings of the Christians in the galleries throughout Europe, especially those of the Annunciation, a lily is always to be observed. In later ages as the original significance of the lotus was lost, any lily came to be substituted. Godfrey Higgins is sure that although the priests of the Romish Church are at the present time ignorant of the true meaning of the lotus, or lily, "it is, like many other very odd things, probably understood at the Vatican, or the Crypt of St. Peter's."[8]

. . . In India the lotus frequently appears among phallic devices in place of the sacred *Yoni*. From the foregoing pages the fact will be observed that the God of the ancients embodied the two creative agencies throughout the universe, but as nothing could exist without a mother, the great Om who was the indivisible God and the Creator of the sun was the mother of these two principles, while the Tree of Life was the original life-giving energy upon the earth, represented in the creation myths of the first man Adam, and the first woman Eve or Adama.

Throughout the ages, this force, or creative agency has been symbolized in various ways, many of which have been noted in the foregoing pages. We have observed that notwithstanding the fact that the supremacy of the male had been established, the sacred *Yoni* and the lotus were still reverenced as symbols of the most exalted God. Finally, when the masculine energy began to be worshipped as the more important agency in reproduction, the female, although still necessary to complete the god-idea, was veiled. . . .

Chapter III. Sun-Worship—Female and Male Energies in the Sun

. . . Underlying all the ancient religions of which we have any account, may be observed the great energizing force throughout Nature recognized and reverenced as the Deity. . . . This God was Light and Life, both of which proceeded from the sun, or more properly speaking were symbolized by the sun. . . .

It is evident that at an early age, both in Egypt and in India, spiritualized conceptions of sun-worship had already been formed. We have seen that Netpe, the Goddess of Light, or Heavenly Wisdom, conferred spiritual life on all who would accept it. The Great Mother of the Gods in India was not only the source whence all blessings flow, but she was the Beginning and the End of all things.

Of "Aditi, the boundless, the yonder, the beyond all and everything," Max Müller says that in later times she "may have become identified with the sky, also with the earth, but originally she was far beyond the sky and the earth."[9] The same writer quotes the following, also from a hymn of the Rig-Veda:

O Mitra and Varuna, you mount your chariot which, at the dawning of the dawn is golden-colored and has iron poles at the setting of the sun; from thence you see Aditi and Diti—that is, what is yonder and what is here, what is infinite and what is finite, what is mortal and what is immortal.[10]

Aditi is the Great *She that Is*, the *Everlasting*. . . . This Goddess, who is designated as the *"Oldest,"* is implored "not only to drive away darkness and enemies that lurk in the dark, but likewise to deliver man from any sin which he may have committed." . . .

Bryant produces numberless etymological proofs to establish the fact that all the early names of the Deity were derived or compounded from some word which originally meant the sun. . . .

During an earlier age of human history, prior to the dissensions which arose over the relative importance of the sexes in reproduction, and at a time when a mother and her child represented the Deity, the sun was worshipped as the female Jove. Everything in the universe was a part of this great God. At that time there had been no division in the god-idea. The Creator constituted a dual but indivisible unity. . . . Jove was the "Great Virgin" whence everything proceeds. . . .

Although the great God of India was female and male, yet we are assured by Forlong that the female energy Maya, Queen of Heaven, even at the present time is more heard of than the male principle.

According to Bryant, the worship of Ham is the most ancient as well as the most universal of any in the world. This writer remarks that Ham, instead of representing an individual, is but a Greek corruption of Om or Aum, the great androgynous God of India, a God which is identical in significance with Aleim, Vesta, and all the other representatives of the early dual, universal power. "In the old language God was called Al, Ale, Alue, and Aleim, more frequently Aleim than any other name." According to the testimony of Higgins, Aleim denotes the feminine plural. . . .

Mitras—the Savior, the great Persian Deity which was worshipped as the 'Preserver," was both female and male. . . . The Divinity Baal was both female and male. The God of the Jews in an early stage of their career was called Baal. The oriental Ormuzd was also dual or androgynous.

Orpheus teaches that the divine nature is both female and male. According to Proclus, Jupiter was an immortal maid, "the Queen of Heaven, and Mother of the Gods." All things were contained within the womb of Jupiter. . . . She was the life-giving, energizing power in Nature, and was identical with Aleim, Om, Astarte, and others. . . .

Originally in Chaldea and in Egypt, only one supreme God was worshipped. This Deity was figured by a mother and her child, as was the great Chinese God. It comprehended the universe and all the attributes of the Deity. It was worshipped thousands of years prior to the birth of Mary, the Mother of Christ, and representations of it are still extant, not only in oriental lands, but in many countries of Europe. . . .

. . . The fact has been observed that *Am* or *Om* was originally a female Deity, within whom was contained the male principle;

when, however, through the changes wrought in the relative positions of the sexes, the male element in the Divinity adored came to be represented as a man instead of a child, he was *Amm-on.* He was the sun, yet notwithstanding the fact that he had drawn to himself the powers of the sun, he was still, himself, only a production of or emanation from the female Deity Om, Mother of the Gods and Queen of Heaven. She it was who had created or brought forth the sun. . . .

It was doubtless at a time when woman constituted the head of the gens, and when the feminine element in the sun, in human beings, and in Nature generally was regarded as the more important, that Latona and her son Apollo were worshipped together. Latona, Apollo, and Diana constituted the triune God. The last two were the female and male energies, the former being the source whence they sprang. . . .

From what appears in the foregoing pages the fact has doubtless been perceived that the worship of a Virgin and Child does not, as is usually supposed, belong exclusively to the Romish Christian Church, but, on the contrary, that it constitutes the most remote idea of a Creator extant. As has been hinted, there is little doubt that the earliest worship of the woman and child was much simpler than was that which came to prevail in later ages, at a time when every religious conception was closely veiled beneath a mixture of astrology and mythology. . . .

Within the churches and in the streets of many cities of Germany are to be observed figures of this traditional Virgin. She is standing, one foot upon a cresent and the other on a serpent's head, in the mouth of which is the sprig of an apple tree on which is an apple. The tail of the serpent is wound about a globe which is partially enveloped in clouds. On one arm of the Virgin is the Child, and in the hand of the other arm she carries the sacred lotus. Her head is encircled with a halo of light similar to the rays of the sun.

One is frequently disposed to query: Do the initiated in the Romish Church regard these images as legitimate representations of Mary, the wife of Joseph and Mother of Christ, or are they aware of their true significance? Certainly the various accessories attached to this figure betray its ancient origin and reveal its identity with the Egyptian, Chaldean, and Phoenician Virgin of the Sphere.

The fact has already been observed that in the original representation of the "Temptation" in the cave temple of India, it is not the woman but the man who is the tempter, and a singular peculiarity observed in connection with this ancient female Deity is that it is *she* and *not her seed* who is trampling on the serpent, thus proving that originally woman and not man was worshipped as the Savior. Another significant feature noticed in connection with this subject is that the oldest figures which represent this Goddess are black, thus proving that she must have belonged to a dark-skinned race. . . .

It seems to be the general belief of all writers whose object is to disclose rather than conceal the ancient mysteries, that until a comparatively recent time the moon was never worshipped as Isis. Until the origin and meaning of the ancient religion had been forgotten, and the ideas underlying the worship of Nature had been lost, the moon was never regarded as representing the female principle.

When man began to regard himself as the only important factor in procreation, and when the sun became masculine and heat or passion constituted the god-idea, the moon was called Isis. The moon represented the absence of heat, it therefore contained little of the recognized god-element. It was, perhaps, under the circumstances, a fitting emblem for woman. . . .

The change noted in the growth of the religious idea by which the male principle assumes the more important position in the Deity may, by a close investigation of the facts at hand, be easily traced, and, as has before been expressed, this change will be found to correspond with that which in an earlier age of the world took place in the relative positions of the sexes. In all the earliest representations of the Deity, the fact is observed that within the mother element is contained the divinity adored, while the male appears as a child and dependent on the ministrations of the female for existence and support. Gradually, however, as the importance of man begins to be recognized in human affairs, we find that the male energy in the Deity, instead of appearing as a child in the arms of its mother, is represented as a man, and that he is of equal importance with the woman; later he is identical with the sun, the woman, although still a necessary factor in the god-idea, being concealed or absorbed within the male. It is no longer woman who is to bruise the serpent's head, but the seed of the woman, or the son. He is Bacchus in Greece, Adonis in Syria, Christna in India. He is indeed the new sun which is born on the 25th of December, or at the time when the solar orb has reached its lowest position and begins to ascend. It is not perhaps necessary to add that he is also the Christ of Bethlehem, the son of the Virgin. . . .

If we bear in mind the fact that the gods of the ancients represented principles and powers, we shall not be surprised to find that Muth, Neith, or Isis, who was creator of the sun, was also the first emanation from the sun. Minerva is Wisdom—the Logos, the Word. She is Perception, Light, etc. At a later stage in the history of religion, all emanations from the Deity are males who are "Saviors."

That the office of the male as a creative agency is dependent on the female, is a fact so patent that for ages the mother principle could not be eliminated from the conception of a Deity, and the homage paid to Athene or Minerva, even after women had become only sexual slaves and household tools, shows the extent to which the idea of female supremacy in Nature and in the Deity had taken root.

Notwithstanding the efforts which during numberless ages were made to dethrone the female principle in the god-idea, the Great Mother, under some one of her various appellations, continued, down to a late period in the history of the human race, to claim the homage and adoration of a large portion of the inhabitants of the globe. And so difficult was it, even after the male element had declared itself supreme, to conceive of a creative force independently of the female principle, that oftentimes, during the earlier ages of their attempted separation, great confusion and obscurity are observed in determining the positions of male deities. Zeus who in later times came to be worshipped as male was formerly represented as "the great dyke, the terrible virgin who breathes out on crime, anger, and death." . . .

As in the old language there was no neuter gender, the gods must always appear either as female or male. For apparent reasons, in all the translations, through the pronouns and adjectives used, the more important ancient deities have all been made to appear as males.

By at least two ancient writers Jupiter is called the Mother of the Gods. In reference to a certain Greek appellation, Bryant observes that it is a masculine name for a feminine deity—a name which is said to be a corruption of Mai, the Hindoo Queen of Heaven.

In process of time, as the world became more and more

masculinized, so important did it become that the male should occupy the more exalted place in the Deity, that even the Great Mother of the Gods, as we have seen, is represented as male.

The androgynous or plural form of the ancient Phoenician God Aleim, the Creator referred to in the opening chapter of Genesis, is clearly apparent. This God, speaking to his counterpart, Wisdom, the female energy, says: "Let us make man in our own image, in our own likeness," and accordingly males and females are produced. By those whose duty it has been in the past to prove that the Deity here represented is composed only of the masculine attributes, we are given to understand that God was really "speaking to himself," and that in his divine cogitations excessive modesty dictated the "polite form of speech"; he did not, therefore, say exactly what he meant, or at least did not mean precisely what he said. We have to bear in mind, however, that as man had not at that time been created, if there were no female element present, this excess of politeness on the part of the "Lord" was wholly lost. Surely, in a matter involving such an enormous stretch of power as the creation of man independently of the female energy, we would scarcely expect to find the high and mighty male potentate which was subsequently worshipped as the Lord of the Israelites laying aside his usual "I the Lord," simply out of deference to the animals.

In Christian countries, during the past eighteen hundred years, the greatest care has been exercised to conceal the fact that sun-worship underlies all forms of religion, and under Protestant Christianity no pains have been spared in eliminating the female element from the god-idea; hence the ignorance which prevails at the present time in relation to the fact that the Creator once comprehended the forces of Nature, which by an older race were worshipped as female.

Chapter V.   Separation of the Female and Male Elements in the Deity

Glimpses of antiquity as far back as human ken can reach reveal the fact that in early ages of human society the physiological question of sex was a theme of the utmost importance, while various proofs are at hand showing that throughout the past the question of the relative importance of the female and male elements in procreation has been a fruitful source of religious contention and strife. These struggles, which from time to time involved the entire habitable globe, were of long duration, subsiding only after the adherents of the one sex or the other had gained sufficient ascendency over the opposite party to successfully erect its altars and compel the worship of its own peculiar gods, which worship usually included a large share of the temporal power. Only since the male sex has gained sufficient influence to control not only human action, but human thought as well, have these contentions subsided.

That religious wars have not been confined to more modern times, and that among an early race the attempt to exalt the male principle met with obstinate resistance which involved mankind in a conflict, the violence of which has never been exceeded, are facts which seem altogether probable. Indeed, there is much evidence going to show that the cause of the original dispersion of a primitive race was the contention which arose respecting their religious faith or regarding the physiological question of the relative importance of the sexes in the function of reproduction; and that the general war indicated in the *Puranas*, which began in India and extended over the entire habitable globe, and which was celebrated by the poets as "the basis of Grecian mythology," originated in this conflict over the precedence of one or the other of the sex-principles contained in the Deity. Although there are no records of these wars in extant history, accounts of them are still preserved in the traditions and religious monuments of oriental countries. . . .

It would seem that the fierce wars which had devastated the land had ceased prior to the beginning of the Tower of Babel. According to the testimony of Moses, the Lord himself declared "Behold the people is one." This unanimity of belief, as is plainly shown, was of short duration, for the Tower arose "upright and defiant," not, however, as an emblem of the primeval dual or triune God in which the female energy was predominant, but as a symbol of male creative power. It was the type of virility which in the subsequent history of religion was to assume the position of the "one only and true God."

It is not improbable that idolatry began with the Tower of Babel. Indeed it has been confidently asserted by certain writers that the earliest idols set up as emblems of the Deity, or as expressions of

the peculiar worship of the Lingajas, were obelisks, columns, or towers, the first of which we have any account being the Tower of Babel, erected probably at Nipur in Chaldea. Until a comparatively recent time, the actual significance of this monument seems to have been little understood. Later research, however, points to the fact that it was a phallic device erected in opposition to a religion which recognized the female element throughout Nature as God. . . .

. . . As the tower typified the Deity worshipped by those who claimed superiority for the male, so the pyramids symbolized the creative agency and peculiar qualities of the female, or of the dual Deity which was worshipped as female. . . .

The Great Mother Cybele, who is represented by the Sphinx, had doubtless been adored as a pure abstraction, her worship being that of the universal female principle in Nature.[11] . . .

From the time when the two religious elements began to separate in the minds of the people, the prophets, seers, and priestesses of the old religion, those who continued to worship the Virgin and Child, had prophesied that a mortal woman, a virgin, would, independently of the male principle, bring forth a child, the fulfilment of which prophecy would vindicate the ancient faith and forever settle the dispute relative to the superiority of the female in the office of reproduction. Thus would the woman "bruise the serpent's head." . . . Finally, with the increasing importance of the male in human society, it is observed that a reconciliation has been effected between the female worshippers and those of the male. Athene herself has acquiesced in the doctrine of male superiority. . . .

. . . Although the female principle is still a necessary factor in the creative processes, and although it is capable of producing gods, the mother element possesses none of the essentials which constitute a Deity. In other words, woman is not a Creator. From the father is derived the soul of the child, while from the mother, or from matter, the body is formed. Hence the prevalence at a certain stage of human history of divine fathers and earthly mothers; for instance, Alexander of Macedon, Julius Caesar, and later the mythical Christ who superseded Jesus, the Judean philosopher and teacher of mankind.

Henceforth, caves, wells, cows, boxes and chests, arks, etc., stand for or symbolize the female power. We are given to understand, however, that for ages these symbols were as holy as the God himself, and among many peoples even more revered and worshipped. . . .

The logic by which the great female principle in the Deity has been eliminated, and the subterfuges which have been and still are employed to construct and sustain a Creator who of himself is powerless to create, is as amusing as it is suggestive, and forcibly recalls to mind *la couvade*, in which, among certain tribes, the father, assuming all the duties of procreation, goes to bed when a child is born.[12]

All mythologies prove conclusively that ages elapsed before human beings were rash enough, or sufficiently blinded by falsehood and superstition, to attempt to construct a creative force unaided by the female principle. . . .

To this separation of the two original elements in the Deity, and the consequent exaltation of one of the factors in the creative processes, is to be traced the beginning of our present false, unnatural, and unphilosophical masculine system of religion—a system under which a father appears as the sole parent of the universe. . . .

With the light which in these later ages science and ethnological research are throwing upon the physiological and religious disputes of the ancients, the correctness of the primitive doctrines elaborated under purer conditions at an age when human beings lived nearer to Nature is being proved—namely, that matter like spirit is eternal and indestructible, and therefore that the one is as difficult of comprehension as the other, and that Nature, instead of being separated from spirit, is filled with it and can not be divorced from it; also that the female is the original organic unit of creation, without which nothing is or can be created.

NOTES

1. Hargrave Jennings, *Phallicism.*

2. *Primitive Culture*, vol. i., p. 295 [Edward Burnett Tylor (London, 1871)].

3. Max Müller, *Origin and Growth of Religion*, p. 279 [London, 1878].

4. Eliza Burt Gamble, *The Evolution of Woman* (New York: G. P. Putnam's Sons, 1894).—Ed.

5. *Rivers of Life*, vol. i., p. 70.

6. Thomas Inman, M.D., *Ancient Faiths Embodied in Ancient Names* (London, Liverpool, 1868, 1869).—Ed.

7. Godfrey Higgins, *Anacalypsis.*—Ed.
8. *Anacalypsis,* book vii., ch. xi.
9. *Origin and Growth of Religion,* p. 221. [Max Müller].
10. Ibid.
11. Hargrave Jennings, *Phallicism,* p. 25.
12. *The Evolution of Woman,* p. 127.

MATHILDE AND MATHIAS VAERTING

Mathilde and Mathias Vaerting, distinguished researchers in Germany in the early part of this century, made contributions in the areas of sociology, psychology, biology, and mathematics. In their prolific studies they covered a wide area of investigation, much of it concerned with social problems pertinent to our own time. For example, they explored male and female psychology, the physiological basis for superior achievement, the character of the peaceful individual, the psychology of power, and the peril posed by the superstate.

The fundamental thesis presented by the Vaertings in *The Dominant Sex* is that dominance and subordination determine traits that each society designates as "masculine" and "feminine." To prove their point they marshal an array of evidence of cultural patterns in societies that they categorize as male dominated, female dominated, or sexually equal. To counter the argument that matriarchal societies remain primitive and never create advanced cultures, they give particular attention to Egypt, Libya, and Sparta, all reputedly highly developed ancient cultures, which they designate as matriarchal. The Vaertings also cite examples of states where relative equality prevailed, and they give detailed evidence indicating that the two sexes in such states resemble one another in numerous characteristics. They hypothesize that in a society of true sex equality the injustice and tyranny practiced by the dominant against the subordinate sex will be eliminated and those character traits that are truly genetic will differentiate the sexes. A corollary of their argument is that neither sex possesses a larger infusion of inborn morality.

The excerpt included here can do no more than propound the Vaertings' basic thesis and illustrate their method of amassing supporting scientific evidence, much of it cropping up unwittingly in the works of masculinist writers. Thus Chapter II, in abridged form, presents an array of investigative reports illustrating sexual patterns in numerous societies in matters of courtship, obedience, fidelity, chastity, power to divorce, the double standard, age differences of marital partners, and celibacy—all tending to confirm the Vaerting argument.

In subsequent chapters, regrettably omitted in our limited space, their basic hypothesis is buttressed by citations from a procession of scientific authorities reporting on attitudes of so-called Men's States and Women's States toward abortion, illegitimacy, prostitution, monogamy, property rights, division of labor, physical prowess, dress and adornment, sexual modesty, sex of deities, priests, and monarchs, and propensity for war. In all instances the authors see what they refer to as the "principle of reversal, of the exchange of sexual roles," related consistently to masculine or feminine dominance.

A skeptical investigator is bound to react to the Vaertings' summation as a little too pat. It is highly unlikely that such a simple formula as theirs could apply universally to the complexity of relationships in the diverse societies on this earth and could be, as they say, "perennial" and "immutable." At times their conclusions strain credulity, as when they explain "couvade" as a practice arising from the obligation of the husband, in caring for the newborn infant, to stay in bed in order to keep the baby warm.[1] However, one need not accept their theory in toto to conclude that most human characteristics cannot be designated as physiologically belonging to one sex and not to the other.

Of particular relevance to the present volume is their compelling exposition in Chapter XVII of the propensity of the Men's State to dispute, as it does today, the possibility that matriarchy ever existed, and to expunge, as it has done, profeminine material from the historical record.

The Dominant Sex

Introduction

From of old the comparative psychology of man and woman has been on a false route, and there it still wanders to-day. The custom

Reprinted by permission from Mathilde and Mathias Vaerting, *The Dominant Sex: A Study in the Sociology of Sex Differentiation*, trans. Eden and Cedar Paul (London: George Allen & Unwin, Ltd., 1923). Selection includes the Introduction, Chapter I, and abridgments of Chapters II and XVII.

is to compare dominant males with females whose position is subordinate or at least inferior in rank, the comparison being thus between groups whose position is fundamentally unequal. But the differences shown to exist between such groups are just as likely to depend upon sociological causes, and to be the outcome of the reciprocal position of the sexes, as to be due to congenital divergencies. It is erroneous, therefore, to do what is usually done at the present time, and to describe the differences in question without further consideration as sexual characters.

The error presumably arises from a not unnatural identification of the male sex with dominance and of the female sex with subordination. The respective associations have been regarded as inseparable. The extant inequality in the positions of men and women has consequently been looked upon as itself an expression of sex differentiation, and a search for additional factors of the inequality has been considered superfluous. Yet the steady advance of the female sex towards the attainment of equal rights has been enough to show that the foregoing assumption is invalid. The course of this investigation will make the fallacy manifest on other grounds.

A new basis of comparison is the essential prerequisite to a precise comparison of man and woman, a comparison which shall enable us to discover the truly congenital differentiae of sex. We must compare the sexes when their position is precisely similar. We must either compare men where masculine dominance prevails with women where feminine dominance prevails; or else we must compare women in a community where men are dominant with men in a community where women are dominant; or else we must compare men and women under conditions where complete equality prevails between the sexes. We must not, as hitherto, compare dominant men with subordinate women; we are only entitled to compare dominant men with dominant women, subordinate men with subordinate women, or the two sexes under absolutely equal rights.

To-day we are still far from any such equivalence of powers. Nominally, indeed, there is an equivalence of rights, but in reality men continue to exercise a notable predominance. Consequently the sexes cannot at present be unreservedly compared. But among quite a number of peoples women have been dominant, and the women and the men of these peoples can be compared with the men and the women of peoples where masculine dominion prevails. A comparison between the sexes when this precaution is observed will throw an entirely new light upon the psychology of men and women respectively. Furthermore and simultaneously, it will furnish remarkable elucidations in the domains of the ethnography, sexology, anthropology, and sociology of the sexes. Our investigation has enabled us to ascertain the extremely important fundamental law that the contemporary peculiarities of women are mainly determined by the existence of the Men's State, and that they are accurately and fully paralleled by the peculiarities of men in the Women's State.

Such is the general thesis we hope to establish in the present volume. To do so, we must proceed to examine the question in detail.

Chapter One.   The Principle of Reversal in Monosexual Dominance

Testimony concerning the dominance of women among various peoples differs greatly in comprehensiveness. As regards the ancient Egyptians such abundant evidence is forthcoming that the existence of feminine dominance as far as this people is concerned has been placed beyond question for all who have studied the matter objectively. In the case of the Spartans the historical traces are perhaps less numerous, but they are so plain as to leave no doubt as to the reality of the dominance of women in that nation. In both instances, therefore, we have proof of the existence of feminine dominance among civilised peoples. As far as savages are concerned, the most detailed reports that have come to hand anent the dominance of women relate to the Kamchadales, the Chamorros, the Iroquois, the Basque-Iberian stocks, the Garos, the Dyaks, and the Balonda. In addition there were, for example, the Libyans, among whom it is demonstrable that the dominance of women was once absolute at a time when they were at least in an intermediate stage between barbarism and civilisation. We find, moreover, fairly definite traces of the dominance of women among numerous races in the most diverse phases of development; for instance in Tibet and in Burma, among the Khonds, the Creeks, etc. Bachofen has shown that matriarchy (the mother-right) existed in Lycia, Crete, Athens, Lemnos, Egypt, India and Central Asia, Orchomenos and Minyae, Elis, Locris, Lesbos, Mantinea, and among the Cantabri. In Bachofen's terminology, matriarchy (Mutterrecht) is synonymous with the dominance of women.

It is of the first importance that we should recognise the hitherto unknown peculiarities of the dominance of women. A comparative study of feminine dominance as it existed among the most diverse peoples and in the most various phases of civilisation shows that the main characteristics of this dominance are perennial and immutable, whether it is encountered among savages or in a race at the highest level of civilisation. Where women rule, woman is the wooer. The man contributes the dowry; the woman expects a pledge of fidelity from her husband, and the woman has the sole right of disposal over the common possessions. She alone is entitled to divorce her partner should he no longer please her. From the husband, chastity and conjugal fidelity are demanded; the man is often severely punished for unfaithfulness; but the obligations of the wife in this respect are less exacting. The husband adopts the name and nationality of the wife. The children are called after the mother and inherit from the mother. The social position of the children depends on that of the mother. The wife's occupations lead her away from the home, whilst the husband attends to domestic affairs. The man adorns himself, but the woman's clothing is comparatively sober. Unmarried men are regarded with contempt. The males are considered kindlier and more benevolent than the females, but less intelligent. Girl children are valued more highly than boys. Where infanticide or the mutilation of children prevails, as among many savage and barbarous peoples, they are practised on boys but not on girls. The parental duty of providing education for the children is imposed upon the dominant sex. The gods, or at least the leading divinities, are for the most part feminine.

These phenomena are characteristic of feminine dominance. A comparison with the phenomena characteristic of masculine dominance shows that the latter are no less perennial and no less immutable among the most diverse peoples and in the most various phases of civilisation. The only difference is that the roles of the sexes are reversed. Where men rule, we find that in love and marriage, in social life and in religion, the man occupies the position which is occupied by the woman in communities where women rule.

Feminine dominance, like masculine dominance, is especially characterised by the fact that, notwithstanding the existence of two sexes, one sex holds sway. Both these varieties of dominance must therefore be described as monosexual. Monosexual dominance invariably allots the same position to the dominant sex, be that sex female or male. But according as man or woman rules, we find a reversal of the relationships, which, but for this reversal, are identical in aspect. The two leading principles of the comparative psychology of the Men's State and the Women's State are therefore: on the one hand, complete conformity in the general laws and limitations of sexual and social duties; and, on the other hand, a reversal of relative positions, an interchange in the roles of the sexes.

As an outcome of the operation of these two principles we find that feminine peculiarities in the Men's State have as their counterpart masculine peculiarities in the Women's State. Conversely, masculine peculiarities in the Men's State are fundamentally identical with feminine pecularities in the Women's State. We shall, in the sequel, show above all that the canons whereby feminine peculiarities are determined in contemporary civilisation are, in all their details, a pure product of the Men's State. We shall show that there is not a single "masculine quality" which cannot be paralleled as a "feminine quality" in the history of one race or another. The more complete our information becomes concerning the phases of the dominance of women, the more fully does it demonstrate the reversal of masculine and feminine peculiarities.

Chapter Two.   The Canons of the Sexual Life
under Monosexual Dominance

The working of the principle of reversal, of the exchange of sexual roles, under masculine and feminine dominance respectively, is extremely conspicuous in connection with love and marriage. Courtship is, for example, to-day regarded as a specifically masculine function, as one for which man is especially adapted by the peculiarites of his nature. But from the love poems of the ancient Egyptians we learn that among them woman was the wooer.[1] In fifteen of the nineteen songs in the so-called London Manuscript the woman courts the man; in four only is man the wooer. We may infer that most of the poems were written by women, although that possibility is not even considered by modern Egyptologists. . . . This Men's-State viewpoint leads Müller so far astray that he minimises the significance of the feminine wooing, although the internal evidence of the poems is too strong for him to be able to deny the reality of the phenomenon. He writes, characteristically enough, that to a modern poet it must seem "as if Egyptian women had been over-ready to play the man's part." . . . Whereas to the Egyptians, in their Women's State, courtship appeared to be a natural womanly function, and whereas they extolled courtship by women in their poems, to Müller, living in a Men's State, and knowing no other canons than those of the Men's State, courtship by women seemed "immorality and the extremity of feminine license." . . .

Not all investigators, of course, take so biased and subjective a view. Reitzenstein,[2] for instance, recognises that in Egypt the women were the wooers. W. von Bissing,[3] too, says: "The peculiarity of these poems is that they always exhibit the girls as taking the initiative; it is they who come to their lovers, or endeavour to catch them." . . .

The following facts likewise contribute to sustain the conviction that the custom of women acting as wooers is the outcome of feminine dominance. The farther back we go in the literature of a people, the more frequent are the indications of women as wooers. But the older a literature, the greater the probability that it arises from phases of an earlier dominance of women, or from times which in manners and customs were at least closely akin to such phases. Among the Lydians, where the reversal of roles in the division of labour is an additional indication that the dominance of women prevailed, the women sought out their mates.[4] In the ancient sagas of Hindustan, wooing by the women plays a notable part. By the *Laws of Manu*, a girl is allowed the free choice of her husband.[5] We are told in the Bible that in the case of the first human couple the woman was the wooer. Jaeckel shows that among primitive folk it is frequently the custom for the women to choose their husbands. In ancient Teutonic poesy, descriptions of wooing by women are not infrequent. Experts in Teutonic lore speak in this connection of the "initiative of woman."[6] . . . From the ninth century onwards, these women's songs were censured by the clergy as immoral. We plainly discern how, as the power of the male sex grew, the practice of courtship by women (surviving from the days of women's dominance) came by degrees to arouse the impression of shamelessness.

Among the Garos, women were dominant, and family groups were of the matriarchal type, tracing descent through the mother. According to Westermarck,[7] the duty of courtship was imposed on the girls as a legal obligation. Should a man play the wooer, he was subject to punishment for his shameless behaviour. . . .

A yet plainer indication that dominance is the origin of the practice of courtship by women is found in the fact that sovereign princesses always woo and choose husbands for themselves. Examples are frequent in history. A like tendency is observable in priestesses whenever they have considerable power.[8]

. . . Typical and psychologically significant is the fact that, when women are the wooers, men are reported to behave in the way that is regarded as proper for women do-day when men are the wooers. Think of the wooing of Joseph by Potiphar's wife. Joseph indignantly repudiates the attempt to seduce him. As a last resort, he runs away in order to preserve his virtue. The story is told, moreover, as an awe-struck commendation of masculine chastity, while the narrator is filled with contempt for the female seducer. These trends are those of countless contemporary tales, with the only difference that in the latter the roles are reversed, as becomes a community where the males are dominant.

Jaeckel[9] speaks of an Indian tribe in Assam (probably the Garos are referred to) among whom the girls are the wooers. The courted male "has to make a vigorous resistance, culminating in flight; he is captured and led back to the nuptial residence amid the lamentations of the parents." Among the Kamchadales, where the dominance of women prevailed and women were the wooers, the women positively fought for the possession of the men (Klemm). . . .

The psychological correspondence between the contemporary masculine peculiarities in the Men's State and the feminine pecularities in the Women's State, is as conspicuous, or even more conspicuous, in the case of marriage. . . . Consider, for example, the fundamental law of Men's-State marriage, that the wife shall obey her husband. . . . The tendency to accept subordination has been described as specifically feminine. . . . Man, on the other hand, we are assured, has a natural inclination to command, so that it is congruent with the male disposition that the husband should exercise dominance over the wife. But if we turn to contemplate marriage in the Women's State, we find the same fundamental law of obedience in action, the only difference being that here the roles of the sexes are reversed. In the Women's State the duty of obedience is incumbent on the husband; the wife holds sway. . . .

The conformity to type displayed by the sexes goes so far that the dominant partner, when entering upon marriage, demands an express pledge of obedience from the chosen mate. To-day men receive from their wives a promise that these will "love, honour, and obey." In ancient Egypt the wife exacted a promise of obedience from the husband. Diodorus[10] says in plain terms: "Among the people,[11] too, the wife has authority over the husband, and in the marriage contract the husband has expressly to pledge himself to obey his wife." . . .

In Sparta, likewise, the men were subject to the women. Plutarch states in several passages[12] that the Spartan women were the only wives who held sway over their husbands. Aristotle,[13] too, says in a phrase quite free from ambiguity: "Contentious and warlike peoples such as the Lacedaemonians always pass under the dominion of women." . . .

To the men of a community where the males are dominant, the accounts of the earlier extensive prevalence of a social system in which the men were subject to the women are as annoying as a red rag to a bull. Witness Meiners,[14] when confronted with the fact of the dominance of women among the Lacedaemonians. He writes that the Spartan women had absolute authority over their "degenerate" husbands. The husbands treated the wives as mistresses, and termed them such. . . .

. . . Subordination of the husband, the imposing of the duty of unconditional obedience upon the husband, are found in all those primitive peoples among whom the dominance of women prevails. Meiners[15] tells us that the sway of the women was unrestricted among the Kamchadales. The men were entirely subordinate to their wives. A husband never secured anything from his wife by force, but "achieved his ends only by the humblest and most persistent petitions and caresses." Among the Chamorros, too, the dominance of women was in force. Waitz[16] declares that the legal status of the women was higher than that of the men, and that the men had practically no legal rights. In the most trifling matters, the wife's consent must be secured. The husband was forbidden to alienate any property without his wife's permission. If the husband failed in due obedience to his wife, the latter would knock him about. Or in some cases the parents would punish the erring husband severely.

Meiners[17] gives a similar description of the complete subordination of the husband in a Chamorro marriage. The Chamorro men, who were famous for their bodily strength, were kept by their wives in a state of abject subjection. The wives ruled, and the husbands could do nothing without their consent. If a man failed to pay due respect to his wife, or if he gave her any other cause for dissatisfaction, she would make him rue it by physical methods. . . .

An additional proof that the subordination of one partner to the other in marriage arises out of monosexual dominance, is supplied by the fact that at all times there have been sovereign princesses no less than sovereign princes who have carried over into conjugal life the despotism exercised by them in the political field. As regards male rulers, instances in which dominance in marriage and subordination of the wife extended to the exercise of the power of life and death over the spouse, are familiar to all. These cases are strictly paralleled in the behaviour of female despots, and the only reason why the phenomenon has not hitherto been generally noted is that the reports concerning the conjugal despotism exercised by female monarchs have never become widely known. A few examples will therefore be given.

Westermarck tells us that among the people of Loango the queens kill their paramours when these allow their affections to stray. From Meiners we quote the following passage concerning the privileges of the women of the reigning house among the Natchez—a people among whom, according to Waitz, the women were greatly honoured, and could discharge the functions of royalty. "They exercised the power of life and death, and could order their guards to put to death summarily any one who was unlucky enough to incur their displeasure. If a queen should do a subject the honour of choosing him as a husband, the latter had to obey his exalted partner in all things, and to preserve inviolable fidelity towards her.

The queen could punish a disobedient or unfaithful husband, just like any other commoner, by ordering his instant execution. But the queens regarded it as their traditional privilege to live precisely as they pleased. Their husbands had no say in the matter, no ground for complaint if the wife were unfaithful, nor any right of punishment."

Meiners reports the exercise of similar unrestricted authority over husbands by the sovereign princesses of many other tribes. In almost all the instances it is expressly stated that this authority included the power of life and death. Jaeckel tells us that in the case of a general social predominance of women, no less than where a woman occupied the throne, conjugal despotism by women went so far that the husbands had to kneel in the presence of their wives, or to adopt some like posture of humility when serving their wives' needs. . . .

This conformity recurs in respect of other exaggerated manifestations of conjugal authority on the part of the dominant sex. At the height of its power, a dominant sex is not satisfied with insisting that in married life the members of the subordinate sex shall obey their partners; in addition it reserves to itself the right of divorce. . . . In ancient Egypt the right is directly specified in marriage contracts belonging to the phase of feminine dominance. Two such contracts dating from the pre-Greek era give assurance of this. Both are reported by Spiegelberg.[18] Although their dates are separated by nearly three hundred years, the clauses of the two agreements cover much the same ground. In the older papyrus, the wife who is entering into the contract says to her husband: "Should I divorce you because I have come to hate you and because I love another more than you, then I will give you, etc., etc." The divorce formula is exactly the same in the later contract. Not a word has been modified, so that we are entitled to infer that we have to do with a legally established form of marriage contract. Among the Balonda, the Iroquois, the Cantabri, the Khonds, etc., during the era of feminine dominance, whilst the wife had the right to divorce her husband, the husband was not entitled to divorce his wife.

Even certain notorious customs connected with the termination of a marriage by the death of the dominant partner are the same whether the deceased was a man or a woman. Every one knows that, in the case of certain ruling princes, when the sovereign died his widow or widows had either to join the husband in the tomb, or else were condemned to practice some extraordinarily harsh form of mourning; every one, too, has heard of the practice of suttee in Hindustan, where the widow was burned alive on the husband's funeral pyre. But, in accordance with the peculiarities of the Men's State ideology, few of our contemporaries are aware that these customs have their obverse where women are endowed with despotic powers. Jaeckel (op. cit., p. 62), for example, tells us that among the Ashantis the husbands of the priestesses had to follow their wives in death. According to Bossu,[19] among the Natchez the princesses of the ruling race could choose as many lovers as they pleased; upon the death of one of these princesses, all her lovers must die. Among certain South American tribes, after a wife's death a prolonged period of severe ceremonial mourning was imposed on the bereaved husband. . . .

Duplex sexual morality, with which we are all familiar as an accompaniment of male predominance, is met with in the reverse form where women rule. . . .

It is a familiar fact that in modern civilised countries under masculine domination a duplex sexual morality prevails, despite the recognition of the monogamic principle. There, in the life of sex, the men have preferential rights. But hitherto it has not been generally recognised that where women rule, sexual morality develops in the inverse sense, so that the women have more sexual freedom than the men. Here likewise there is an infringement of the monogamic principle, but this time in favour of the wife. . . . During the most flourishing period of Sparta, monogamy became the recognised form of marriage in that country. Herodotus[20] tells us that among the Spartans a man had only one wife. According to Plutarch[21] there were no male adulterers in Lacedaemon. But as regards the fidelity of Spartan wives, history tells a very different tale. Meyer[22] declares that polyandry was common in Sparta. The Spartan women were never faithful to the marriage bond. Plutarch[23] relates that adultery on the part of women was even considered commendable. By the laws of Lycurgus the position of women in regard to adultery was much more favoured than that of men. Euripides[24] goes so far as to say that despite her best endeavours no Spartan woman could possibly lead a chaste and virtuous life. Plato animadverts upon the loose morals of the Lacedaemonian women. According to Nicolaus Damascenus a

Spartan wife was entitled to have herself impregnated by the handsomest man she could find, whether native or foreigner. . . .

We still possess but little information concerning the sexual life of the ancient Egyptians in the period when the dominance of women was complete. . . .

Among primitive folk where the dominance of women prevailed, there was the same tendency towards the maintenance of a duplex code of sexual morality, according to which the duty of conjugal fidelity was enforced on men only. Women could follow their own bent in sexual matters. In the case of the Chamorros conjugal infidelity was severely punished in men, even when the offence was merely suspected, not proved. The accused husband was dealt with by the women of the neighbourhood. But if the wife proved unfaithful, her husband had no right to lay a finger on her. Meiners declares that among the Chamorros it was only the women who were privileged libertines. This phrase gives us a clear insight into the characteristics of family life among this people.[25]

Conditions were precisely similar among the Kamchadales. Meiners[26] tells us that the married men of this race had to conceal their amours with extreme care. But wives bestowed their favours quite openly, not considering it worth while to hide their infidelities from their husbands. . . . Among the Mingrelians and the Circassians, where women were likewise predominant, a woman was more honoured in proportion to the number of her lovers. In many cases, duplex sexual morality takes the form of a one-sided development of polyandry or polygamy. Polyandry invariably presupposes the dominance of women; polygamy presupposes the dominance of men. The connexion between these institutions has not hitherto been recognised. But in many Women's States the existence of polyandry has been expressly recorded: among the Garos, the Nayars, the Tlingits, the Eskimos, the Sakai; in Tibet and Burma. In the case of the Iroquois, polyandry was permissible to women, but polygamy was forbidden to men (Westermarck). A characteristic fact is that we are often told how well the numerous husbands of one woman got on together.

Among the Arabs, too, in the days when women were dominant, polyandry prevailed.[27] Even in Mohammed's time, the Arab woman was essentially polyandrous. According to Reitzenstein, Mohammed once exhorted a married woman to be faithful to her husband, and admonished her not to indulge in whoredom. She made answer: "A free woman does not practise whoredom." The implication was that a free woman might have carnal relations with as many men as she liked. Children born out of wedlock secured full recognition, and were not regarded as bastards. On the Malabar coast, where also women were dominant, polyandry was practised, not only by the queens, but throughout the population. Among the Cascovins, where the women were dominant, a wife usually had, in addition to her husband-in-chief, a supplementary husband to whom various duties were assigned.

In like manner, the value placed upon pre-conjugal chastity in men and women respectively is sharply contrasted in the Men's State and the Women's State. Only in the Men's State is feminine continence before marriage highly esteemed; in the Women's State the unmarried girls enjoy (openly or secretly) sexual freedom, just as unmarried men do in the Men's State. Meiners[28] writes of the Kamchadales that they do not prize virginity at all. "The greatest recommendation an unmarried girl can have, is that she has bestowed her favours upon an exceptionally large number of lovers. Such a girl is supposed to have exceptionally good grounds for expecting that she will be able to count upon the love of her future husband, since she has given plain proof of her experience in love."
. . .

. . . Among the Iroquois, where the women were dominant, the sexual life of the young unmarried men was kept under very strict control. Intercourse with the girls was absolutely forbidden; the youths were not even allowed to converse with them in public. Marriages were arranged for young men by their mothers. Similar conditions obtained in other Women's States. In Sparta, the boys were brought up to be far chaster and more bashful than the girls. Xenophon tells us that it is easier to make a pillar of stone speak or a marble statue move its eyes, than a Spartan boy. The boys, he says, are more bashful than the girls. Among the Garos the contrast was even greater. The young males were strictly segregated in a domicile for youths; the young women led free lives, and the obligation of chastity was not imposed on them (Friedenthal).

. . . In another respect, sexual customs prove to be wholly dependent upon the wielding of power. Dominant males and dominant females have harems whenever this accords with the established code of sexual morals. The resemblance between the respective practices of the male and the female owners of harems is so close as to seem almost incredible. In the male harems of negro queens, for instance, we find the precise counterparts of the female harems of the rulers of Persia.[29] The same aberrations of jealousy and the same abuses of power are encountered in both cases. The negro queens could choose for their harems any men that took their fancy. No man could refuse the queen's favour, except at the risk of liberty or life. The men were the slaves and the prisoners, rather than the spouses, of their distinguished wives. The men in the harem were rigidly secluded from the other sex. They were not allowed even a glimpse of any woman except their queen-wife. They could only go out under a strong escort, whose duty it was to keep the streets clear of girls and women. If any strange woman, disregarding the regulations, ventured near the strictly guarded husbands, or if a woman should even catch sight of one of them, her life was infallibly forfeit, and she was executed in ignominious fashion. The same punishment awaited any husband who should be unfaithful to his queen-wife. . . .

Seeing that the vagaries of love in the two sexes, when these respectively hold sway, are so closely akin psychologically, are indeed indentical, all over the world, we can no longer doubt that sex differentiation is merely the outcome of the position of dominance or subjection, and is not a product of inborn biological characteristics. . . .

Again, the customary relationship between husband and wife in the matter of age, far from being dependent upon biological and psychical sexual differentiation, is simply a consequence of mono-sexual dominance. The supremacy of either sex tends to establish a particular age relationship between husband and wife, the rule being that in marriage the member of the dominant sex is in almost all cases considerably older than the member of the subordinate sex. Where men dominate, therefore, husbands are older than their wives; and where women dominate, wives are older than their husbands. The chief determinant here is the duty of providing for the spouse, inasmuch as we shall see that this duty devolves upon the dominant sex.

In Egypt, for instance, it was the young man, not the maiden, who was exhorted to marry early. Müller translates from the Bulak papyrus: "Get thyself a wife while thou art young, so that thou mayst procreate a son in thine own likeness. If she bear thee a child while thou art still young, that is as it should be."

Among the Iroquois, where the women were dominant, the wife was usually older than her husband. Waitz[30] reports that a young man was often assigned by his mother to a wife older than himself—for the mothers were supreme in matrimonial arrangements. There have been many other peoples among which, during the phase of feminine dominance, the marriage of a young man to an older woman was customary. Jaeckel[31] gives numerous instances of this. In some cases, 15 was regarded as the best age for a young man to marry, and 19 for a young woman. "Youths who have not married before they are 16 are derided, whereas it is no shame to a girl to remain unmarried until she is 20 or more." The age contrast that obtains between husband and wife in the contemporary Men's State is here faithfully reflected, of course with the usual reversal of roles; the same remark applies to the one-sided social valuation of early marriage, for we see that it is always the members of the subordinate sex that must be married off while still quite young.

Among the Otomacos of South America the young men were first wedded to elderly women; and subsequently, after these had died, to young girls. Among the Fuegians, "the young men would rather marry an experienced woman of a certain age, than a young and even beautiful girl." Among the Khonds, the father usually chooses for his son a wife about six years older than the lad. In Burma, the difference is even greater, for here the wife is apt to be from ten to fifteen years older than her husband. . . .

In bringing to a close our account of the differential psychology of love and marriage in the Men's State and the Women's State, a reference may be made to the valuation of celibacy. In this matter, also, opinion receives its stamp from monosexual dominance. It is always the members of the subordinate sex who are derided for being unmarried. A one-sided contempt for the "old maid" is purely a product of the Men's State. Where women rule, it is the "old bachelor" who is an object of derision, the target of popular wit—though attention has not hitherto been directed to the fact. Among the Koreans a lad is already subjected to ridicule if he reaches the age of 16 without being married. Such an "old bachelor" is refused the title of man, and receives the contumelious name of "jatua." Who can fail to be reminded of our Men's-State usage of the term "old maid"?

Among the Santals, unmarried men are similarly scorned. They are regarded with contempt by both sexes, and are compared with thieves and witches. They are "not men." In Sparta, during the days of the dominance of women, unmarried men were utterly despised. A Spartan bachelor was actually deprived of civil rights. At certain times in winter he had to walk through the market place totally nude, singing a song descriptive of his own shame, and admitting that it was a just punishment for having despised marriage. Herein we see the precise counterpart of the institutions of the Men's State, where the old maid is the subject of contumely, and completely loses caste.

But the unmarried are only contemned when they belong to the subordinate sex. This one-sided restriction of scorn to members of the subject sex is doubtless connected with the division of labour that obtains under monosexual dominance, and also perhaps with the consequent differentiation in social position. The fuller consideration of this topic must be deferred. . . .

Chapter Seventeen. The Campaign against the Historical Vestiges of the Dominance of Women

Under monosexual dominance there necessarily and invariably prevails a powerful inclination to obliterate all traces of any earlier dominance exercised by the sex that is now subordinate. . . . The members of the ruling sex feel affronted by every reminder of the fact that in former days their sex was under tutelage, and the sentiment is accentuated by the reflection that rule was then exercised by those who are now subordinate. Monosexual dominance, therefore, at its zenith, is always characterised by the spread of a tradition that the hegemony of the sex actually in power is eternal and unalterable. All the historical vestiges that conflict with this tradition are deliberately or unconsciously expunged from the record. Sometimes they are glossed over or falsified; sometimes they are erased; sometimes they are ignored. . . .

. . . Now; almost universally, men are still the dominant sex, and for a considerable period in the past their dominance has been practically unchallenged. Indications that in still earlier days women held sway arouse an unpleasant sense of instability, and claim from us the recognition that the prevailing opinion is unsound. . . .

Not merely do we argue from ourselves to others; we also argue from our own times to all earlier epochs. The pictures from the past have to adapt themselves to the minds formed by the present in which we live. . . .

A glance at some of the studies made during recent decades will show how strong has been the influence of the Men's-State prejudices characteristic of the society in which the investigators happen to have been born. They take it as self-evident that they are entitled to measure with the yardstick of their own days, epochs that lie thousands of years back in the past. For example, Breysig, E. Meyer, and many others, try to prove the impossibility of the dominance of women even in the earliest periods of human history on the ground that, precisely in those ruder times, men must have been more ruthless in taking advantage of their superior bodily strength. . . . We have shown, however, that the ratios between the stature of men and women are not constants, but vary concomitantly with changes in the relationships of power between the sexes. We have shown that among many peoples the women were stronger than the men, and that this occurred in periods when women were dominant. . . .

Curtius makes the same mistake of measuring the past by the standards of the present when he writes that the tracing of descent through the mother "must be regarded as the vestige of an imperfectly developed condition of society and of family life, a condition that passed away when more orderly conditions became established." The influence of the present in prejudicing Curtius' mind is rendered conspicuous by his own mention of the fact that early writers had held other views. . . . More recent discoveries in Egypt have proved Curtius' theory to be unfounded. In ancient Egypt descent was traced through the mother alone for thousands of years. Nor did this happen during "an imperfectly developed condition of society and family life," but in an era when social life was very highly evolved, when Egyptian civilisation was at its acme, and when family institutions were of an advanced character and were based on monogamic marriage.

Again, Lewis Morgan's opinion, that paternal authority was at first weak, but that its growth steadily advanced as the family became more and more individualised, so that finally paternal authority "became fully established under monogamy,"[32] is the typical utterance of one whose judgments are unduly swayed by the spirit of his own time. . . . But our information regarding marriage among many of the peoples who lived under the dominance of women suffices to invalidate this theory. The Egyptians, the Chamorros, and the Cantabri were all strict monogamists, and nevertheless in their married life maternal authority was supreme.

Besides, as we have learned, Diodorus tells us in so many words that the women of Egypt ruled their husbands, for the husbands had to give a pledge of obedience when they married. This passage from Diodorus is a very sore point with our Men's-State investigators, for there is no ambiguity about its implication that wives were absolutely supreme. In many German works on ancient Egypt the passage is completely ignored. . . .

It is most characteristic that modern authors should have no hesitation in reproducing marriage formulas wherein the wife promises to obey the husband. . . . the marriage formulas of the Women's State, which conflict with the time spirit of the Men's State, are received with the utmost incredulity.

These conflicting standards are almost universally apparent in the reports concerning marriage contracts. The marriage contracts belonging to the pre-Ptolemaic era, when women were dominant, are known to us from the reports of Spiegelberg.[33] They show that women alone had the right to divorce a sexual partner, and that this could be exercised on payment of an indemnity, and upon the refund of half the dowry which the husband had brought into the marriage. Although in the earlier Egyptian records no evidence has been discovered of any contract giving similar rights to the husband, most investigators have endeavoured to represent matters as if such contracts had existed. . . .

The marriage contracts of the pre-Ptolemaic era, as made known to us by Spiegelberg, contain another clause which seems incomprehensible or repugnant to those whose minds are dominated by Men's-State ideology. In both these documents the woman promises the man that in the event of divorce she will not merely return to him half the dowry, but she says "in addition I will pay

you a share of everything I may have earned in conjunction with you during the time in which you will have been married to me."
. . . Egyptologists have either ignored the passage, or else have interpreted it in a way which plainly betrays their Men's-State prejudices. For instance, Wilckens[34] writes: "Let me remark in passing that I consider somewhat puzzling the phrase in the Libbey papyrus 'one-third of the property which I may have earned in conjunction with you,' for a woman does not usually earn anything. She must have been engaged in trade of some sort." It becomes all the more obvious that the authorities' doubt as to the accuracy of the text was the outcome of their Men's-State ideology when we recall that there is ample documentary evidence, not merely that the women of Egypt took part in the earning of income, but that they definitely occupied a dominant position. The phrase "everything I may have earned in conjunction with you" is not only found in the Libbey papyrus, but also, we learn from Spiegelberg, in the Berlin papyrus. We read, moreover, in a marriage contract of about 117 B.C., that the children are to have "everything that belongs to me, and everything that I earn in conjunction with you."[35]

Viktor Marx,[36] who studied the position of women in Babylonia from the days of Nebuchadnezzar to those of Darius (604–485 B.C.), furnishes a similar example. He translates a document in which an unmarried girl has the disposal of a large sum of money, and adds: "It is rather difficult to understand how a Babylonian girl could possess a sum of money and dispose of it as she pleased." Yet Viktor Marx himself tells us that married women and girls of this land and time could enter into contracts as independent persons. He would presumably have accepted without demur a document in which an unmarried man was represented as an independent property owner!

In Plato's *Menexenus* we read that Aspasia was the teacher of many famous orators, and above all of one of the most noted personalities in ancient Greece, Pericles, son of Xanthippus. But Diehlmann[37] assures us that "the irony is manifest" when, in Plato's *Menexenus*, Aspasia is described as training Pericles in oratory and as even writing his speeches for him. Still more trenchantly does Karl Steinhart[38] endeavour to show that there can have been no warrant for Aspasia's reputation in this matter. He writes: "The idle chatter to the effect that Aspasia used to help Pericles prepare his speeches was doubtless a popular witticism, the outcome of the universal inclination to take the shine off a splendid reputation." To possess a "splendid reputation" is self-evidently a purely masculine prerogative, and it is mortifying to the male sentiment of dominance that any mention should be made of feminine achievements which seem to put those of a man into the shade. Steinhart does not realise that he is himself playing the detractor's part that he ascribes to the common people, is himself taking the shine off a splendid reputation. According to the testimony of the ancients, Aspasia was fully Pericles' equal in capacity, her genius being no less outstanding than his. Ebers says of her: "But for the aid of her wings, Pericles would never have reached the heights which in her company and partly through her help he was able to attain." . . .

Strabo[39] records that in his day there were numerous nations in which the division of labour between the sexes was the reverse of that with which we are familiar to-day and which prevailed in the geographer's own land. The women, he says, worked away from the home, whilst the men attended to domestic affairs. The present authors have never come across any comment on this observation. It has been utterly ignored.

Here is another instance. Plutarch, in his account of the prosecution of Phocion, tells us that recourse was had to the law by which women voted as well as men. It follows that at that date women must still to a degree have functioned as co-rulers in Greece. But modern histories of Hellas are silent as to the point; Bachofen, the jurist, is the only writer who refers to it. A similar silence prevails anent the participation of women in the popular assemblies under Cecrops. It is noteworthy, by contrast, that the writers of much earlier days, when the phase of the dominance of women was less remote, did not fail to allude to the matter. For example, there is a reference to it in Augustine's *De Civitate Dei*. The philosopher Meiners, who published his *Geschichte des weiblichen Geschlects* in 1788, at a time when male dominance was at its height, does indeed record the fact, but only to refute it. No subsequent writer considered it worth mentioning until it was disinterred by Bachofen. . . .

Even more dangerous to the recognition that women were formerly dominant is the distortion of meaning in the translation of ancient texts. To misinterpret is worse than to ignore. Here is an instructive illustration. Strabo[40] reports that among the Medes, not only did the kings have a plurality of wives, but the custom of polygamy prevailed also among the common people, and that it was considered desirable for a man to have at least five wives. But Strabo goes on to say that it was likewise a point of honour with the women to have many husbands, and that a woman who had fewer than five husbands deemed herself unfortunate. Now Groskurd, the German translator of Strabo, holds that "it is an unheard of custom in the East that women should, as it were, keep male harems." He therefore twists the passage in Strabo to give it a sense more accordant with his own Men's-State ideology, and makes it run as follows: "Likewise the women deem it an honour to them that the *men* should have numerous wives, and they consider it unfortunate that there should be less than five." Groskurd actually tells us in a footnote that he has followed other translators in reading πλείστας for πλείστους. That is to say, he has arbitrarily substituted the feminine for the masculine of the original text, and has interpolated τοὺς before ἄνδρας, "so that it may be made plainer that men are spoken of and not women." Thus translators do not shrink from modifying their texts, as by changing an object into a subject, in order to give the translation a sense which harmonises with Men's-State prejudices, even though the amended version be absurd. . . .

Another instructive example of a Men's-State gloss is found in the writings of Erman.[41] He says: "Once only does a king of Egypt give us any light on the life of his wives. In the portico of the great temple of Medeenet Haboo, King Rameses III had himself depicted with his wives. The ladies, like their lord, are clad only in sandals and necklace. Their hair is dressed like that of the children of the royal house, and for this reason some have considered that the figures represent the king's daughters. But why should Rameses III want to depict his daughters while ignoring his sons? Besides, it was not the Egyptian custom to represent members of the royal family without giving their names." Erman goes on to say that for the foregoing reasons he feels entitled "with a good conscience" to describe the female figures in this picture as those of ladies of the harem. Although the way the hair of the two girls is dressed shows plainly that they were children of the royal house, and although their lineaments are definitely those of children, Erman cannot admit them to have been the king's daughters, for the king would never have thought of depicting his daughters and ignoring his sons!

. . . There is abundant evidence that, in the days of Rameses III, Egyptian girls were, to say the least of it, the equals of Egyptian boys. Erman's second reason for transforming the king's daughters into ladies of the harem is that it was contrary to Egyptian custom to depict members of the royal family without giving their names. Yet by Erman's own showing it would have been just as much a breach of etiquette to depict the king with ladies of the harem. We have Erman's word for it that once only does a king of Egypt give a glimpse into the life of his wives—and that is the case we are now considering. . . .

Among some of the peoples where women held sway, the mothers chose wives for their sons without consulting the latter. Bancroft remarks in this connexion that it seems incredible the sons should have complied. . . .

Wilkinson and Westermarck both question the accuracy of Herodotus' statement that in Egypt sons were not responsible for the maintenance of their parents. Inasmuch as filial duties were held in high regard, we may assume (say these modern critics) that sons in especial were educated to respect the obligation. But it would not have occurred to Wilkinson or Westermarck to express any doubt if Herodotus had written that daughters were under no obligation to maintain their parents. . . .

Let us give another instance. Bunsen[42] says that according to the hieroglyphs "Osiris" signified "Hes-Iri," that is, "the Eye of Isis." "But in this case the chief deity, the leading embodiment of the divine spirit, would be named after Isis. Thus Isis would take precedence of Osiris, although she can have been nothing more than the female complement of his personality. This would be preposterous and unprecedented." . . . Goddesses perforce occupy a subordinate position as mere complements of the masculine deity. Any other view is absurd and therefore incredible!

Still more misleading than the suppressions and misinterpretation of facts that bear witness to unfamiliar relationships of power between the sexes, is the way in which reports that bear a Women's-State complexion are filled out in the spirit of the Men's-State ideology. In such cases it is extremely difficult to get at the truth. When an author who tendentiously expands his reports is good enough to mention the original sources, an independent examination of these is possible. Thus Max Müller[43] writes of the Egyptians: "The Greeks mockingly relate concerning the common people that the women left their homes on business affairs, for petty trade presumably, whilst the men did the housework." In a footnote Max Müller adds: "Cf. the description of this topsy-turvy world in Herodotus, ii. 35." When we turn up the passage in the original we find, first, that there is no trace of mockery, and, secondly, that there is not a word to show that the historian is speaking only of "the common people." Both of these are interpolations by Max Müller, but it would have been difficult, nay impossible, to prove the fact had he failed to refer his readers to the original. . . .

A few typical examples may be adduced, in conclusion, to show how quickly, when men become dominant, the memories of the antecedent dominance of women are expunged. By the time of Aristophanes, the remembrance that women had once held sway in Athens was so utterly extinct that the dramatist assures us in his *Ecclesiazusa* (The Parliament of Women) that gynecocracy was the only "cracy" which Athens had never known. Bachofen's comment is: "Gynecocracy had in fact been the first form of rule in Athens." We learn from Meiners (who wrote, it will be remembered, in 1788) that women were then dominant among the Kamchadales. Kennan[44] when he visited Kamchatka about a century later, found among the Kamchadales "a far more chivalrous regard for the wishes and views of the fair sex than might have been expected in such a condition of society." The memory of the absolute dominance of women that prevailed in Meiners' day had been so completely obliterated (at any rate to the eye of the foreign observer) at the time of Kennan's visit that the latter could discern nothing more than an unexpected chivalry in the men's attitude towards the women.

We may learn another very important lesson from the foregoing incident. It shows how imperfectly travellers are able at times to understand the characteristics of the peoples they are studying, for the simple reason that they measure all manners and customs by their Men's-State standards. . . . Take Kennan's remark, that he was surprised to find so much chivalry towards women in such a condition of society, and recall the fact that the aforesaid chivalry is known to have been the sequel of a phase in which women held absolute sway! . . .

Kennan is merely voicing a general opinion when he implies that the chivalry of men towards women is the outcome of advanced civilisation. What we know of the Kamchadales is enough to prove the theory erroneous. The "chivalry" displayed by one sex towards the other is quite independent of the level of civilisation. It is a product of monosexual dominance, and it varies as power waxes or wanes.

The instances we have given of the campaign which is carried on during the phase of masculine dominance for the obliteration of the vestiges of feminine dominance will give an idea of the difficulties encountered in founding the new science of the comparative psychology of monosexual dominance. The elements of this science are based upon a comparison between the respective peculiarities of masculine and feminine dominance. The characteristics of masculine dominance are familiar to us from actual experience, and still more from the records of a very recent past. But it is extremely difficult to study the characteristics of feminine dominance, for the ascendancy of males is accompanied by a tendency to obliterate the traces of the converse type of monosexual rule. . . . The aphorism of Bacon[45] applies to all human wisdom: "Human reason is not a pure light, but is clouded by caprice and emotion. Consequently it makes of the sciences what it will."

. . . By a psychological determinism, male dominants perforce demand of history that it shall be the history of male dominance. Perchance this is why extant historical records extend back for so few thousand years. Winckler[46] has shown that history really began much earlier than we usually suppose: "Every one inclines to look for the beginnings of civilised States in that grey primal age (3000 B.C.), which is in fact the limit to which our knowledge extends as far as it is based upon written documents, so that we naturally incline to regard it as the initial period in the development of State systems and civilised communities. But such a view is erroneous, for the period in question was not the beginning but the end of the first era of civilised life to which history bears witness." Inasmuch as it seems to be a law of monosexual dominance that there is a slow but sure movement in the direction of obliterating the historical traces of an antecedent obverse type of monosexual dominance, we see that monosexual dominance definitely imperils the general integrity of the historical record.

NOTES

1. Wilhelm Max Müller, *Die Liebespoesie der alten Aegypter*, Leipzig, 1899.—The practice of courtship by women continued as late as 1400 B.C., if we accept Müller's estimate of the date when the poems were written. Some Egyptologists, however, regard them as of much earlier date.

2. Ferdinand Emil Reitzenstein, *Liebe und Ehe im alten Orient*.

3. Friedrich Wilhelm von Bissing, *Die Kultur des alten Aegypten*, 2nd edition, Leipzig, 1919, p. 39.

4. Herodotus, *The History of Herodotus*, translated by George Rawlinson, 2 vols., Everyman's Library, 1910, i. 93.

5. Cf. Valeska Jaeckel, *Studien zur vergleichenden Völkerkunde*, Berlin, 1901, p. 65.

6. Cf., among others, Karl Schmeing, *Flucht und Werbungssagen in der Legende*, Münster (Westphalia), 1911.

7. Edward Alexander Westermarck, *The History of Human Marriage*, 5th ed., rewritten, 3 vols., Macmillan, London, 1921.

8. Cf., among others, Christoph Meiners, *Geschichte des weiblichen Geschlechts*, 4 vols., Hanover, 1788–1800, vol. i; also Franz C. Müller-Lyer, *Die Familie*, 1912, being vol. iv. of *Die Entwicklungsstufen der Menschheit*, Lehmann, Munich.

9. Jaeckel, op. cit., p. 62.

10. Diodorus Siculus, *Bibliotheca Historica*, I. 27. The accuracy of the passage has been confirmed by recently discovered papyri. . . .

11. That is to say, not only in the royal family, whose customs in this respect he has already described.

12. Lycurgus. *Spartan Apophthegms*.

13. Aristotle, *Politica*. Cf. *Aristotle's Politics*, translated by B. Jowett, Clarendon Press, Oxford, 1905, II. 6. 6.

14. Meiners, *Geschichte*, vol. i. pp. 355 et seq.; English transl., vol. i. pp. 291 et seq.

15. Ibid., vol. i. pp. 19 et seq.; Eng. transl., vol. i. pp. 17 et seq.

16. Theodor Waitz, *Anthropologie der Naturvölker*, 6 parts, Leipzig, 1859–1872, vol. v. p. 107.

17. Meiners, *Vermischte philosophische Schriften*, 3 Teile, Leipzig, 1775–1776, p. 267.

18. Wilhelm Spiegelberg, Der Papyrus Libbey, ein ägyptischer Heiratsvertrag, Strasburg, 1907 (Schriften der wissenschaftlichen Gesellschaft in Strasburg).

19. N. Bossu, *Nouveaux vogages aux Indes occidentales*, 2 vols., Paris, 1768; Amsterdam, 1769, vol. ii. p. 44.

20. Herodotus, V. 39.

21. Plutarch, I. 196.

22. Eduard Meyer, *Geschichte des Altertums*, Stuttgart, 1884, vol. i. p. 28.

23. Plutarch, *Life of Pyrrhus*.

24. Euripides, *Andromache*, 596.

25. Meiners, *Geschichte*, vol. i. pp. 105 et seq.; English translation by F. Shobert, *History of the Female Sex*, 4 vols., London, 1808, vol. i. pp. 89 et seq.

26. Ibid., vol. i. pp. 19 et seq. and vol. i. pp. 17 et seq.

27. Strabo, *Geographica*, xii. 31.

28. Meiners, *Vermischte philosophische Schriften*, p. 174.

29. Meiners, *Geschichte*, vol. i. pp. 74 et seq. and pp. 160 et seq.; *History*, pp. 62 et seq., and pp. 134 et seq. It need hardly be said that Meiners himself fails to note the resemblance.

30. Waitz, op. cit., p. 102.

31. V. Jaeckel, op. cit., p. 60.

32. Lewis Henry Morgan, *Ancient Society*, New York, 1877, p. 466.

33. Spiegelberg, op. cit.
34. Ulrich Wilckens, *Grundzüge und Chrestomathie der Papyruskunde*, vol. ii. p. 211.
35. Spiegelberg, op. cit., p. 9.
36. Viktor Marx, *Beiträge zur Assyriologie*, vol. iv.
37. Diehlmann, *Forschungen auf dem Gebiete der Geschichte*.
38. Karl Steinhart, Einleitung zu Platons Werke (Platon's sämmtliche Werke mit Einleitung begleitet von K. Steinhart, 1850, etc.).
39. Strabo, IV. 3.
40. Ibid., XI. 13.
41. Adolf Erman, *Aegypten und ägyptisches Leben im Altertum*, 1896, vol. i. p. 115.
42. Christian Carl Josias Bunsen, *Aegyptens Stelle in der Weltgeschichte*, 1845–1857. English translation by C. H. Cottrell, *Egypt's Place in Universal History*, 5 vols., London, 1848–1867.
43. Müller, op. cit., p. 6.
44. George Kennan, *Tent Life in Siberia*, Putnam, New York and London, 1910.
45. Francis Bacon, *Novum Organum*.
46. Hugo Winckler, *Altorientalische Forschungen*, Leipzig, 1893–1906, p. 76.

PART 3

History as Related to Women

LYDIA MARIA CHILD (1802–1880)

When I first discovered Child's *Brief History of the Condition of Women*, I had never heard of the author. A clue to her view regarding women was offered by a quotation from Byron's *Corsair* that she chose for her title page:

> I am a slave, a favored slave
> At best, to share his splendor, and seem very blest;
> When weary of these fleeting charms and me,
> There yawns the sack, and yonder rolls the sea.
> What! am I then a toy for dotard's play,
> To wear but till the gilding frets away?

My search for further knowledge of this author revealed that Lydia Maria Child was a prolific writer, probably the most popular woman writer in America of her day, whose works embraced an amazing variety of subjects. More than forty publications included stories for children, books for young girls, guides on housewifery, nursing, and mothering, biographies of famous women, books on outstanding men, novels, poems, and letters. In a contrasting vein she wrote extensively on the condition of the American Indians, and above all, on the evils of slavery. She and her husband, David Lee Child, were among the first in New England to throw themselves into the struggle for emancipation of the slaves. Of this struggle, John Greenleaf Whittier wrote, "Thenceforth her life was a battle; a constant rowing hard against the stream of popular prejudice and hatred. And through it all—pecuniary privation, loss of friends and position."[1] And further, "While faithful to the great duty which she felt was laid upon her in an especial manner, she was by no means a reformer of one idea, but her interest was manifested in every question affecting the welfare of humanity. Peace, temperance, education, prison reform, and equality of civil rights, irrespective of sex, engaged her attention."[2]

This brief introduction cannot begin to give an adequate picture of this remarkably versatile woman. To compile the *History*, with the prodigious research it involved, would seem enough to take up the major part of a lifetime, yet it was only a small part of her total

135

literary productivity, to say nothing of the time she devoted to social causes.

The *History* first appeared in 1835, when Mrs. Child was only thirty-three years old. With a minimum of polemics, confining herself largely to description and recital of events, the author nevertheless succeeds in presenting a telling picture of woman's debased status through most of recorded history.

The few condensed excerpts given here are gleaned from a two-volume compendium of information drawn from the Bible, the Koran, the Shastra or Hindu Bible, and ancient historians and poets, including Herodotus, Tacitus, Pausanias, Plutarch, Thucydides, Euripides, Menander, Eustathius, and others. Her specificity in regard to local customs among a great variety of peoples of the world suggests a familiarity with reports of her contemporaries who traveled to exotic lands.

A careful perusal of this work yields some fascinating items for speculation. For example, in respect to the origin of the Hindu custom of suttee the author cites "a tradition that women many centuries ago frequently murdered their husbands; and the Bramins [*sic*] . . . put an effectual check to it by saying it was the will of the gods that widows should be burned on the funeral pile of their husbands."[3] Similarly, she relates that the custom of binding the feet of Chinese women "originated several centuries ago, when a numerous body of women combined together to overthrow the government; and to prevent the recurrence of a similar event it was ordained that female infants should wear wooden shoes, so small as to cramp their feet and render them useless."[4] Shades of Amazonism! The author is reporting, with no interpretive inferences, ancient myths consistent with theories of other investigators that an age of matriarchy existed at some early time which was overthrown by a patriarchal revolution. These reports fit neatly into later speculations of Bachofen, Ward, and others.

The reader whose attitude toward women has possibly been conditioned by the stories of Potiphar's wife and Phaedre may find piquant the tale included here of the rajah's wife and the prime minister, which reverses the sex roles in regard to the attempted seduction and the false witness.

One of the shortcomings of the *History* is the failure to provide systematic documentation of source material. While references to sources abound within the narrative, the pattern is inconsistent and incomplete. Thus, to my chagrin, the references for the three significant anecdotes related above are missing.

Although Lydia Maria Child was not an active participant in the Women's Rights Movement, the position of women was of major concern to her. Thanking George Curtis for his Women's Rights speeches, she wrote:

> I thank you, in the name of the crippled class to which I belong, for trying to ennable us to walk without crutches. My disabilities as a woman have annoyed me more than I have told you. When my friend Ellis Gray Loring wanted to entertain himself with seeing my face flush and my eyes kindle, he used to repeat, "A married woman's dead in the eyes of the law." To *me* who felt so very much alive. . . .[5]

The few samplings offered here can give only a little of the flavor of the wealth of fascinating detail of the customs and traditions, the sufferings and the glories, in the lives of women in the far corners of the world, as reflected in this *History.*

Brief History of the Condition of Women

[Jewish Women]

The ancient patriarchs led a quiet pastoral life, far removed from those excitements which kindle the avarice and ambition of men in modern times. Their chief care was to increase their flocks; and for this purpose they removed their tents, from time to time, near the most verdant pastures and abundant fountains. Their habits and manners partook of the simplicity of their occupations; of this there is sufficient proof in the story of Jacob's courtship and marriage.

In those times, when the earth was thinly peopled, an increase of laborers was an increase of wealth. . . . To be the mother of a numerous family was the most honorable distinction of women; and the birth of a son was regarded as a far more fortunate event than the birth of a daughter. Under such circumstances, women were

From Lydia Maria Child, *Brief History of the Condition of Women,* 2 vols. (1835; New York: C. S. Francis & Co., 1845).

naturally considered in the light of property; and whoever wished for a wife must pay the parents for her, or perform a stipulated period of service, as Jacob did for Rachel. Sometimes, when parents were desirous to unite their families, the parties were solemnly betrothed in childhood, and the price of the bride stipulated. Marriage in those primitive times consisted merely in a formal bargain between the bridegroom and the father of the maiden, solemnized by a feast. . . .

Among the Israelites, as well as among the nations with whom they sojourned, innocence was by no means universal. The world seems very soon to have grown old in sin. . . . The deception practised by Abraham and his son Isaac, lest the beauty of their wives should be the occasion of their own death, betrays habits and manners sufficiently violent and profligate. That the husbands of Sarah and Rebecca should have been willing thus to consult their own safety, at the risk of exposing them to insult, is by no means extraordinary among a people where polygamy prevailed; for in all such countries the value placed upon women has an origin essentially low and depraved. We are told that Sarah herself consented to pass for the sister of her husband; and both in Egypt and in Gerar the handsome stranger was ordered into the household of the king. That marriage was acknowledged as a protection, and that the concealment of it left her defenceless, is shown by Pharoah's earnest expostulation with Abraham: "What hast thou done unto me? Why saidst thou, She is my sister? Why didst thou not tell me she was thy wife?" . . .

Jewish husbands seem to have had a discretionary power of divorcing their wives; and no bargain or vow made by a woman was binding, unless made in the presence of her father or husband, and with their sanction.

Before the time of Moses, women appear to have been incapable of inheriting the estates of their fathers, even when he died without other heirs. The daughters of Zelophead brought before Moses, the priests, the princes, and the congregation a petition, setting forth that their father had died in the wilderness without sons; on which account they thought themselves entitled to a share of his possessions. Moses granted the petition, and ordained that in future, when a man died without sons, his inheritance should descend to the daughters. . . .

In the patriarchal ages the Jewish women must have enjoyed a large share of personal freedom; for we read of all ranks engaged in the labors of the field, and going out of the cities to draw water. That they were not usually secluded from visiters [*sic*] seems to be implied by the question which the strangers asked Abraham, "Where is Sarah, thy wife?" Indeed, living as they did in tents, and removing so frequently, it would have been no easy matter to have preserved the complete privacy that exists in the seraglios of the East. But as the Jews grew more numerous and wealthy, the higher ranks indulged in a much greater number of wives, and kept them more carefully secluded. Solomon had seven hundred wives, and three hundred mistresses; but these, like horses and chariots, were probably valued merely as the appendages of ostentatious grandeur. To prevent the increasing tendency to polygamy, a law was made forbidding any man who took a new wife to diminish the food and raiment of his other wives, or in any respect to treat them with less attention. . . .

That women sometimes transacted business and made bargains in their own name, seems to be implied in the Proverbs: "She considereth a field and buyeth it; with the fruit of her hands she planteth a vineyard. She maketh fine linen and selleth it. She delivereth girdles to the merchant." It is likewise certain that women went with their husbands to Jerusalem, and worshipped in the temple on solemn festivals.

Even in those days there was no dearth of invective against the follies and vices of the sex. Solomon praises good women in the most exalted terms; but he implies their extreme rarity by the question, "Who can *find* a virtuous woman?" The son of Sirach says, "All wickedness is but little to the wickedness of a woman." "From garments cometh a moth, and from women wickedness." "A loud crying woman and a scold shall be sought out to drive away the enemies." "A drunken woman and a gadder abroad causeth great anger." . . .

. . . among the Jews, as well as other nations, we find a strong tendency to believe that women were in more immediate connection with Heaven, than men. Miriam, the sister of Aaron, was a prophetess, and seems to have possessed great influence. Deborah, the wife of Lapidoth, was not only a prophetess, but for many years a judge in Israel; and we are told that Barak refused to go up with his army against Sisera, unless she went up with him. At a later period, there was Anna the prophetess, who for many years remained in the temple of the Lord, night and day, in fasting and prayer. . . . The belief in women who were under the influence of evil spirits, is shown by the story of the witch of Endor.

That women were imbued with the sternness which marked the barbarous character of men, is evident in the story of Jael, who drove the nail through the temples of Sisera, her sleeping guest; and of Judith, who deliberately bewitched the senses of Holofernes, that she might gain an opportunity to sever his head from his shoulders. . . .

[Babylonian Women]

Little is known of ancient Assyria, and of Babylonia, which was at first a part of Assyria. Being a wealthy and luxurious nation, their women were of course treated with a degree of consideration unknown among savage tribes. . . .

. . . With regard to marriages, they had a yearly custom of a peculiar kind. In every district three men, respectable for their virtue, were chosen to conduct all the marriageable girls to the public assembly. Here they were put up at auction by the public crier, while the magistrates presided over the sales. The most beautiful were sold first, and the rich contended eagerly for a choice. The most ugly or deformed girl was sold next in succession to the handsomest, and assigned to any person who would take her with the least sum of money. The price given for the beautiful was divided into dowries for the homely. Poor people, who cared less for personal endowments, were well content to receive a plain wife for the sake of a moderate portion. . . .

When the Babylonians were besieged by the Persians, they strangled all the women except their mothers, and one other in each family, to bake their bread. This was done to prevent famine; and the lot fell upon women because they were of less importance in carrying on the war.

It is not known whether females were admitted into the priesthood; but a woman always slept in the temple of Jupiter Belus, whom the Chaldean priests declared to have been chosen by the deity as his especial favorite from among all the nation.

Two remarkable women are mentioned in the brief records we have of Assyria and Babylon. Their names are Semiramis and Nitocris.

When Ninus, king of Assyria, besieged Bactria, it is said the attempt would not have been successful, had it not been for the assistance of Semiramis, who was at that time the wife of one of his principal officers. She planned so skilful a method of attack, that victory was insured. Ninus became a passionate lover of the sagacious lady, and her husband committed suicide. Soon after this she became queen. Some say she requested the monarch to invest her with uncontrolled power merely for the space of five days; and as soon as a decree to this effect had been made public, she caused him to be put to death; but other authors deny this. She succeeded Ninus in the government of the Assyrian empire, and to render her name immortal, she built the great city of Babylon in one year. Two millions of men were constantly employed upon it. Certain dykes built by order of the queen, to defend the city from inundations, are spoken of as admirable.

Altars were built and divine honors paid to the memory of Semiramis.

The other celebrated queen was Nitocris, wife of Nabonadius, who in the Scripture is called Evil Merodach. She was a woman of great endowments. While her voluptuous husband gave himself up to what the world calls pleasure, she managed the affairs of state with extraordinary judgment and sagacity. She was particularly famous for the canals and bridges which she caused to be made for the improvement of Babylon.

Such instances as these do not indicate a degraded condition of women. Yet the Assyrian monarchs had seraglios, at least in times later than Nitocris; for we are told that the effeminate Sardanapalus spent his chief time in the apartments of his women, learning to handle the distaff, and imitating their voice and manners. . . .

[Lycian Women]

The ancient Lycians, supposed to be descendants of the Cretans, always took their names from their mothers, and not from their fathers. When any one was asked to give an account of his ancestors, he mentioned the female branches only. If a free woman married a slave, the children were free; but if a citizen married a concubine or a foreigner, his children could not attain to any political dignity. The inheritance descended to daughters, and sons were excluded. . . . A woman presided over the different companies into which the Cretans were divided, had the entire management of the household, and at table gave the choicest food to those who had most distinguished themselves. . . . The Lycian men mourned for the dead by assuming female garments.

[Carian Women]

Artemisia, queen of Caria, so famous for her wisdom and bravery, was descended from the Cretans on the mother's side. By the death of her husband she was left with the government of the kingdom, until her son should be of age. She served with Xerxes in his expedition against Greece, and furnished five of the best ships in the fleet. She endeavored to dissuade the Persian monarch from venturing a naval battle at Salamis; but her judicious advice not being accepted, she commanded her portion of the fleet, and fought with the utmost bravery. When her vessel was pointed out to Xerxes, he exclaimed, "The men on this occasion behave like women, and the women like men." The Athenian conquerors considered themselves so much disgraced by having a female antagonist, that they pursued her with the utmost vengeance, and offered ten thousand drachmae to whoever would take her alive. But she escaped in safety to her own kingdom by means of an artifice; for having attacked one of her own allies, with whom she was displeased, the Greeks supposed her vessel to be one friendly to their cause. . . .

[Ionian Women]

The Asiatic Greeks, particularly those of Ionia, were distinguished for voluptuous refinement, and the beauty and gracefulness of their women. The celebrated Aspasia, first the mistress, and afterwards the wife of Pericles, was of Ionia. Her wit and eloquence must have equalled her beauty; for we are told that

Plato loved to discourse philosophy with her, and that Pericles sought her advice in great political emergencies.

[Asiatic Women]

Zenobia, queen of Palmyra and the East, is the most remarkable among Asiatic women. Her genius struggled with, and overcame, all the obstacles presented by oriental laws and customs. She is said to have been as beautiful as Cleopatra, from whom she claimed descent. She knew the Latin, Greek, Syriac, and Egyptian languages; had drawn up, for her own use, an abridgement of oriental history; and read Homer and Plato under the tuition of Longinus. She was the companion and friend of her husband, and accompanied him on his hunting excursions with eagerness and courage equal to his own. She despised the effeminacy of a covered carriage, and often appeared on horseback in military costume. Sometimes she marched several miles on foot, at the head of the troops. Having revenged the murder of her husband, she ascended the throne, and for five years governed Palmyra, Syria, and the East, with wonderful steadiness and wisdom. After a long and desperate resistance she was conquered by the Roman emperor Aurelian, who had grown jealous of the increasing wealth and power of his rival. . . .

[Arabian Women]

The Arabs, though Mohammedans, seldom have more than one wife. Divorces rarely take place, unless for misconduct, or for not being the mother of children. If the Arabian women are fortunate enough to have several sons, they are almost idolized by their husbands. The little girls are fair, but they are almost universally exposed to hardships, which soon spoil the complexion. . . .

The Bedouins live in tents, divided into three apartments, one for the men, one for the women, and one for the cattle. . . .

The Bedouins consider their wives as slaves, and exercise arbitrary power in punishing them for any fault. One of them is said to have beat his wife to death merely because she had lent his knife without permission, though she begged pardon and offered in the humblest manner to go and bring it for him. Being called before a council of the chief men of the tribe, he acknowledged the offence; saying he had told the deceased never to meddle with any thing of his, and he was determined to have a wife who would obey him better. The chief reproved him for not first making a complaint to him; adding that if his wife should, after such a step, be guilty of disobedience, he had a right to kill her if he pleased. The murderer was ordered to pay four sheep, as a penalty for not making application to the sheik or chief; and soon after he married another woman. . . .

. . . the Arabs are in general extremely jealous of the honor of their women. They would immediately stab a wife or daughter, who was supposed to have disgraced herself. A single life is considered so disrespectable, that a woman, in order to avoid it, will marry a man very much her inferior, or even consent to be the second wife of one already married. . . .

The Kereks are not so kind to their wives as the Bedouins, with whom they often intermarry. A woman cannot inherit the merest trifle of her husband's property. Even during his lifetime he does not supply her with necessary clothing; she is obliged to beg of her father, or steal her husband's wheat, and sell it clandestinely. No greater insult can be offered to a Kerek than to tell him he sleeps under the same blanket with his wife; for they do not allow the women to share their apartments. When a wife is ill, they send her back to her parents, saying they paid for a healthy woman, and cannot have the expense of an invalid. . . .

[Persian Women]

The Persians seem to have been remarkable among the ancient nations for a savage jealousy of women, which led them to keep the objects of their love perpetually imprisoned and guarded. . . .

A Persian woman, under the dominion of the kindest master, is treated in much the same manner as a favorite animal. To vary her personal graces for his pleasure is the sole end and aim of existence. . . . They are allowed to learn a little reading, writing, and embroidery; but their reading is confined to the Koran, and even that they generally read very imperfectly. . . .

The Persian women are kept continually shut up in the *harem,* which they rarely leave from the cradle to the grave. They are visited only by female relations, or female teachers, hired to furnish them their scanty apparatus of knowledge. The mother instructs her daughter in all the voluptuous coquetry by which she herself acquired precarious ascendency over her absolute master; but all that is truly estimable in female character is neglected, as it ever must be where nothing like free and kind companionship exists between the sexes. . . .

The contempt in which women are held is singularly exemplified by a Persian law, which requires the testimony of four of them in cases where the declaration of two men would be deemed sufficient. While talking with a person of rank, it would be considered grossly impolite to make the most remote allusion to the female part of his family; even if his beloved wife were on her death-bed, it would be deemed an almost unpardonable insult to make any inquiries concerning her. . . .

[Hindoo Women]

The architectural remains and ancient literature of Hindostan give a high idea of their knowledge and refinement in remote ages. According to their old poets, women were then regarded with a kind of chivalrous gallantry, and enjoyed a degree of personal freedom, to which modern Asiatic women are entire strangers: Sacontalu, the adopted daughter of a holy Bramin, is the heroine of an interesting old drama, in which she is mentioned as receiving strangers with the most graceful hospitality; and when Dusmantha was absent from his capital, his mother governed in his stead. Women were then admitted as witnesses in courts of justice, and where the accused was a female, their evidence was even preferred.

Malabar boasts of her seven sages, and four of them were women. The celebrated Avyar, one of the most ancient of these sages, probably lived more than a thousand years ago. . . .

The Mohammedan creed, which everywhere produces a miserable effect on the destiny of women, has considerably changed their condition in Hindostan. The higher classes among the Hindoos, without adopting the religion of the Mussulmans, copied their jealous precautions with regard to females.

Wives are numerous, according to the wealth and character of their owners. A petty Hindoo chief has been known to have several hundred female slaves shut up in his zananah.[1] Under these unnatural circumstances, we cannot wonder at the character of women given by one of their pundits, as the Braminical expositors of law are called: he says, "Women are characterized, first, by an inordinate love of jewels, fine clothes, handsome furniture, and dainty food; second, by unbounded profligacy; third, by violent anger and deep resentment, no one knowing the sentiments that lie concealed in their hearts; fourth, another person's good appears evil in their eyes." This is but one among many instances wherein men have reproached the objects of their tyranny with the very degradation and vices which their own contempt and oppression have produced. How can it be wondered at that women, with all the feelings and faculties of human nature, and unnaturally deprived of objects for their passions, affections, or thoughts, should seek excitement in petty stratagem and restless intrigue?

No Hindoo woman is allowed to give evidence in courts of justice. The Bramins have power to put their wives to death for unfaithfulness; but it is said that milder punishments are more usually inflicted. . . .

This crime in Hindoo women is generally punished by expulsion from their caste, a heavy fine, and the bastinado. It is considered a still more disgraceful penalty to have the hair cut off. This is rarely inflicted, except upon very abandoned females, who are afterward plastered with filth, and led about on a donkey, accompanied with the sound of tamtams.

Instances of extreme injustice sometimes occur, as must always be the case where human beings are invested with arbitrary power.

One of the rajahs of Hindostan had a beautiful wife, whom he loved better than all the rest of his women. A young man, who was originally his barber, gained his confidence to such a degree that nothing could be done but through his interest. The rajah, having accepted an invitation to an annual festival held at a great distance, trusted every thing to the integrity of this prime minister. Before his master had been gone a week, the villain dared to make love to his favorite wife. She treated him with indignation and scorn, and threatened, if he continued to repeat professions of his love, that she would expose his baseness. He knew the rajah had a most fiery and impetuous temper, and he at once resolved how to escape danger, and to be revenged upon his virtuous victim. He sought an interview with his master the very first moment he returned, and by a tissue of plausible falsehoods, made him believe that his favorite wife was a faithless creature, entirely unworthy of his confidence. The rajah, in a fit of blind fury, flew into the zananah, and without speaking a word, murdered the beautiful object of his recent attachment. . . .

The Nairs, on the coast of Malabar, have very extraordinary customs, for the origin of which it is difficult to account. They are usually married before they are ten years of age; but it would be deemed exceedingly indecorous for the husband to live with his wife, or even to visit her, except as an acquaintance. She lives with her mother, and prides herself on the number of her lovers, especially if they be Bramins or rajahs; but if any of them were her inferiors, she would be immediately expelled from her caste, which is the greatest misfortune that can befall a Hindoo. Owing to these strange customs, a Nair has much more affection for his sister's children than for those of his wife, and no one is offended at being asked who is his father. . . . Sons inherit the fortune of the maternal grandfather. The heir apparent to the throne of Travancore is not the son of the rajah's wife, but of his oldest sister, who is treated as queen.

The Nairs treat their mothers with the utmost respect, and have a filial regard for maternal uncles and aunts; but they scarcely notice their fathers, and have little affection for brothers and sisters. . . .

Truly, in no part of the world does the condition of women appear more dreary than in Hindostan. The arbitrary power of a father disposes of them in childhood; if the boy to whom they are betrothed dies before the completion of the marriage, they are condemned forever after to perpetual celibacy; under these restraints, if their affections become interested and lead them into any imprudence, they are punished with irretrievable disgrace, and in many districts with death; if married, their husbands have despotic control over them; if unable to support them, they can lend or sell them to a neighbor; and in the Hindoo rage for gambling, wives and children are frequently staked and lost; if they survive their husbands, they must pay implicit obedience to the oldest son; if they have no sons, the nearest male relative holds them in subjection; and if there happen to be no kinsmen, they must be dependent on the chief of the tribe. . . .

The self-immolation of widows is of great antiquity. The natives have a tradition that women many centuries ago frequently murdered their husbands; and the Bramins, finding the severest punishments of no avail, put an effectual check to it, by saying it was the will of the gods, that widows should be burned on the funeral pile of their husbands. . . .

The custom of murdering female infants, which formerly prevailed throughout several districts in India, is so unnatural that it could not be believed, if it were not proved beyond all possibility of doubt. The horrid act was generally done by the mothers themselves, either by administering opium as soon as a child was born, smothering it, or neglecting the precautions necessary to preserve life. Now and then a wealthy man saved one daughter, especially if he had no sons; but the practice of infanticide was so general, that when the young men wanted wives, they were obliged to seek them in such neighboring tribes as their laws permitted them to marry. The marquis of Wellesley, during his government of India, made great exertions to have this abominable custom abolished; but the natives were very stubborn in their prejudices. They urged the natural inferiority of females, the great responsibility which attended their bringing up, and the expense incident upon their marriages. . . .

[Chinese Women]

A foot unnaturally small is considered a great beauty. In order to attain this, the higher classes bind tight bandages round the feet of female infants, so that none but the great toe is suffered to retain its natural position. This compression is continued until the foot ceases to grow. It is than a misshapen little stump, four or five inches long, with all the smaller toes adhering firmly to the sole. The growth thus cruelly checked in its proper place, increases the ankle to such a clumsy size, that it almost entirely conceals the foot. When the ladies attempt to walk, they seem to be moving on stumps, and hobble along in the most awkward manner imaginable. Their little shoes are as fine as tinsel and embroidery can make them.

According to Chinese history, this custom originated several centuries ago, when a numerous body of women combined together to overthrow the government; and to prevent the recurrence of a similar event it was ordained that female infants should wear wooden shoes, so small as to cramp their feet and render them useless. . . .

. . . The apartments of the women are separated from those of the men by a wall, at which a guard is stationed. The wife is never allowed to eat with her husband; she cannot quit her apartments without permission; and he does not enter hers without first asking leave. Brothers are entirely separated from their sisters at the age of nine or ten years.

Divorces are allowed in cases of criminality, mutual dislike, jealousy, incompatibility of temper, or too much loquacity on the part of the wife.

The Chinese character is grave, ceremonious, and taciturn. It is said that women are in the habit of answering concisely, and seldom speak unless spoken to; nevertheless the Chinese proverb declares, "What women have lost in their feet they have gained in their tongues." If female loquacity be a ground for divorce, it may render the marriage contract very precarious, even in China. A husband can neither put away his wife, nor sell her, until a divorce is legally obtained. If she leaves him, he may immediately commence an action at law, by the sentence of which she becomes his slave, and he is at liberty to sell her to whom he pleases. . . .

A husband has always a right to sell an unfaithful wife for a slave. Women do not inherit property, but it may be left to them by will.

Next to submission, industry is inculcated as the greatest of female virtues. The following are extracts from a Chinese ballad: "Employment is the guardian of female innocence; do not allow women time to be idle; let them be the first dressed, and the last undressed, all the year round." . . .

The custom of exposing infants, principally daughters, prevails in China, as well as in some parts of Hindostan. . . .

In the mountainous districts of China is a singular tribe called the Miao-Tse. They live together in the utmost harmony, under the government of elders. The men and women dress almost exactly alike. The men wear ear-rings, and the women carry a sword. Both go barefoot, and climb the sharpest rocks with the swiftness of mountain goats. . . . One of these women defended a fort against

Chinese troops, for more than two months after every other being but herself was killed. She contrived to fire several muskets in such a manner as to deceive them with regard to the strength of the garrison; and at every moment of leisure she collected heaps of large stones, to hurl down upon them from different places with her foot. . . .

NOTE

1. The Hindoo word for harem.

LADY SYDNEY MORGAN (1776?–1859)

It was perhaps characteristic of Lady Sydney Morgan's flair for the provocative that she gave the satirical title *Woman and Her Master* to her history of woman. With this work she "brought her long train of creative literary efforts to a singularly beautiful and effective close."[1]

Rising from obscure beginnings as the daughter of an Irish actor, Lady Morgan had won both acclaim and notoriety with earlier works, both fiction and nonfiction, which had addressed themselves to Irish national grievances against England and to the rights of the common people in France and Italy. Because of her liberal views she was subjected to virulent criticism and savage personal attack by both the Whig and the Tory press. She was branded a revolutionary and an atheist, though she was hardly either. Her response to the onslaught of criticism was chivalrously summed up by her biographer, William J. Fitzpatrick: ". . . with her own fragile female hand she parried undauntedly the assaults of a furious and organized host of Critic-Cut-Throats, and finally hurled them, one by one, to the ground, where the teeth that had been sharpened to gnaw this brilliant woman's heart, impotently bit the dust beneath her feet."[2]

The report of her biographer as well as her personal memoirs reveal a woman of vivacity and good humor, of eloquence and charm, brisk and captivating, and withal a courageous champion of freedom and equality. Shortly before her death the influential journal the *Athenaeum* was generous enough to write: "Through more years than we care to say, her name was as signs among the combatants, her voice sounded as a trumpet through Whig and

Tory camps, and a new book from her hand drummed a host of enemies and friends to arms. She wrote, too, in an age when, to be a woman, was to be without defence, and to be a patriot, was to be a criminal."[3]

In preparing *Woman and Her Master* Lady Morgan carried out a laborious investigation of the records of the past. In regard to biblical events, she traces the role of women, extracting from the scant information given in historical sources perceptive inferences regarding the intellect, the wisdom, the inspiration, and the relative compassion of a gallery of forceful women—Eve, Sarah, Rebecca, Miriam, the daughters of Zelophehad, Deborah, Naomi, Ruth, Hannah, the witch of Endor, Abigail, Michal, the wise woman of Tekoah, the wise woman of Abel in Bethmaachah, the Queen of Sheba, the Alexandras, Esther, and others. In regard to such anathematized characters as Jezebel and Athalia, she has the courage to scrutinize and interpret the scriptural statements, and to present a version of their cases showing that they were courageous, indomitable women, possibly more sinned against than sinning. Throughout the text of the Bible she extracts phrases which reveal that in an increasingly patriarchal society the influence and power of women survived. She was still too tied to the tenents of Judeo-Christian religion to suspect, as a modern feminist might, that the writers of the Bible, as arbiters of good and evil, portrayed as villainesses those women who opposed the patriarchal theocracy. In the time frame in which she lived, and already maligned as an atheist, she could hardly be expected to speculate, as a modern feminist might, that the continuing ascription of the power of prophesy to women as well as the ever-recurring execration of those who worshipped former deities (often female) intimated the ongoing struggle against an earlier matriarchal society, which constantly threatened to revive.

The few pages from her voluminous work are included here to give the reader a slight acquaintance with this dynamic, courageous woman. Chapter I serves as an introduction and a statement of her thesis, and following it are a few illustrative short excerpts from the body of the work.

The two completed volumes follow the history of woman down to the period just before the fall of the Roman Empire. Failing sight interfered with the work and probably prevented its continuation to a later period.

Woman and Her Master

Book I, Chapter I

The chronicles of six thousand years, the records of the known world, lie open for the benefit of mankind, preserving, in pages indited by the lights of their respective times, monuments of the ignorance, the timidity, and the credulity, of successive generations. . . .

. . . In the great and general progress of knowledge, much has been neglected, much overstepped; and, amidst the most beneficial reforms and sagacious improvements, great moral incoherences still linger, which require to be eliminated, before the interests of humanity can be based upon a system, consonant with nature, and conducive to general happiness.

But where lies the oversight? Can it be one, astounding in its obviousness, and all-important in its mischiefs? While codes have been reformed, institutes rationalized, and the interests of orders and classes have been minutely attended to, has one half of the human species been left, even to the present moment, where the first rude arrangements of a barbarous society and its barbarous laws had placed it. Is woman still a thing of sufferance and not of rights, as in the ignorant infancy of early aggregation, when the law of the strongest[1] was the only law acted on? and in the great impulsion to a regenerating reform, has that most applicable and intelligible instrument of social improvement and national well-being, has Woman, been forgotten?

Even now, when supremacy has been transferred from muscle to mind, has that most subtle spirit, that being of most mobile fibre, that most sensitive and apprehensive organization—has *she*, whom God has placed, to be a "mate and a help to man," at the head of his creation, the foundress of nations, the embellisher of races, has she alone been left behind, at the very starting-post of civilization, while around her all progresses and improves? And is man still "the master," and does he, by a misdirected self-love, still perpetuate her ignorance and her dependence, when her emancipation and

---

From Lady Sydney Morgan, *Woman and Her Master* (1840; London: David Bryce, 1855).

improvement are most wanting, as the crowning element of his own happiness? If, in the progress of refinement, he has brightened instead of breaking the chain of his slave, he has only linked a more shewy nucleus of evil to his own destiny, and bound up, with his noblest views of national and social development, a principle that too often thwarts the progress and enfeebles the results of his best reforms.

If, in the first era of society, woman was the victim of man's physical superiority, she is still, in the last, the subject of laws, in the enactment of which she has had no voice—amenable to the penalties of a code, from which she derives but little protection. While man, in his first crude attempts at jurisprudence, has surrounded the sex with restraints and disabilities, he has left its natural rights unguarded, and its liberty unacknowledged. Merging the very existence of woman in his own, he has allowed her no separate interest, assigned her no independent possessions: "for," says the law—the law of man—"the husband is the head of the wife, and all that she has belongs to him."[2] Even the fruit of her own labour is torn from her, unless she is protected by the solitary blessedness of a derided but innocent celibacy, or by an infamous frailty. . . .

But in vain has opinion, the new depository of power, the antagonist of physical force, opened its tribunals to the wrongs of the aggrieved! Even there her master meets her, citing against her what *he* calls philosophy and science; and if, even while these lines are tracing, a scanty measure of partial and reluctant amelioration has been wrung from the legislature, the exceptional fact has only been made an occasion for the sterner assertion of the outrageous principle. The natural dependence of the sex on its master, its imputed inaptitude for the higher intellectual pursuits, and presumed incapacity for concentration, are still insisted upon; and, while woman is permitted to cultivate the arts which merely please, and which frequently corrupt, she is denounced as a thing unsexed, a *lusus naturae*, if she directs her thoughts to pursuits which aspire to serve, and which never fail to elevate.

Educating her for the Harem, but calling on her for the practices of the Portico, man expects from his odalisque the firmness of the stoic, and demands from his servant the exercise of those virtues which, placing the *élite* of his own sex at the head of its muster-roll, give immortality to the master. He tells her "that obscurity is *her* true glory, insignificance her distinction, ignorance her lot, and passive obedience the perfection of her nature"; yet he expects from her, as the daily and hourly habit of her existence, that conquest over the passions by the strength of reason, that triumph of moral energy over the senses and their appetites, and that endurance of personal privations and self-denials, which with him (even under all the excitements of ambition and incentives to renown) are qualities of rare exception, the practices of most painful acquirement.

Such has been the destiny of woman amongst the most highly-organized and intellectual of the human races, and in the regions most favourable to their moral development. . . .

But how has this Pariah of the species, this alien to law, this dupe of fictions and subject of force—how has she felt, how acted, how borne the destiny assigned her? Has she bowed her head to the yoke with tame acquiescence, as one for whose nature it was fitted and adapted? or has she, as slave, concubine, or wife, felt and protested? Has she not, under the corrupting influence of oppression, sometimes converted those qualities of her sex, which were designed as the supplement of the intellectual system of the species, as an aid to man in his war with the elements, into weapons against him? Has not her quick apprehension often degenerated into cunning under his misrule? Has she not, in discovering how little was to be hoped from his justice, succeeded in founding an empire over his passions? And has not man, who denies every right that interferes with his own supremacy, submitted to the spell which undermines it; and, by thus giving influence, direct or indirect, where he has withheld knowledge and denied rights, established an insidious, ignorant tyranny that perpetually thwarts his own designs, injures the best interests of society, and retards its progress to reform?

Still, notwithstanding her false position, woman has struggled through all disabilities and degradations, has justified the intentions of Nature in her behalf, and demonstrated her claim to share in the moral agency of the world. In all outbursts of mind, in every forward rush of the great march of improvement, she has borne a part; permitting herself to be used as an instrument, without hope of reward, and faithfully fulfilling her mission, without expectation of acknowledgement. She has, in various ages, given her secret services to her task-master, without partaking in his triumph, or sharing in his success. Her subtlety has insinuated views which man has shrank from exposing, and her adroitness found favour for doctrines, which he had the genius to conceive, but not the art to divulge. Priestess, prophetess, the oracle of the tripod, the sibyl of the cave, the veiled idol of the temple, the shrouded teacher of the academy, the martyr or missionary of a spiritual truth, the armed champion of a political cause, she has been covertly used for every purpose, by which man, when he has failed to reason his species into truth, has endeavoured to fanaticise it into good; whenever mind has triumphed by indirect means over the inertia of masses.

In all moral impulsions, woman has aided and been adopted; but, her efficient utility accomplished, the temporary part assigned her for temporary purposes performed, she has been ever hurled back into her natural obscurity, and conventional insignificance: no law against her has been repealed, no injury redressed, no right admitted. Alluded to, rather as an incident than a principal in the chronicles of nations, her influence, which cannot be denied, has been turned into a reproach; her genius, which could not be concealed, has been treated as a phenomenon, when not considered as monstrosity!

But where exist the evidences of these merits unacknowledged, of these penalties unrepealed? They are to be found carelessly scattered through all that is known in the written history of mankind, from the first to the last of its indited pages. They may be detected in the habits of the untamed savage, in the traditions of the semi-civilized barbarian! and in those fragments of the antiquity of our antiquity, scattered through undated epochs,—monuments of some great moral *débris*, which, like the fossil remains of long-imbedded and unknown species, serve to found a theory, or to establish a fact.

Wherever woman has been, there has she left the track of her humanity, to mark her passage—incidentally impressing the seal of her sensibility and her wrongs upon every phasis of society, and in every religion, "from Indus to the Pole."

Humbly but "fearlessly" to plead her cause, and to illustrate her agency, by traits more graphic than didactic, is the object of the following pages.

Book I, Chapter III

. . . there are fragments of the history of . . . nations, which, like the lingering fires of expiring volcanoes, throw up, here and there, flashes to brighten the darkness of woman's destiny, and show her able and prompt to justify the original intention of nature in her favour. It is related in the brief story of the Cretans and of the Syrians, that their national genealogy was carried on from mother to daughter, the bearers and bestowers of the family cognomen, and the inheritors of its wealth.

Woman, too, in ancient Crete, presided over the companies into which the population was divided. In the time of Xerxes . . . the prejudice in favour of the Cretan women was so great, that Artemisia (who could prove her Cretan descent from the mother's side) was accepted as a leader in the army of Xerxes, and a member of his council. Her sagacious advice to the headlong prince might have saved him at Salamis, had he adopted it; and it was in watching her efforts at the head of his fleet, that he exclaimed, "The men have this day behaved like women, and the women are behaving like men."[3]

When the existence of Troy itself remains a mystery and a doubt, the tale of Cassandra, her genius and her fate, cannot be cited as a direct proof of the position of the Asiatic women in that city. Still, as a mere poetical conception, embodying an ancient tradition, it may be adopted as implying a prevalent opinion of wisdom and forethought in the sex, to which it assigns the divine honours of prophecy; and as an impersonation of the female character, according to the notions imported into Greece by the Asiatic colonies. . . .

Egypt, that land where man was wisest,—Egypt, from whose intellectual fires[4] Greece and Rome borrowed the lights, by which worlds then unguessed at, and races then unknown, have since learned the laws of Nature and the philosophy of morals,—Egypt, from her remotest existence, assumed the female form, as the representative of a superintending Providence; and gave to Isis a homage, which the assigned co-partner of her divinity, Osiris, never received.

The image of a young mother, with her child on her bosom, Isis, suckling the infant Horus, was to the initiated of the Egyptians a personification of Nature; or rather, this worship offered to the "queen of Heaven," the "mother of the universe," of "gods and men,"[5] was addressed to the great source of the imperishable elements, the essence of life itself. . . . After an interval of many thousand years, the sublime fragments of the Temple of Tentyra, as they rise, in their ruined magnificence, on the boundless horizon of the vast and dreary solitudes they glorify, attest to this day the religious associations of the Egyptians with their reverence for motherhood. . . .

. . . the last and greatest of the Cleopatras was she who closed the heroic history of her country with her own. The glory of Egypt, and the intellectual powers of her women, sunk together in the tomb of the daughter and successor of Ptolemy-Auletes. Accused, by the eulogists and parasites of her enemies, of crimes most prevalent in the age, and in the caste to which she belonged, the halo of her patriotism still threw a redeeming light over the shadow of her faults, brightening, if it did not efface them. Cleopatra loved Egypt better than the Caesars loved Rome, and struggled to the last for the independence of *her* country, as they had done against the liberty of theirs. Opposed to the most able and powerful men that ever lived, she finally conquered the world's conquerors, by the brilliant qualities of her mind, and the seductive influence of her charms. She successively subdued Julius, enslaved Antony, and outwitted Augustus. When proclaimed the partner of the Imperator of Rome, and when her statue was placed in the temple of its gods, she only used her power over the hearts of "the world's great masters," to save Egypt and to increase her dominions.[6] From a fugitive princess, wronged, friendless, dethroned, and hunted to the death by unnatural kindred, she made herself an independent sovereign queen, and raised the decaying capital of her kingdom to be the intellectual metropolis of the universe; a shrine to which the wise men of all nations brought their tributes.

Never was Egypt so rich in wealth, power, and civilization, as under the reign of this last of its queens, who made knowledge the basis of national supremacy, who reconstructed that precious library, which man in his madness had destroyed; and who, when the treasures of the Roman empire were made disposable at her will, (by the prodigality of the enamoured Antony) replied to his offers:—"the treasures I want are two hundred thousand volumes from Pergamus, for my library of Alexandria."

Cleopatra encouraged science, loved the arts, cultivated letters, and was irresistibly eloquent in seven different languages, all of which she spoke with the purity of her mother tongue. . . .

Book II, Chapter III

. . . whenever they [Hebrew women] do appear, as queens, stateswomen, champions, or patriots, they come forth in illuminated characters, brightening the page they occupy; sometimes indeed sharing the crimes of the men, but oftener surpassing them in intellectual device, and fearless volitions.

Even the characters of the dauntless and guilty queen of Ahab, king of Israel, the anathematized Jezebel and her immortal daughter Athaliah, held forth by the Jewish priesthood, for the express execration of their own times, and of posterity,—bold and bad as they were, still rose superior to the weak and wicked men who surrounded and opposed them.

The powerful king of Israel, Ahab, returning home "heavy and displeased," because he had been frustrated in an act of puerile despotism, by the sturdy independence of Naboth, who refused to part with his vineyard for money, Jezebel meets her royal husband with a wife's anxiety, and a woman's quick perception; and asks, "Why is thy spirit so sad that thou eatest not bread?" "Because (he replies) I spake unto Naboth the Jezreelite, and said unto him, Give me thy vineyard for money, or else, if it please thee, I will give thee another vineyard." "And Jezebel his wife said unto him, dost thou now govern the kingdom of Israel! arise, and eat bread, and let thy heart be merry, *I* will give thee the vineyard of Naboth the Jezreelite."

So she wrote letters in Ahab's name, and sealed them with his seal, and sent the letters to the nobles, and to the elders, that were in his city dwelling with Naboth. And she wrote in the letters, saying "Proclaim a fast, and set Naboth on high among the people," etc. etc. etc.[7]

The crime of Jezebel was enormous, and though Ahab, in profiting by it, shared the criminality, he wanted the hardihood and decision which urged his guilty wife to perpetrate the deed. Her equal in guilt, he was her inferior in device and courage.

But still the greatest error attributed to Jezebel was her

resistance to the Jewish priesthood: for she was the daughter of the king of Tyre, and, professing the religion of her fathers, had her own temple raised, by Joab's permission, with her own priests, to the number of four hundred. All these were massacred by the state hierarchy of Judah, with her husband Ahab's offspring, and her own damsels, together with many of Ahab's great men, and his kinsfolk, and his priests, all of whom were put to death, until none "were left remaining."

This was an awful retribution. Jehu, the instrument of this priestly vengeance, the anointed usurper of her husband's throne, the destroyer of her family, of her friends, her kindred and her partizans, excused his outrage by the prophecy of Elijah, by whom the death of the proud Jezebel herself was predicted, even to its minutest and most ferocious detail.

Throughout all the history of this bold and bad woman, she appears to have been superior in firmness of purpose to the weak and vacillating man to whom she was united, and upon an equality in courage with the bad men against whom she was opposed.

Her genius, her prowess, and her misfortunes were inherited by her ill-starred daughter Athaliah, by her marriage, queen of Judah. . . . Athaliah was not, like her mother, a Tyrian princess, "the daughter of a strange land." She was a Hebrew, the daughter of Ahab king of Israel. . . . Certainly no little toleration must have been admitted in Israel, when the queen Jezebel was allowed to raise an altar in its capital to Baal, the god of the Tyrians, to surround it with delicious groves and gardens, and to establish her own priesthood in Samaria.

At this altar worshipped also Athaliah, the daughter of Ahab and Jezebel. But when the young apostate Jewess, brought up in her mother's faith, became the wife of Joram, king of the orthodox Judah, and had the art, or persuasion, to pervert her husband (the seventh descendant from David), the hope of the Jewish hierarchy, the son of the most devoted of their flock (the pious Jehoshaphat), —the consequence was widely different. "Joram (says Josephus), not content with imitating the impiety of the kings of Israel, his predecessors, learnt from Athaliah, his wife, to pay to her strange gods sacrilegious adorations; and, though, owing to the promises made to David, God did not exterminate him and his race," no such promise protected Athaliah, or her father, (Israelites and apostates, like Joram). No vengeance, therefore, was spared that could afflict and outrage the unfortunate queen of Judah, until the extermination of her family, prophesied by Elijah the prophet, was fully and fearfully accomplished.

The agent of this dreadful prediction, the cruel and treacherous Jehu,[8] "slew all that remained of the house of Ahab, and all his great men, and all his kinsfolk, and his friends, and he left him none remaining—none in Israel!" One, however, there was in Judah, who had survived parents, brothers, son, friends, who knew that the dogs had eaten the flesh, and lapped the blood of her mother, in the streets of her own capital, and that the heads of her brothers ("of the king's sons") had been sent in baskets, by Jehu, to Jezreel, and that the perpetrator of these deeds of blood, the murderer of her family (upheld by the powerful hierarchy of her own Jerusalem), was seated on her father's throne.[9]

This remnant of a once numerous and powerful family, was Athaliah, queen of Judah, the widowed and childless sovereign of Jerusalem, a woman of powerful passions and indomitable spirit, who, "when she saw that her son Ahaziah was dead, (murdered with the rest), arose and destroyed the seed royal," and "continued to reign over Judah"—to reign miserable and wicked, and wicked because she was miserable. But she reigned not long: the rescue of the infant Joas from the vengeance of the infuriated Athaliah by his aunt, the wife of the High Priest Jehoiada, still saved the race of David for the great destiny prepared for it. . . . The infant Joas . . . was suddenly brought forth, when he had attained his eighth year; and . . . was presented to the people as the sole remaining scion of the house of David, and as the legitimate king of Judah.

Joas was crowned and anointed in the temple, amidst the shouts of "God save the king"; and these shouts brought Athaliah from her palace to the temple, by that royal way which the fated queen had still a right to pass. . . . The instant command of the High Priest (Jehoiada) for the death of the solitary and bereaved woman, who then presented herself boldly in the midst of her armed enemies, . . . her murder, which instantly followed, near the torrent of Cedron, are traits that render the story one of those grand tragedies of fact, which fiction but faintly imitates, and never surpasses. . . .

Book II, Chapter IV

Artaxerxes, king of Persia, the Ahasuerus of scriptural story, having given a royal feast in the capital of his empire to the representatives of many strange nations, his beautiful and beloved queen Vashti refused to attend, on the plea that the law of Persia forbade women to show themselves before strangers. Her disobedience became a subject of state enquiry; the seven magi, the interpreters of the Persian laws, were summoned, and their decisions taken. The queen was pronounced guilty of a greater crime than violating the laws of the land, of a violation of the law of nature, by the resistance of woman to the divine-righted power of man! "The Magi urged (says the Jewish historian) the danger of Vashti's example to the women of Persia, and the domestic insubordination and public evil it might produce."[10]

Vashti was, in consequence, repudiated. . . .

Book III, Chapter II

. . . what did the reason and justice of the Greeks effect, for the encouragement of virtue in the wife and mother? The Egyptian Cecrops, the early legislator of Athens, abolished polygamy, and ordained that marriage, a consecrated union with one woman, should be dissoluble only by death, or a legal divorce. He even admitted the wives of the free citizens to something like political rights; allowing them to attend all public meetings in which the affairs of state were discussed.

But Solon . . . treated the sex with less esteem. Marriage, indeed, he left on its original footing; but by considering woman less as a member than as a ward of the state,—as a being whose intellectual capacity would never attain to majority—he took the shortest and most effectual means for providing that she never should. Multifarious as were his laws for the education of the male youth, for the development of their every faculty,—for the utmost cultivation of every natural endowment, he was contemptuously silent on the moral and intellectual education of females. He, who provided for the elegant texture of the courtesan's drapery, left to chance the instruction of the Athenian daughters; or rather, perhaps, designedly forbade the cultivation of their minds, lest their aspirations after knowledge should diminish their aptitude for domestic drudgery and monotonous seclusion.

Whatever laws were framed in reference to the sex, were provisions of restraint, not of protection. They considered the free women, as they did the slaves, only as members of the family, not as constituents of the republic. The paramount object of the lawgiver was the legitimacy of the infant citizen; and to obtain that, his coarse agency sought only the incarceration of the neglected mother, who, condemned to the solitude of the Gynoecium (the homeliest and remotest apartment of her husband's sumptuous mansion) seldom saw the lord of her destiny, or associated with her male relations.

Even that model of Athenian husbands, the wise and virtuous Ischomachus, the friend of Socrates, is quoted as saying, that "there were few men with whom he had conversed so seldom, or of whom he had seen so little, as he had of his own wife." "Yet," observes Xenophon, "his regard for her was as great as it was virtuous." The Athenian of later times, indeed, could no longer sell his daughter or sister; but, whatever her age, the unmarried woman was placed under the absolute tutelage and control of her male relations. Fathers, grandfathers, and brothers, contracted the marriages of the better classes of women, without their knowledge or consent: and when no such relation existed, "let her marry," (says Solon) "whom the laws shall appoint." . . .

In the Greek drama (and the drama has been the mirror of manners of all times), the destiny of the Greek wives, their wrongs and oppressions, are subjects of constant complaint and reproach. The splendid Medea of Euripides ascribes the crimes and misfortunes of her sex to laws, which obliged women to purchase husbands with large fortunes, only to become their slaves and victims.[11] Even in the best age of Athens, the daughters of persons of distinction were brought up with no other society or instructors than ignorant mothers and corrupt slaves; dress was their sole science, embroidery their sole acquirement, ignorance their portion, and privation their penalty. . . .

One dogma only was conveyed to the undeveloped mind of the sex—"to be faithful to their masters"; a command which embraced all the privations of the stoic, and anticipated all the virtues of the Christian: for what was obedience to such a law, but to return good for evil, and service for neglect; to maintain faith to the faithless, to offer devotion to the selfish, and love to the unloving! . . .

Innocent, however, or offending, injuring or wronged, the low estimate of the sex has been notified to posterity, in the contemptuous language of the finest of the Greek poets, and of the most spiritual of the Greek philosophers: and Euripides and Plato, however elevated their ideas of the capacity of the sex, stand alike accused as the unwearied traducers and unsparing calumniators of their contemporary women. . . .

NOTES

1. "The husband, by the old law, might give his wife moderate correction; for as he is to answer for her misbehaviour, the *law thought reasonable* to intrust him with this power of restraining her by domestic chastisement, allowing him—flagellis et fustibus acriter verberare uxorem," etc.—*Blackstone.*

2. "The very being or legal existence of the woman is suspended during the marriage, or, at least, is incorporated or consolidated into that of the husband, under whose wing, protection, and cover, she performs every thing (and is therefore called, in our law-French, a feme coverte, or covert Baron, or, under the protection and influence of her husband, her Baron, or Lord; and her condition during her marriage is called her coverture)."—*Blackstone.*

3. The fragment of a society, so constituted, still survives on the coast of Malabar, in the military tribes of Nairs, where the succession follows the female line. In the battle of Assaye, fought by the Duke of Wellington, in 1803, against the Marhattas, a female, the begum of Lumroom, fought with the enemy, at the head of her cavalry;—a strange anomaly, in that quarter of the globe, where the sex is most despised and trampled on.

4. In the Egyptian Pantheon, Athor, Neith, and Isis, are placed in equality with Osiris, Amon, and Anubis.

5. Athor and Isis; the one so often named the "queen of Heaven," the other the "mother of the universe."

6. By the addition of Cyprus, Cilicia, Judea, and Syria.

7. I Kings, Chap. xxi. This is one of the earliest instances of female letter-writing on record. [Morgan is referring to Jezebel's contriving that an accusation of heresy and treason be brought against Naboth, and ordering that he be stoned.]

8. II Kings, Chap. ix, x.

9. Jehu, after he had collected all the worshippers of Baal by a stratagem, murdered them in cold blood. The translator of Josephus, in the heads of his chapters of the ninth book, thus sums up the murders committed by Jehu, after his anointment:—"Jehu killed with his own hand Joram, king of Israel, and Ochosias (the Ahaziah of Scriptures), king of Judah (the brother and son of Athaliah), and put to death Jezebel, seventy sons of Ahab, all the relatives of this prince, forty-two relatives of Ochosias, nearly all the priests of Baal, the god of the Tyrians, to whom Ahab had raised a temple." . . .

10. Josephus.

11. Potter.—Vol. ii., p. 297.

OTIS TUFTON MASON (1838–1908)

In his anthropological studies of primitive cultures Otis Tufton Mason appears to have carried on a love affair with his subject. He was astonished at the ingenuity and achievements of primitive people and filled with admiration, perhaps even exaltation, over the remarkable accomplishments of the women. Immediate insight into his orientation toward the female sex is evident on the title page of *Women's Share in Primitive Culture:*

> To All Good Women, living or dead,
> who with their brains or by their toil
> have aided the progress of the World
> I dedicate this book.

Here, as with most of the authors represented in this book, the condensed excerpts can convey only an intimation of the mass of illustrative data the author has offered, with obvious affection and reverence, as a tribute to the women of all ages.

Mason was convinced not only that primitive women were responsible for most of the work involved in carrying on daily life, but also that it was they in the main who had made the discoveries and inventions associated with agriculture, domestication of animals, medicinal aids, pottery making, skin dressing, weaving, basket making, tool making, aesthetic and language arts, religion, and social amenities, to say nothing of cooking and sewing.

In candor it must be said that Mason conceived of woman's primary role as that of child bearer, home keeper, and willing servant. Yet he recognized that she was fit for the most challenging societal roles, and, were he living today, in a time of pressure for population control, he would surely not have wished her to be denied opportunities at the highest levels of the social organization. Witness his statement:

> Brilliant examples of women skilled and potent in statecraft are not wanting among all civilized nations. The testimony of the best observers is to the effect that in primitive society there were queens in fact if not in name. Nothing is more natural than that the author of parental government, the

165

founder of tribal kinship, the organizer of industrialism, should have much to say about the form of housekeeping called public economy.[1]

Otis Tufton Mason was curator of the department of ethnology in the United States National Museum, Smithsonian Institution, Washington, D.C.

Woman's Share in Primitive Culture

Chapter I. Introduction

Of the billion and a half human beings on the earth, one half, or about seven hundred million, are females. What this vast multitude are doing in the world's activities and what share their mothers and grandmothers, to the remotest generation backward, have had in originating and developing culture, is a question which concerns the whole race. The answer to this inquiry will benefit the living in many ways, especially if it can be shown that the achievements of women have been in the past worthy of honour and imitation and have laid the foundation for arts of which all are now justly proud. . . . In the present work . . . the effort is made to set forth woman's share in the culture of the world by her works. . . .

Militancy and industrialism—these are the two periods into which Herbert Spencer divides the life history of civilization. First came the period of militancy, of savagery and barbarism, of warring between man and man, between man and Nature. After that succeeded the period of industrialism, when peoples settled down to the great occupations that dignify the most advanced nations.

Without calling in question this classification, the inquiry is here made whether these two words, in the early history of our species at least, did not mark a sexual division—whether, instead of an *age*, we should not rather say a *sex* of militancy and a *sex* of industrialism. Certainly there was never an age in which there was a more active armament, larger battle ships, more destructive

From Otis Tufton Mason, *Woman's Share in Primitive Culture* (New York: D. Appleton & Co., 1894).

explosives and cannon, and vaster establishments for the creation of engines and implements of death than in our own. From all these women are excluded, save now and then a few poor girls may be allowed for a pittance to fill cartridges; save that, as in the days of Tacitus, women carry food and cheers to their husbands on battlefields; save that the good sisters of the Red Cross bind up the wounds and minister to the wants of the unfortunate victims. In contact with the animal world, and ever taking lessons from them, men watched the tiger, the bear, the fox, the falcon—learned their language and imitated them in ceremonial dances.

But women were instructed by the spiders, the nest builders, the storers of food and the workers in clay like the mud wasp and the termites. It is not meant that these creatures set up schools to teach dull women how to work, but that their quick minds were on the alert for hints coming from these sources. Even though we disarm our soldiery, we do not seem to be able to dissociate men from the works that bring violent death. It is in the apotheosis of industrialism that woman has borne her part so persistently and well. . . .

How comfortless, however, was the first woman who stood upon this planet! How economical her dowry! Her body was singularly devoid of comfortable hair, her teeth and jaws were the feeblest, her arm was less powerful than that of any creature of her size, she had no wings like the birds, she could not see into the night like the owl, the timid hare was fleeter of foot then she. Her inventive genius and cunning fingers had not yet devised the sheltering tent or the comfortable clothing. As yet she had no tools of peaceful industry nor experience. Society had not then formed its body politic around her as a nucleus. She had poor ways of expressing her thoughts or her sense of beauty. So many secrets were held back from her by Nature, who knew so much and told so little. . . . As yet her magic touch had not even begun to cover the earth with waving grainfields or golden cornfields, or luscious fruit. . . . The road from her to my fair reader in the midst of many comforts is long indeed. But even this poorly equipped woman had more brain than was sufficient to meet the demands of bodily existence, and in this fact lay the promise of her future achievements. The maternal instinct, the strong back, the deft hand, the aversion to aggressive employment, the conservative spirit, were there in flower.

Her shop was ample enough, for it was the vaulted sky; but her tools and materials and methods were of the simplest kind. What we do in hours she accomplished in years. But if you could from some exalted position take in the exploitation of the earth and sea, the transformation of raw material into things of use, the transportation of these products in all directions, the commercial transactions involved in the sale of these commodities, you would be astonished to know how many of these wheels were set agoing by women in prehistoric times. . . .

In many books of travels woman among savage tribes is pictured to us as an abject creature born under an evil star, the brutalized slave of man, to be kicked or killed at his pleasure. . . .

It is not reasonable to suppose that any species or variety of animals would survive in which the helpless, maternal half is subjected to outrageous cruelty as a rule. According to the law of survival of the fittest, a tribe or stock of human beings in which brutality of this sort has place simply chooses the downward road and disappears. . . .

. . . Of one of the most primitive peoples E. H. Man says: "It is incorrect to say that among the Andamanese marriage is nothing more than taking a female slave, for one of the striking features of their social relation is the marked equality and affection which subsists between husband and wife. Careful observations extended over many years prove that not only is the husband's authority more or less nominal, but that it is not at all an uncommon occurrence for Andamanese Benedicts to be considerably at the beck and call of their better halves."[1]

From Africa we have the testimony of Livingstone upon the same subject. He offered one of Nyakoba's men a hoe to be his guide, which the man agreed to, and went off to show the hoe to his wife. He soon returned and said his wife would not let him go. After much chaffing the doctor was told: "Oh, that is the custom in these parts—the wives are masters."[2]

Among the Guiana Indians, says Im Thurn, an excellent observer, there is an equal division of labour, though that of the men is accomplished more fitfully than that of the women. No different distribution ever entered into the thoughts of Indians, and the women do their share willingly, without question and without compulsion. The women in a quiet way have a considerable amount of influence with the men; and even if the men were

—though that is contrary to their nature—inclined to treat them cruelly, public opinion would prevent this. Moreover, the women, just because they have been accustomed to hard labour all their lives, are little weaker than the men. If a contest arose between an average man and an average woman, it is very doubtful with which the victory would be.[3] . . .

Another popular error concerning the division of labour in savagery is the assertion that all woman's work is degrading to man and all man's work tabooed to women.

It is not denied that the taboo is in full force among primitive races. There are occasions in all aboriginal tribes when it would be fatal and ill-starred for a woman even to touch or to look upon objects to be used in men's activities. There are also occupations of women in which men think themselves degraded to engage. But nothing is more common than to see the sexes lending a helping hand in bearing the burdens of life. Men were the hunters and fishermen, but women went hunting and fishing. Women have been the spinners and weavers the world over, but there are occasions when men have to weave. . . .

We may close this introductory chapter with the significant words of Plutarch: "Concerning the virtues of women, O Clean-thes, I am not of the same mind with Thucydides. For he would prove that she is the best woman concerning whom there is the least discourse made by people abroad, either to her praise or dispraise; judging that, as the person, so the very name of a good woman ought to be retired and not gad abroad. But to us Gorgias seems more accurate, who requires that not only the face but the fame of a woman should be known to many. For the Roman law seems exceeding good, which permits due praises to be given publicly both to men and to women after death.

"Neither can a man truly any way better learn the resemblance and difference between feminine and virile virtue than by compar-ing together lives with lives, exploits with exploits, as the product of some great art; duly considering whether the magnanimity of Semiramis carries with it the same character and impression with that of Sesostris, or the cunning of Tanaquil the same with that of King Servius, or the discretion of Porcia the same with that of Brutus, or that of Pelopidas with Timoclea, regarding that quality of these virtues wherein lie their chiefest point and force."[4]

Chapter II. The Food Bringer

In this chapter we are to note the multiplicity of industries set agoing by woman in prehistoric times for the supply of aliment to mankind, in which she brings food and drink, and even medicine, to the use of her family.

To feed the flock under her immediate care, woman had to become an inventor, and it is in this activity of her mind that she is specially interesting here. . . .

In her exploitation of the vegetable world woman first appears as taking from the hands of Nature those fruits and other parts of the plant that are ready for consumption without further preparation. On the next journey she ventured a step further. With digging stick and carrying basket she went to search out roots and such other parts of plants as might be prepared for consumption by roasting or perhaps by boiling with hot stones. On her third journey she gathered seeds of all kinds, but especially the seeds of grasses, which at her hand were to undergo a multitude of transformations. Wherever tribes of mankind have gone women have found out by and by that great staple productions were to be their chief reliance. In Polynesia it is taro and bread fruit. In Africa it is the palm and tapioca, the millet and yams. In Asia it is rice, in Europe the cereals, and in America corn and potatoes, and acorns or piñons in some places. The whole industrial life of woman is built up around these staples. From the first journey on foot to procure the raw material until the food is served and eaten there is a line of trades that are continuous and that are born of the environment. The occupations necessarily grouped around any vegetal industry are the gathering of the plant or parts to be utilized, the transportation of the harvest from the field to the place of storage, the activities necessary to change a raw foodstuff into an elaborated product, and, lastly, the cooking and serving of the meal. It may be stated with much certitude, though there are noteworthy exceptions, that all of these processes in savagery were the function of woman, and in their performance she includes within herself a multitude of callings, some of which now belong largely to men. . . .

In [the] *rôle* of inventing the granary and protecting food from vermin the world has to thank woman for the domestication of the cat. There may be some dispute as to who has the honour of subduing the dog and the milk- and fleece-yielding animals. But woman tamed the wild-cat for the protection of her granaries. Of the time when this heartless beast laid down its arms and enlisted in her service no one knoweth. Already at the dawn of written history in Egypt the cat was sacred to Sekhet, or Pasht, daughter of Ra and wife of Ptah. Then as now the cat and the goddess had among their other qualifications the faculty of seeing in the dark. Her method of domestication was to secure the young wild-cats and rear them about her household as playthings for her children, and to gratify them in their instincts of prowling and seizing.

There is abundant proof among . . . divisions of humanity still living in [primitive conditions] . . . that women were the builders and owners of the first caches, granaries, and storehouse of provisions. A stroll through any market house will be convincing that they still keep up the very ancient custom of guarding bread.

When the time came to grind her seeds the woman discovered two implements, one of which is now exalted to the service of the apothecary, and may be seen any day over his door covered with gold leaf; the other holds its own as the implement of the miller.

Mortars are common enough in savagery, occurring in the forms of stone with stone pestles, of wood with wooden pestles, of wood with stone pestles, but stone mortars with wooden pestles are rare. For the fabrication of these woman was entirely competent. . . .

The second class of implements for grinding seeds were in the nature of mills—and women grinding at a mill have passed into a proverb. . . .

It is again the woman, ransacking the vegetal kingdom, who learns to know the drinks that Nature yields. . . .

There are in many lands plants which in the natural state are poisonous or extremely acrid or pungent. The women of these lands have all discovered independently that boiling or heating drives off the poisonous or disagreeable element. . . .

The exploitation of the mineral kingdom by women in savagery was chiefly in the search and care for water. Their habitations were erected near to springs or streams, and from these to the domestic hearth an uninterrupted caravan has marched since the uses of fire. In the discussion of other employments will appear the multitudinous inventions for carrying, storing, and using water. The effect of environment in deciding whether the vessel shall be of skin, or bark, or wood, or pottery is worthy of attention. . . .

The scraping out of a spring deeper and deeper forms a well, and the lengthening of a conducting pipe converts it into an aqueduct or a conduit. Both of these industries had very humble origins at the hands of women. . . .

The men of those early times made weapons and all the paraphernalia of their daily use, and so did their female companions chip off the spall or flake of flinty rock to make their knives withal. They each carried at their sides a hard bit of bone, answering in every respect to the butcher's steel, and gave therewith from time to time new edge to their homely cutlery. . . .

Every savage knows that stones heated and brought in contact with water are fractured hopelessly. But there is an exception to this rule in the class of rocks usually called soapstone, steatite, potstone. The aboriginal mineralogist, after scouring the earth, discovered this fact. All over Eskimo land both lamps and cooking pots are made of this material. . . . The steatite pots found in southern California, among the graves of the extinct tribes of the Santa Barbara islands are almost globular, the mouths are only a few inches in diameter, the walls are in many examples less than an inch in thickness. Many are capable of holding several gallons, and numbers of them show long-continued exposure to fire. . . .

The earliest pots had no legs, but were propped up by loose stones against the base, serving the twofold purpose of preventing the tipping of the vessel and of lifting it up to allow the air to circulate thereunder and to create a draught.

One sunny day a company of savage women were alternately chatting and chipping in a soapstone quarry, when it occurred to one of them to leave a bit of the stone projecting here and there for legs. Happy thought! No sooner said than done. And after that all soapstone pots had legs. . . .

There are among ethnologists opposing schools of interpreting this simple act, some minimizing the poor woman's share therein, others giving her all the praise and Nature none.

Before dismissing the patient creature who all this time has been practicing for our instruction a multiplicity of arts it may not be amiss to ask her what is done with the fish and flesh that is not immediately to be cooked. To this she would reply, "This portion will be smoked, another will be sun-dried and ground and packed in marrow. . . ."

These same people dried clams, oysters, fish, and meat. . . .

Chapter III.   The Weaver

There is no work of woman's fingers that furnishes a better opportunity for the study of techno-geography, or the relationship existing between an industry and the region where it may have been developed, than the textile art. Suppose a certain kind of raw material to abound in any area or country: you may be sure that savage women searched it out and developed it in their crude way. . . .

It is customary to divide woman's textile industry in savagery into basket work and weaving. . . .

Subsidiary to these chief divisions of the textile art as practiced by women in savagery are spinning, netting, looping, braiding, sewing, and embroidery. . . .

Each and all of these require tools which the work-women must fashion for themselves. And, though the earth had the raw materials in abundance, it did not yield them without a search which would do honour to the manufacturers of our day.

. . . There are no savages on earth so rude that they have no form of basketry. The birds and beasts are basket-makers, and some fishes construct for themselves little retreats where they may hide. Long before the fire maker, the potter, or even the cook, came the mothers of the Fates, spinning threads, drawing them out, and cutting them off. . . . With few exceptions, women, the wide world over, are the basket-makers, netters, and weavers. . . .

. . . Aboriginal woman's basketry excites the admiration of all lovers of fine work. It is difficult to say which receives the most praise—the forms, the colouring, the patterns, or the delicacy of manipulation. . . .

A careful study of all woman's work in basketry, as well as in weaving and embroidery, reveals the fact that both in the woven and in the sewed or coil ware each stitch takes up the very same area of surface. When women invented basketry, therefore, they made art possible. Along with this fact, that each stitch on the same basket made of uniform material occupies the same number of square millimetres, goes another fact—that most savage women can count ten at least. The production of geometric figures on the surface of a basket or a blanket, therefore, is a matter of counting. If the enumeration is correct each time the figures will be uniform.

Now, many of the figures on savage basketry contain intricate series of numbers, to remember which cost much mental effort and use of numerals. This constant, every day and hour use of numerals developed a facility in them, and coupled with form in ornament, made geometry possible. The ever-present geometrician of savagery is the woman basket-maker. . . . She knew lines, triangles, squares, polygons of all sorts, meanders and a set of cycloidal curves. . . .

. . . Many savage basket-makers, . . . in trying to represent birds and clouds and the human form on their geometric material, conventionalized them, and then abridged these conventionalities, until they produced forms that might be the envy of Cairene rug weavers. . . .

Chapter IX. The Linguist

There have been many ways imagined for the beginnings of speech. The chief among them are the emotional or interjectional, the imitative or mimetic, and the responsive or intuitive, utterance of thought, will, and feeling.

When the true origin of language shall be explained, all of these theories and others will have to be taken into account, and in any event women will receive their share of credit. . . .

. . . It must not be forgotten that language is one of the great classes of human inventions, created just as were tools, processes of activity, artistic designs, institutions, and even worships. The invention of language has followed the line of evolution pursued in other activities, beginning with almost purposeless changes, and ending with cooperative and purposeful modifications. The earliest language . . . was made up of brief sentence terms, in which thoughts and emotions and wishes were couched in a single complex utterance, which was elucidated and enforced by accentuation and by gestures of the body. . . . The savage tribes, the primitive men and women, invented these utterances, and, leaving out the common expressions, the very nature of the case is convincing that women developed and owned more than half of the sentence terms that were not common property.

Women, having the whole round of industrial arts on their minds all day and every day, must be held to have invented and fixed the language of the same. . . .

If women in savagery had to do with butchering and tanning, and gleaning and carrying, and milling and cooking, and the interminable list of drudgeries before mentioned then women's continual mockings or chatterings or stammerings or ejaculations thereabout, repeated and repeated to one another and to their daughters, and even to their infant sons, became a considerable addition to the general stock of speech. Furthermore, women have invented terms for men to use—at least have put expressions into the mouths of their male infants to become a part of their stock. . . .

. . . the Mexicans say, "A woman is the best dictionary."[5] This unpremeditated confession is based upon an early induction made by the aborigines of that country centuries ago. Savage men, in hunting and fishing, are much alone, and have to be quiet, hence their taciturnity; but women are together, and chatter all day long. Away from the centers of culture women are still the best dictionaries, talkers, and letter writers. . . .

. . . The infinite number of gestures which are believed to be necessary for *the enforcement* of any thought must surely conform to woman's special employments. The pantomine of conversation is always in harmony with the subject, and so is the drama of ceremony. Men imitate the animals they hunt; women, both by voice and gesture, imitate what is theirs. . . . This last suggestion leads on to that inquiry how far women have helped to the selection and preservation of language through onomatopoeia. The female vocal apparatus is singularly adapted to the imitation of many natural sounds, and the female ear is correspondingly quick to catch the sounds within the compass of the voice. . . . Indeed, the attempt to catch the sounds easily within woman's capabilities has necessitated the cultivation of the falsetto voice in men.

The same rule holds true with regard to the whole series of poetic figures. As every one knows, analogy lies at the basis of most savage reasoning, and is the source of many applications of words. But for one moment consider that analogy is for some fancied resemblance the applying of a term with which we are familiar to some thing with which it is not generally associated. The poet who compared life to a weaver's shuttle drew his inspiration from woman's work. In the use of simile and metaphor, especially all through the daily ministrations, necessarily the tropes will conform to the easiest imagery of the speaker. Whole hosts of sound combinations are constantly acquiring special meanings in the minds and in the language of women for this very reason. Many of these survive to swell the general stock of language and to add to its richness. . . .

The fact is that women are naturally more voluble than men, have more things to talk about, are captured and carried about more, and spread the seeds of new words and their underlying thoughts. In an equally remarkable degree women have been the conservators of speech. . . . Women very early invented industries which were to last until the end of time. That they worked at them day in and day out without talking about them is not to be supposed. They did prattle about them, and gave names to them and to all the raw materials and tools and apparatus and methods and rules and productions and their thousand and one uses. As all these were to endure, the words and sentences which were attached to them became an integral part and symbols of them, and had the best chance of preservation. . . .

Chapter XII. Conclusion

Civilization is the composite result of progress from the purely natural life of the animal to the purely artificial life of the most enlightened individuals and peoples. This progress has always been made along the lines of satisfying human needs, of gratifying human desires. . . . Nature . . . has occupied the position of almoner, prompter, teacher, and friend, saying at first what she says now: Occupy the earth, dress and keep it.

The human race faced this duty in the beginning with endowments that seemed to be entirely inadequate from a zoölogical point of view, but with more brain and mind than the mere bodily wants demanded. . . . With this extraordinary capital the man and the woman set forth hand in hand, the former to fight and outwit, the latter to conserve and elaborate the results of victory; the former to explore and wander, the latter to settle down and congregate; the former becoming dispersive or centrifugal, the latter unifying and centripetal; the former developing the militant spirit, the latter the industrial spirit. Many thousands of books have been written to set forth the gallant deeds of men, and these have stirred a noble emulation in youthful minds; but few books have been devoted to the patience and energy of the other actor in the drama.

To accomplish the object in view in this work there has been no necessity of eulogizing or depreciating the author's own sex. The past has been a mixture of good and evil, of light and darkness, of justice and injustice, of knowledge and ignorance. . . . There is at the present time a great awakening among women as to their own attributes and functions and capabilities. They are seriously inquiring for the roads that will conduct them to their largest and noblest development. With eager eyes they look ahead to see whether they can discern the true outlines and character of that good life that is to be. . . .

It matters not whether we regard the history of the remotest past or the diverse civilizations of the present, the emancipation and exaltation of women are the synonym of progress. . . .

To sum up the results of our study, women in primitive life had their share in determining the relation of geography to history, in the conquest of the three kingdoms of Nature, in the substitution of other forces to do the work of human muscles, in the elaboration of industrial and aesthetic arts, in the creation of social order, in the production of language, in the development of religion. I mean that they had a peculiar part, aside from that they would have to play merely as human beings. . . .

Dealing with the mineral kingdom, it was woman's early function, using the same materials and means that men employed for their industries, to invent cutlery, hardware, mills, and the like. Of the four treatments of stone—chipping, battering, cutting and grinding—they were familiar with the first for making knives and scrapers; with the second in the manufacture of mortars and other grinding stone; but the cutting and polishing of stone were the legitimate work of men. Women almost wholly were the patrons of water springs and wells. . . . Women were the first salt-makers and extracted nitre from the ashes of certain plants. They also understood thoroughly the quarrying and manipulation of potter's clay, mineral paint, and soapstone.

There is no end to woman's connection with the vegetal kingdom. It is peculiarly hers. Of the four main uses of plants as food, fibre, timber, and in landscape gardening, only a moment's thought is necessary to discern woman's varied relations. It was her duty to gather the roots, the fruits, and the seeds, to transport and store them, to cook and serve them. No one ever heard of savage men having aught to do with the food-plant industry. The same is true of plant medicines. The first empirical physicians were not the sorcerers, but the herb women. They gathered the first materia medica.

These good women made another journey. It was to collect flexible grasses and barks and roots and woods for basketry and cloth, to put this material through the tedious processes of dyeing, splitting, twisting, weaving, netting, embroidery. They laid the foundation of the great modern textile institutions. . . .

Women wrought in wood or timber sparingly. It is true that they gathered faggots, cut down tent poles, and made dishes of bark and logs by hollowing them, but the makers of dugout boats and the carvers of war clubs were more frequently men than women.

But it would be a reprehensible oversight to pass by the beginnings of agriculture and gardening. In point of fact, in the great savage areas at this very moment women are just beginning to discover that they can raise plants cheaper than they can gather the wild ones.

Of the animals woman was not generally the slayer, though she was expert in fishing and in the taking of land animals alive. But she was the butcher, the skin dresser, the curer and packer, the cook and the server, and all men and women now engaged in such work must look back to savage women as the founders of their craft. The whole clan of bonnet-makers, dressmakers, tailors, furriers, were originally of the gentler sex, and woman was the original St. Crispin. Domestic animals were first tamed not for men to ride, but for the service of women—for their fleece and milk and strong backs. The most eminent of these animals have a double and perhaps a triple function. The horse, camel, cow, ass, dog, llama, and reindeer are burden bearers, on to whose backs women shifted a portion of their wearisome loads. The first four also yielded milk, the dog assisted in hunting, and all of them had good skins, which the women at first converted into some form of leather. As for the sheep and the goat, they still live for spinners and dairy-women and cooks. The discovery that the horse, the camel, the cow, the ass, the goat, and the reindeer would yield milk was one of the most useful ever made. . . .

All the social fabrics of the world are built around women. The first stable society was a mother and her helpless infant, and this

little group is the grandest phenomenon in society still. To attach
the man permanently to this group for the good of the kind has
been the struggle of the ages. No wonder that the mother goddess
exists in all theologies, that savages worship the all-producing earth
as mother, that maternity has been accorded the highest place in
prayer and adoration, that the Buddhists of China have changed
one of the chief Bodhisattvas into the adorable goddess Kwan-yin,
or Manifested Voice.[6] . . .

For the highest ideals in civilization, in humanitarianism,
education, and government the way was prepared in savagery by
mothers and by the female clan groups, and the most commanding
positions are at this moment in women's possession. Pedagogy and
the body politic had their foundations laid there. Bebel says that
"woman was the first human being that tasted bondage. Woman
was a slave before the slave existed."[7] But this expression takes all
the aroma from her fragrant life. She made a servant of herself, and
willingly, before there was any slavery. The emancipation of
woman is from a self-imposed bondage, as everybody knows. . . .

If women now sit on thrones, if the most beautiful painting in the
world is of a mother and her child, if the image of a woman crowns
the dome of the American Capitol, if in allegory and metaphor and
painting and sculpture the highest ideals are women, it is because
they have a right to be there. . . .

In the World's Columbian Exposition the place of honour was
occupied by the colossal statue of a young woman represented in
burnished gold. In one hand she held the world, in the other the
cap of emancipation or liberty. Upon her right hand stood the
building devoted to manufactures and liberal arts, upon her left
hand the temple of agriculture. In the distance the dairy, the
leather, and the horticultural buildings. In the anthropological
building, at the extreme south of the grounds, was an exhibit from
the cemetery of Ancon, in Peru. One figure was of especial interest
in this connection—the skeleton of an ancient Peruvian woman. It
was in a crouching attitude, wrapped in the customary grave
clothes, and about it were the spindles, cradle frame, pottery, and
dishes of vegetables with which she was familiar in her life and
from which her spirit was not to be separated in her death.
Spontaneously the thoughtful mind connected this crouching figure
with the statue in the place of honour, and with the noble buildings
and scenes about her. How wonderful the transformation, wrought

by no magic or legerdemain, but with woman's hands and heart and ingenuity!

It is not here avowed that women may not pursue any path in life they choose, that they have no right to turn aside from old highways to wander in unbeaten tracks. But before it is decided to do that there is no harm in looking backward over the honourable achievements of the sex. All this is stored capital, accumulated experience and energy. If all mankind to come should be better born and nurtured, better instructed in morals and conduct at the start, better clothed and fed and housed all their lives, better married and encompassed and refined, the old ratios of progress would be decupled. All this beneficent labour is the birthright of women, and much of it of women alone. Past glory therein is secure, and it only remains to be seen how far the future will add to its lustre in the preservation of holy ideals.

NOTES

1. [E. H. Man], The Andamanese Islanders, London, 1883. . . .

2. [David Livingstone], Travels in South Africa, New York, 1858, p. 667.

3. Im Thurn, Indians of British Guiana, p. 215. . . .

4. Plutarch, Concerning the Virtues of Women. Morals, Boston, 1870, Little, Brown & Co., vol. i, pp. 340, 341.

5. [Edward John Payne], Hist. of America, New York, 1892, vol. i, p. 307.

6. Samuel Johnson, Oriental Religions, China, p. 817.

7. August Bebel, quoted by Helen Campbell, the Arena, Boston, 1893, vol. vii, p. 153.

EUGENE A. HECKER (1880–1959)

Hecker's historical review traces the evolution of women's rights from the days of Augustus to the beginning of the twentieth century. The reader will note that in the excerpts presented here every statement dependent on evidence is referred to a primary source. The writer's extensive scholarship can be imagined when the reader is advised that these excerpts represent but a skeletal abstract of the whole text. For the sake of economy many fascinating illustrations, fully annotated, of social practices and authoritative comment have regrettably been deleted. In order to emphasize the early historical aspects, the better-known material on English and United States laws and practices has been omitted.

All I could learn about Eugene A. Hecker is that he was Master in the Roxbury Latin School, author of *The Teaching of Latin in Secondary Schools,* and married. I can only ponder with disbelief that way back in 1910 a secondary school Latin teacher came to write such a learned and sympathetic history of the condition of women. Before I was born, he favored such a radical idea as equal wages for equal work, while I as an adult in the thirties and forties accepted the cultural axiom that a working woman was depriving a man—and his family—of a livelihood.

This account reveals that even within recorded history women's rights have not followed one course, that is, from a very low point to a steadily improving condition. It is apparent that in some respects woman's condition was better in Roman times and with some so-called "barbaric" peoples than for a long period of the Christian era.

A Short History of Women's Rights

Chapter I. Women's Rights under Roman Law, from Augustus to Justinian—27 B.C. to 527 A.D.

The age of legal capability for the Roman woman was after the twelfth year, at which period she was permitted to make a will.[1] However, she was by no means allowed to do so entirely on her own account, but only under supervision.[2] This superintendence was vested in the father or, if he was dead, in a guardian;[3] if the woman was married, the power belonged to the husband. The consent of such supervision, whether of father, husband, or guardian, was essential, as Ulpian informs us,[4] under these circumstances: if the woman entered into any legal action, obligation, or civil contract; if she wished her freedwoman to cohabit with another's slave; if she desired to free a slave; if she sold any things *mancipi*, that is, such as estates on Italian soil, houses, rights of road or aqueduct, slaves, and beasts of burden. Throughout her life a woman was supposed to remain absolutely under the power[5] of father, husband, or guardian, and to do nothing without their consent. In ancient times, indeed, this authority was so great that the father and husband could, after calling a family council, put the woman to death without public trial.[6] The reason that women were so subjected to guardianship was "on account of their unsteadiness of character,"[7] "the weakness of the sex," and their "ignorance of legal matters."[8] Under certain circumstances, however, women become *sui iuris* or entirely independent: I. By the birth of three children (a freedwoman by four);[9] II. By becoming a Vestal Virgin, of whom there were but six;[10] III. By a formal emancipation, which took place rarely, and then often only with a view of transferring the power from one guardian to another.[11] Even when *sui iuris* a woman could not acquire power over any one, not even over her own children;[12] for these an agnate—a male relative on the father's side—was appointed guardian, and the mother was obliged to render him and her children an account of any property which she had managed for them.[13] On the other hand, her children were bound to support her.[14]

From Eugene Hecker, *A Short History of Women's Rights* (New York: G. P. Putnam's Sons, 1910; 2d ed. revised, with additions, Westport, Conn.: Greenwood Press, 1914).

So much for the laws on the subject. They seem rigorous enough, and in early times were doubtless executed with strictness. A marked feature, however, of the Roman character, a peculiarity which at once strikes the student of their history as compared with that of the Greeks, was their great respect for the home and the *materfamilias.* The stories of Lucretia, Cloelia, Virginia, Cornelia, Arria, and the like, familiar to every Roman schoolboy, must have raised greatly the esteem in which women were held. . . . The political influence wielded by women[15] was as great during the first three centuries after Christ as it has ever been at any period of the world's history; and the powers of a Livia, an Agrippina, a Plotina, did not fail to show pointedly what a woman could do. . . .

. . . All Roman historians speak with great admiration of the many heroic deeds performed by women and are fond of citing conspicuous examples of conjugal affection.[16] . . . In the numerous provisions for the public education at the state's expense girls were given the same opportunities and privileges as boys; there were five thousand boys and girls educated by Trajan alone.[17] . . .

. . . The woman's parents or guardians were accustomed to arrange a match for her,[18] as they still do in many parts of Europe. Yet the power of the father to coerce his daughter was limited. Her consent was important . . . yet . . . she had not complete free will in the matter: . . . The consent of the father was always necessary for a valid marriage.[19] . . . A daughter passed completely out of the power of her father only if she became *sui iuris* by the birth of three children or if she became a Vestal, or again if she married a special priest of Jupiter . . . , in which case, however, she passed completely into the power of her husband. . . .

The Roman marriage was a purely civil contract based on consent.[20] The definition given by the law was a noble one. "Marriage is the union of a man and a woman and a partnership of all life; a mutual sharing of laws human and divine."[21] The power of the husband over the wife was called *manus;* and the wife stood in the same position as a daughter.[22] No husband was allowed to have a concubine.[23] He was bound to support his wife adequately, look out for her interests,[24] and strictly to avenge any insult or injury offered her;[25] any abusive treatment of the wife by the husband was punished by an action for damages.[26] A wife was compelled by law to go into solemn mourning for a space of ten months upon the death of a husband.[27] . . . But a husband was not compelled to do any legal mourning for the death of his wife.[28]

The wife was, as I have said, in the power of her husband. Originally, no doubt, this power was absolute; the husband could even put his wife to death without a public trial. But the world was progressing, and that during the first three centuries after Christ the power of the husband was reduced in practice to absolute nullity I shall make clear in the following pages. I shall, accordingly, first investigate the rights of the wife over her dowry, that is, the right of managing her own property.

Even from earliest times it is clear that the wife had complete control of her dowry. The henpecked husband who is afraid of offending his wealthy wife is a not uncommon figure in the comedies of Plautus and Terence; and Cato the Censor growled in his usual amiable manner at the fact that wives even in his day controlled completely their own property.[29] . . . A wife could use her dowry during marriage to support herself, if necessary, or her kindred, to buy a suitable estate, to help an exiled parent, or to assist a needy husband, brother or sister. . . .

When the woman died, her dowry, if it had been given by the father . . . returned to the latter. . . .

A further confirmation of the power of the wife over her property is the law that prohibited gifts between husband and wife; obviously, a woman could not be said to have the power of making a gift if she had no right of property of her own. The object of the law mentioned was to prevent the husband and wife from receiving any lasting damage to his or her property by giving of it under the impulse of conjugal affection.[30] This statute acted powerfully to prevent a husband from wheedling a wife out of her goods; and in case the latter happened to be of a grasping disposition the law was a protection to the husband and hence to the children, his heirs, for whose interests the Roman law constantly provided.

Gifts between husband and wife were nevertheless valid under certain conditions. It was permissible to make a present of clothing and to bestow various tokens of affection, such as ornaments. . . .

The laws on adultery are rather more lenient to the woman than to the man. In the first place, the Roman law insisted that it was unfair for a husband to demand chastity on the part of his wife if he himself was guilty of infidelity or did not set her an example of good conduct,[31]—a maxim which present day lawyers may reflect upon with profit. A father was permitted to put to death his daughter and her paramour if she was still in his power and if he caught her in the act at his own house or that of his son-in-law; otherwise he could not.[32] He must, however, put both man and woman to death at once, when caught in the act; to reserve punishment to a later date was unlawful. The husband was not permitted to kill his wife; he might kill her paramour if the latter was a man of low estate, such as an actor, slave, or freedman, or had been convicted on some criminal charge involving loss of citizenship.[33] . . . He must at once divorce a wife guilty of adultery; otherwise he was punished as a pander, and that meant loss of citizenship.[34] Women convicted of adultery were, when not put to death, punished by the loss of half their dowry, a third part of their other goods, and relegation to an island; guilty men suffered the loss of half of their possessions and similar relegation to an island; but the guilty parties were never confined in the same place.[35] . . .

Now, all this seems rigorous enough; but . . . we must beware of imagining that a statute is enforced simply because it stands in the code. As a matter of fact, public sentiment had grown so humane in the first three centuries after Christ that it did not for a moment tolerate that a father should kill his daughter, no matter how guilty she was; and in all our records of that period no instance occurs. As to husbands, we have repeated complaints in the literature of the day that they had grown so complaisant towards erring wives that they could not be induced to prosecute them.[36] . . .

Gradually . . . the status of women changed and they were given greater and greater liberty. Inasmuch as Roman marriage was a civil contract based on consent, strict justice had to allow that on this basis either party to the contract might annul the marriage at his or her pleasure. The result was that during the first three centuries after Christ the wife had absolute freedom to take the initiative and send her husband a divorce whenever and for whatever reason she wished. . . .

Married women, spinsters, and widows had as much freedom as men in disposing of property by will. If there were children, the Roman law put certain limitations on the testator's powers, whether man or woman. . . .

Women engaged freely in all business pursuits. We find them in all kinds of retail trade and commerce,[37] as members of guilds,[38] in medicine,[39] innkeeping,[40] in vaudeville;[41] there were even female barbers[42] and charioteers.[43] . . .

When so many women were engaged in business, occasions for lawsuits would naturally arise; we shall see next what power the woman had to sue. It was a standing maxim of the law that a woman by herself could not conduct a case in court.[44] She had to act through her agent, if she was independent, otherwise through her guardian. . . . But in this case again custom and the law were at variance. . . .

We read of many cases of women pleading publicly and bringing suit. Indeed, according to Juvenal—who is, however, a pessimist by profession—the ladies found legal proceedings so interesting that bringing suit became a passion with them as strong as it had once been among the Athenians.[45] . . .

The rights of women to inherit under Roman law deserve some mention. . . . A daughter was considered a natural heir no less than a son and had equal privileges in succession;[46] and so women were bound to receive some inheritance at least. . . . It is a sad commentary on Christian rulers that for many ages they allowed the crimes of the father to be visited upon his children and by their bills of attainder confiscated to the state the goods of condemned offenders. Now, the Roman law stated positively that "the crime or punishment of a father can inflict no stigma on his child."[47] . . .

Rape of a woman was punished by death; accessories to the crime merited the same penalty.[48] . . . Temporary exile was visited upon those guilty of abortion themselves. . . . If the victim died, the person who caused the abortion was put to death.[49]

The rights of women to an education were not questioned. That Sulpicia could publish amatory poems in honour of her husband and receive eulogies from writers like Martial[50] shows that she and ladies like her occupied somewhat the same position as Olympia Morata and Tarquinia Molza later in Italy during the Renaissance, or like some of the celebrated Frenchwomen, such as Madame de Staël. Seneca addresses a *Dialogue on Consolation* to one Marcia; such an idea would have made the hair of any Athenian gentleman in the time of Socrates stand on end. Aspasia was obliged to be a courtesan in order to become educated and to frequent cultivated society;[51] Sulpicia was a noble matron in good standing. The world had not stood still since Socrates had requested some one to take Xantippe home, lest he be burdened by her sympathy in his last moments. Pains were taken that the Roman girl of wealth should have special tutors.[52] . . .

According to Juvenal, who, as an orthodox satirist, was not fond of the weaker sex, women sometimes became over-educated. He growls as follows:[53] "That woman is a worse nuisance than usual who, as soon as she goes to bed, praises Vergil; makes excuses for doomed Dido; pits bards against one another and compares them; and weighs Homer and Maro in the balance. Teachers of literature give way, professors are vanquished, the whole mob is hushed, and no lawyer or auctioneer will speak, nor any other woman." The prospect of a learned wife filled the orthodox Roman with peculiar horror.[54] No Roman woman ever became a public professor as did Hypatia or, ages later, Bitisia Gozzadina, who, in the thirteenth century, became doctor of canon and civil law at the University of Bologna.

I have been speaking of women of the wealthier classes; but the poor were not neglected. As far back as the time of the Twelve Tables—450 B.C.—parents of moderate means were accustomed to club together and hire a schoolroom and a teacher who would instruct the children, girls no less than boys, in at least the proverbial three R's. . . .

The position of women in slavery merits some attention, in view of the huge multitudes that were held in bondage. Roman law acknowledged no legal rights on the part of slaves.[55] The master had absolute power of life and death.[56] . . . If a master was killed, every slave of his household and even his freedmen and freedwomen were put to torture, although the culprit may already have been discovered, in order to ascertain the instigator of the plot and his remotest accessories.[57]

The earlier history of Rome leaves no doubt that before the Republic fell these laws were carried out with inhuman severity. With the growth of Rome into a world power and the consequent rise of humanitarianism[58] a strong public feeling against gratuitous cruelty towards slaves sprang up. . . . Measures were gradually introduced for alleviating the hardships and cruelties of slavery. . . .

. . . the laws that mitigated slavery under the Empire . . . were not ideal; but they would in more respects than one compare favourably with the similar legislation that was in force, prior to the Civil War, in the American Slave States.

Chapter II. Women and the Early Christian Church

. . . I shall inquire next into the position of women under Christianity. . . .

The direct words of Christ so far as they relate to women and as we have them in the Gospels concern themselves wholly to bring about purity in the relation of the sexes. . . . Christ was content to lay down great ethical principles, not minute regulations. Of any inferiority on the part of women he says nothing, nor does he concern himself with giving any directions about their social or legal rights. He blessed the marriage at Cana; and to the woman taken in adultery he showed his usual clemency. For the rest, his relations with women have an atmosphere of rare sympathy, gentleness, and charm.

But as soon as we leave the Gospels and read the Apostles we are in a different sphere. The Apostles were for the most part men of humble position, and their whole lives were directed by inherited beliefs which were distinctly Jewish and Oriental or Greek; not Western. In the Orient woman has from the dawn of history to the present day occupied a position exceedingly low. Indeed, in Mohammedan countries she is regarded merely as a tool for the man's sensual passions and she is not allowed to have even a soul. In Greece women were confined to their houses, were uneducated, and had few public rights and less moral latitude; their husbands had unlimited license.[59] The Jewish ideal is by no means a lofty one and cannot for a moment compare with the honour accorded the Roman matron under the Empire. According to *Genesis* a woman is the cause of all the woes of mankind. *Ecclesiasticus* declares that the badness of men is better than the goodness of women.[60] In *Leviticus*[61] we read that the period of purification customary after the birth of a child is to be twice as long in the case of a female as in a male. The inferiority of women was strongly felt; and this conception would be doubly operative on men of humble station who never travelled, who had received little education, and whose ideas were naturally bounded by the horizon of their native localities. We are to remember also that the East is the home of asceticism, a conviction alien to the Western mind. There is no parallel in Western Europe to St. Simeon Stylites.

We would, therefore, expect to find in the teachings of the

Apostles an expression of Jewish, i.e., Eastern ideals on the subject of women; and we do so find them. Following the express commands of Christ, they exhorted to sexual purity and reiterated his injunctions on the matter of divorce. They went much farther and began to legislate on more minute details. Paul allows second marriages to women;[62] but thinks it better for a widow to remain as she is.[63] It is better to marry than to burn; yet would he prefer that men and women should remain in celibacy.[64] . . . the words of Paul make it clear that it was now to be a Christian precept that a father could determine on his own responsibility whether his daughter should remain a virgin.[65] Wives are to be in subjection to their husbands, and "let the wife see that she fear her husband."[66] Woman is the weaker vessel;[67] she is to be silent in church; if she desires to learn anything, she should ask her husband at home.[68] Furthermore: "I permit not a woman to teach, nor to have dominion over a man, but to be in quietness. For Adam was first formed, then Eve; and Adam was not beguiled, but the woman being beguiled hath fallen into transgression; but she shall be saved through childbearing, if they continue in faith and love and sanctification with sobriety."[69] . . .

If now, we examine the writings of the Church Fathers, we shall see these ideas elaborated with all the vehemence of religious zeal. . . .

. . . St. Jerome held that women were naturally weaker, physically and morally, than men.[70] The same saint proves that all evils spring from women;[71] and in another passage he opines that marriage is indeed a lottery and the vices of women are too great to make it worth while.[72] "The sex is practiced in deceiving," observes St. Maximus.[73] St. Augustine disputes subtly whether woman is the image of God as well as man. He says no, and proves it thus:[74] The Apostle commands that a man should not veil his head, because he is the image of God; but the woman must veil hers, according to the same Apostle; therefore the woman is not the image of God. . . . Bishop Marbodius calls woman a "pleasant evil, at once a honeycomb and a poison" and indicts the sex,[75] something on the order of Juvenal or Jonathan Swift, by citing the cases of Eve, the daughters of Lot, Delilah, Herodias, Clytemnestra, and Progne. . . .

Marriage was looked upon as a necessary evil, permitted, indeed, as a concession to the weakness of mankind, but to be avoided if possible. "Celibacy is to be preferred to marriage," says St. Augustine.[76] . . .

As for second marriages, the Montanist and the Novatian sects condemned them absolutely, on the ground that if God has removed a wife or husband he has thereby signified his will to end the marrying of the parties. . . .

As soon as the Church begins to exercise an influence upon law, we shall expect to see the legal position of women changed. . . .

. . . the Church referred everything to one unchanging authoritative source, the Gospels and the writings of the Apostles; . . . any attempt to question the injunctions of the Bible was regarded as an act of impiety, to be punished accordingly. . . .

Chapter III. Rights of Women as Modified by the Christian Emperors

Christianity became the state religion under Constantine, who issued the Edict of Milan, giving toleration to the Christians, in the year 313. The emperors from Constantine through Justinian (527–565) modified the various laws pertaining to the rights of women in various ways. . . .

. . . the power of divorce was given for the following reasons alone: adultery, murder, treason, sacrilege, robbery; unchaste conduct of a husband with a woman not his wife and vice-versa; if a wife attended public games without her husband's permission; and extreme physical violence of either party. . . .

Justinian made more minute regulations on the subject of divorce. . . . Abortion committed by the wife or bathing with other men than her husband or inveigling other men to be her paramours—these offences on the part of the wife gave her husband the right of divorce.[77] . . .

Justin, the nephew and successor of Justinian, reaffirmed the right to divorce by mutual consent, thus abrogating the laws of his predecessors.[78] . . . Nothing can more clearly illustrate than his decree how small a power the Church still possessed to mould the tenor of the law; for such a thing as divorce by mutual consent, without any necessary reason, was a serious misdemeanour in the eyes of the Church Fathers, who passed upon it their severest censures. . . .

The consent of the father or, if he was dead, of near relatives was emphatically declared necessary by the Christian emperors for a marriage and the woman had practically no will of her own although, if several suitors were proposed to her, she might be requested to name which one she preferred.[79] Marriage with a Jew was treated as adultery.[80] Women who belonged to heretical sects were to have no privileges.[81] . . .

The Christian emperors permitted widows to be guardians over their children if they promised on oath not to marry again and gave security against fraud.[82] Justinian forbade women to act by themselves in any legal matters.[83]

Arcadius and Honorius (397 A.D.) enacted some particularly savage bills of attainder, which were in painful contrast to the clemency of their pagan predecessors. Those guilty of high treason were decapitated and their goods escheated to the crown. "To the sons of such a man [i.e., one condemned for high treason]," write these amiable Christians,[84] "we allow their lives out of special royal mercy—for they ought really to be put to death along with their fathers—but they are to receive no inheritances. Let them be paupers forever; let the infamy of their father ever follow them; they may never aspire to office; in their lasting poverty let death be a relief and life a punishment. Finally, any one who tries to intercede for these with us is also to be infamous."[85] However, to the daughters of the condemned these emperors graciously granted one fourth of their mother's but not any of their father's goods. . . . Constantine decreed that a wife's property was not to be affected by the condemnation of her husband.[86]

Ravishers of women, even of slaves and freedwomen, were punished by Justinian with death; but in the case of freeborn women only did the property of the guilty man and his abettors become forfeit to the outraged victim. A woman no longer had the privilege of demanding her assailant in marriage.[87]

Chapter IV. Women among the Germanic Peoples

A second world force had now come into its own. The new power was the Germanic peoples, those wandering tribes who, after shattering the Roman Empire, were destined to form the modern nations of Europe and to find in Christianity the religion most admirably adapted to fill their spiritual needs and shape their ideals. In the year 476 the barbarian Odoacer ascended the throne of the Caesars. . . .

In western Europe, then, new races with new ideals were forming the nations that to-day are England, Germany, France, Spain, Italy, and Austria. It is interesting to note what some of these barbarians thought about women and what place they assigned them.

Our earliest authorities on the subject are Julius Caesar and Tacitus. Caesar informs us[88] that among the Gauls marriage was a well recognized institution. The husband contributed of his own goods the same amount that his wife brought by way of dowry; the combined property and its income were enjoyed on equal terms by husband and wife. If husband or wife died, all the property became the possession of the surviving partner. Yet the husband had full power of life and death over his wife as over his children; and if, upon the decease of a noble, there were suspicions regarding the manner of his death, his wife was put to inquisitorial torture and was burnt at the stake when adjudged guilty of murder. Among the Germans women seem to have been held in somewhat greater respect. German matrons were esteemed as prophetesses and no battle was entered upon unless they had first consulted the lots and given assurance that the fight would be successful.[89] As for the British, who were not a Germanic people, Caesar says that they practiced polygamy and near relatives were accustomed to have wives in common.[90]

Tacitus wrote a century and a half after Julius Caesar, when the tribes had become better known to the Romans; hence we get from him more detailed information. From him we learn that both the Sitones—a people of northern Germany—and the British often bestowed the royal power on women, a circumstance which aroused the strong contempt of Tacitus, who was in this respect of a conservative mind.[91] The Romans had, indeed, good reason to remember with sorrow the valiant Boadicea, queen of the Britons.[92] Regarding the Germans Tacitus wrote a whole book in which he idealises that nation as a contrast to the lax morality of civilised Rome, much as Rousseau in the eighteenth century extolled the virtues of savages in a state of nature. . . . From

Tacitus we learn that the Germans believed something divine resided in women;[93] hence their respect for them as prophetesses.[94] One Velaeda by her soothsaying ruled the tribe of Bructeri completely[95] and was regarded as a goddess,[96] as were many others. The German warrior fought his best that he might protect and please his wife.[97] . . . The dowry was brought not by the wife to the husband, but to the wife by the husband—evidently a survival of the custom of wife purchase; but the wife was accustomed to present her husband with arms and the accoutrements of war.[98] . . . A woman guilty of adultery was shorn and her husband drove her naked through the village with blows.[99] . . .

. . . the woman was under the perpetual guardianship of a male relative and must do nothing without his consent, under penalty of losing her property.[100] Her guardian arranged her marriage for her as he wished,[101] . . .

The feeling of caste was very strong; a woman must not marry below her station.[102] By a law of the Visigoths she who tried to marry her own slave was to be burned alive;[103] . . .

The woman on marrying passed into the power of her husband, . . . and the husband thereupon acquired the lordship of all her property.[104] . . .

Adultery was not only a legal cause for divorce, but also a grave crime. All the barbarian peoples are agreed in so regarding it, but their penalties vary according as they were more or less affected by proximity to Italy, where the power of the Church was naturally strongest. . . .

It is always to be remembered that although the statutes were severe enough, yet during this period, as indeed throughout all history, they were defied with impunity. Charlemagne, for example, the most Christian monarch, had a large number of concubines and divorced a wife who did not please him; yet his biographer Einhard, pious monk as he was, has no word of censure for his monarch's irregularities;[105] . . .

Criminal law among these half civilised nations could not but be a crude affair. . . . They were content to fix the penalties for such outrages as murder, rape, insult, assault, and the like in money; . . .

. . . Fines were not paid to the state, but to the injured parties or, if these did not survive, to the nearest kin. . . .

Another peculiar feature of the Germanic law was the appeal to

God to decide a moot point by various ordeals. For example, by the laws of the Angles and Werini, if a woman was accused of murdering her husband, she would ask a male relative to assert her innocence by a solemn oath[106] or, if necessary, by fighting for her as her champion in the lists. God was supposed to give the victory to the champion who defended an innocent party. If she could find no champion, she was permitted to walk barefoot over nine red-hot ploughshares;[107] and if she was innocent, God would not, of course, allow her to suffer any injury in the act. . . .

Chapter V. Digression on the Later History of Roman Law

With Charlemagne, who was crowned Emperor by the Pope in the year 800, began the definite union of Church and State and the Church's temporal power. Henceforth for seven centuries, until the Reformation, we shall have to reckon with canon law as a supreme force in determining the question of the position of women. . . .

Before we enter the question of women's rights during the Middle Ages, we must take a general survey of the character of that period; . . . In the first place, . . . the Church was everywhere triumphant and its ideals governed legislation completely on such matters as marriage. The civil law of Rome, as drawn up first by the epitomisers and later studied more carefully at Bologna, served to indicate general principles in cases to which canon law did not apply; but there was little jurisdiction in which the powers ecclesiastical could not contrive to take a hand. At the same time Germanic ideals and customs continued a powerful force. For a long time after the partition of the vast empire of Charlemagne government was in a state of chaos and transition from which eventually the various distinct states arose. A struggle between kings and nobles for supremacy dragged along for many generations; and as during that contest each feudal lord was master in his own domain, there was no consistent code of laws for all countries or, indeed for the same country. . . . Beginning with the twelfth century city life began to exert a political influence; and this . . . did not fail to have an effect on the status of women. Of any participation of women in intellectual life there could be no question until the Renaissance, although we do meet here and there with isolated exceptions, a few ladies of high degree like Roswitha of Gandersheim and Hadwig, Duchess of Swabia, niece of Otto the Great, and Heloise. The learning was exclusively scholastic, and from any share in that women were barred. When people are kept in ignorance, there is less inducement for them to believe that they have any rights or to assert them if they do think so.

We shall do well to bear in mind, in noting the laws relative to women, that theory is one thing and practice quite another. Hence, although the doctrines of the Church on various matters touching the female sex were characterised by the greatest purity, we shall see that in practice they were not strictly executed. . . .

Chapter VI. The Canon Law and the Attitude of the Roman Catholic Church

The canon law reaffirms woman's subjection to man in no uncertain terms. The wife must be submissive and obedient to her husband.[108] She must never, under penalty of excommunication, cut off her hair, because "God has given it to her as a veil and as a sign of her subjection."[109] A woman who assumed men's garments was accursed;[110] it will be remembered that the breaking of this law was one of the charges which brought Joan of Arc to the stake. However learned and holy, woman must never presume to teach men publicly.[111] She was not allowed to bring a criminal action except in cases of high treason or to avenge the death of near relatives.[112] Parents could dedicate a daughter to God while she was yet an infant; and this parental vow bound her to the nunnery when she was mature, whether she was willing or not.[113] . . .

The most important effect of the canon law was on marriage, which was now a sacrament and had its sanction not in the laws of men, but in the express decrees of God. . . . Free consent of both man and woman was necessary for matrimony.[114] . . . About every form connected with the marriage service the Church threw its halo of mystery and symbol to emphasise the sacred character of the union. Thus:[115] "Women are veiled during the marriage ceremony for this reason, that they may know they are lowly and in subjection to their husbands. . . ."

The Church is seen in its fairest light in its provisions to protect the wife from sexual brutality on the part of her husband. . . .

It has always been and still is the boast of the Roman Catholic Church that it has been the supreme protector of women on account of its stand on divorce. . . .

On the subject of divorce the Roman Catholic Church took the decided position which it continues to maintain at the present day. Marriage when entered upon under all the conditions demanded by the Church for a valid union is indissoluble.[116] . . .

All this seems pretty rigorous; but in actual practice the Church makes its protection of the wife void in certain instances by its insistence on two special doctrines: "diriment impediments" and "dispensations." . . .

By the doctrine of "diriment impediments" the Pope or a duly constituted representative of his can declare that a marriage has been null and void from the very beginning because of some impediment defined in the canon law. Canon IV of the twenty-fourth session of the Council of Trent anathematises any one who shall say that the Church cannot constitute impediments dissolving marriage, or that she has erred in constituting them. The impediments which can annul marriage and leave the parties free to marry again are chiefly affinity and consanguinity. . . . The minute and far-fetched subtleties which the Church has employed in the interpretation of these relationships make escape from the marital tie feasible for the man who is eager to disencumber himself of his life's partner. . . .

Under the canon law . . . resources are open for the man who is tired of his wife; by the doctrine, namely, of "spiritual fornication." Adultery is, of course, recognised as the cause that admits a separation. But the canon law remarks that idolatry and all harmful superstition—by which is meant any doctrine that does not agree with that of the Church—is fornication; that avarice is also idolatry and hence fornication; that in fact no vice can be separated from idolatry and hence all vices can be classed as fornication; so that if a husband only tried a little bit, he could without much trouble find some "vice" in his wife that would entitle him to a separation.[117]

When all these fail, recourse can be had to a dispensation. . . .

History is full of instances to prove that the great and wealthy have been able at all times, by working one or more of these doctrines, to reduce the theory of the Roman Church to nullity in practice. . . . The case of Louis XII of France will at once occur. That monarch, having fallen in love with Anne of Brittany, suddenly discovered that his wife was his fourth cousin, that she was deformed, and that her father had been his god-father; and for this the Bishop of Rome gave him a dispensation and his legitimate wife was sent away. The wife of Louis XIV, to take another instance, never heard a word of censure directed by the Pope against her spouse for committing adultery successively with Louise de la Vallière and Madame de Montespan, . . . The Catholic clergy occasionally point with pride to a case like that of Philip Augustus of France as a case in point where the Pope protected an injured wife: but they forget that the matrimonial relations of Philip's contemporary, John of England, were considerably more rotten and never received any censure. . . .

The attitude of the Roman Catholic Church towards women's rights at the present day is practically the same as it has been for eighteen centuries. It still insists on the subjection of the woman to the man, . . . This position is so well illustrated by an article of the Rev. David Barry in the Roman Catholic paper, the Dublin *Irish Ecclesiastical Review,* that I cannot do better than quote some of it. "It seems plain enough," he says, "that allowing women the right of suffrage is incompatible with the high Catholic ideal of the unity of domestic life. Even those who do not hold the high and rigid ideal of the unity of the family that the Catholic Church clings to must recognise some authority in the family, as in every other society. Is this authority the conjoint privilege of husband and wife? If so, which of them is to yield, if a difference of opinion arises? Surely the most uncompromising suffragette must admit that the wife ought to give way in such a case. That is to say, every one will admit that the wife's domestic authority is subordinate to that of her husband. But is she to be accorded an autonomy in outside affairs that is denied her in the home? Her authority is subject to her husband's in domestic matters—her special sphere; is it to be considered co-ordinate with his in regulating the affairs of the State? Furthermore, there is an argument that applies universally, even in the case of those women who are not subject to the care and protection of a husband, and even, I do not hesitate to say, where the matters to be decided on would come specially within their cognisance, and where their judgment would, therefore, be more reliable than that of men. It is this, that in the noise and turmoil of party politics, or in the narrow, but rancorous arena of local factions, it must needs fare ill with what may be called the passive virtues of humility, patience, meekness, forbearance, and self-repression. These are looked on by the Church as the special prerogative and endowment of the female soul. . . . But these virtues would soon become sullied and tarnished in the dust and turmoil of a contested election; and their absence would soon be disagreeably in evidence in the character of women, who are, at the same time, almost constitutionally debarred from preeminence in the more robust virtues for which the soul of man is specially adapted." . . .

Chapter IX. General Considerations

It is twenty-three centuries since Plato gave to the world his magnificent treatise on the State. The dream of the Greek philosopher of equal rights for all intelligent citizens, among whom he includes women, has in large part been realised; but much is yet wanting to bring society to the standard of the Ideal Republic. In not a few States of the world the conditions affecting property rights are inequitable; in all but very few States woman is still barred from the field of politics and from the legitimate rights of citizenship; and the day seems far distant when the States possessing a representative government will be prepared to accept the woman citizen as eligible for administrative positions. . . .

The opposition to the granting of equal suffrage is . . . based mainly upon five classes of contentions:

    I.   The theological.
    II. The physiological.
    III. The social or political.
    IV. The intellectual.
    V. The moral. . . .

I. The theological argument is based upon the distinctly evil conception of woman, presented in *Genesis*, as the cause of misery in this world and upon the subordinate position assigned to her by Paul and Peter. Christ himself has left us no teachings on the subject. The Hebrew and Oriental creed of woman's sphere permeated the West as Christianity expanded and forced to extinction the Roman principle of equality. Only within fifty years, has the female sex regained the rights enjoyed by women under the law of the Empire seventeen centuries ago. The Apostolic theory of complete subordination gained strength with each succeeding age. . . . recall that when, early in the nineteenth century, chloroform was first used to help women in childbirth, a number of Protestant divines denounced the practice as a sin against the Creator, who had expressly commanded that woman should bring forth in sorrow and tribulation. Yet times have so far changed within two decades that the theological argument is practically obsolete among Protestants, although it is still influential in the Roman Catholic Church, which holds fast to the doctrine laid down by the Apostles. We may say, however, that of all the objections, the theological has, in practice, the least weight among the bulk of the population. The word *obey* in the clerical formula *love, honour,* and *obey* provokes a smile.

II. The physiological argument is more powerful. Its supporters assert that the constitution of woman is too delicate, too finely wrought to compete with man in his chosen fields. The physiological argument makes its appearance most persistently in the statement that woman should have no vote because she could not defend her property or her country in time of war. . . .

. . . the cause of woman's rights will suffer no harm by a frank admission that women are not, in general, the peers of men in brute force. . . . however, . . . in war, as it is practised to-day, physical force is of little significance compared with strategy which is a product of the intellect. . . .

. . . under stress or the need of making a livelihood women in many instances show physical endurance equal to that of men. Women who are expert ballet dancers and those who are skilled acrobats can hardly be termed physiological weaklings. In Berlin, you may see women staggering along with huge loads on their backs; in Munich, women are street-cleaners and hod-carriers; on the island of Capri, the trunk of the tourist is lifted by two men onto the shoulder of a woman, who carries it up the steep road to the village. . . . In all countries and in all ages there have been examples of women who, disguised as men, have fought side by side with the male and with equal efficiency. The case of Joan of Arc will at once occur to the reader; and those who are curious about this subject may, by consulting the records of our Civil War, find exciting material in the story of "Belle Boyd," "Frank Miller," and "Major Cushman."[118] . . .

It should be borne in mind, in connection with the contention that the privileges of a citizen ought to be accorded only to those persons who are physically capable of helping to defend the community by force, that no such principle is applied in fixing the existing qualifications for male citizenship. A large number of the voters of every community are, on the ground either of advanced years or of invalidism, physically disqualified for service as soldiers, sailors, or policemen. This group of citizens includes a very large proportion of the thinking power of the community. No intelligently directed state would, however, be prepared to deprive itself of the counsels, of the active political co-operation, and of the service from time to time in the responsibility of office, of men of the type of Gladstone (at the age of seventy-five), of John Stuart Mill (always a physical weakling), of Washington (serving as President after he was sixty), on the ground that these citizens were no longer capable of carrying muskets in the ranks. . . .

III. According to the social or political argument, if woman is given equal rights with man, the basis of family life, and hence the foundation of the state itself, is undermined, as a house divided against itself cannot stand. It is said that (1) there must be some one authority in a household and that this should be the man; (2) woman will neglect the home if she is left free to enter politics or a profession; (3) politics will degrade her; (4) when independent and self-asserting she will lose her influence over man; and (5) most women do not want to vote or to enter politics. . . .

It is said that there must be some one supreme authority; but this depends on the view taken of marriage. Under the old Common Law, the personality of the wife was merged completely in that of her husband; marriage was an absolute despotism. Under the Canon Law, woman is man's obedient and unquestioning subject; marriage is a benevolent despotism. To-day people are more inclined to look upon matrimony as a partnership of equal duties, rights, and privileges. . . .

Closely connected with the "one authority" argument is the old contention, so often resorted to and relied upon, that women, if they are permitted to vote, will neglect the home, and that, if the professions are opened to them, they will find these too absorbingly attractive. . . . The great leaders of the woman suffrage movement from Mrs. Stanton to Mrs. Snowden have in their home circle led lives as beautiful and have raised families as large and as well equipped morally and intellectually as those who are content to sit by the fire and spin.

Thus far I have argued from the orthodox view, that matrimony ought to be the goal of every woman's ambition. But if a woman wishes to remain single and devote herself exclusively to the realisation of some ideal, it is hard to see why she should not. Men who take this course are eulogised for their noble self-sacrifice in immolating themselves for the advancement of the cause of civilisation; women who do precisely the same thing are sometimes unthinkingly spoken of in terms of contempt or with that complacent pity which is far worse. It is difficult for us to realise adequately what talented women like Rosa Bonheur had to undergo because of this curious attitude of humanity.

"The home is woman's sphere." This shibboleth is the logical result of the attitude mentioned. Doubtless, the home is woman's sphere; but the home includes all that pertains to it—city, politics and taxes, laws relating to the protection of minors, municipal rottenness which may corrupt children, schools and playgrounds and museums which may educate them. Few doctrines have been productive of more pain than the "woman's sphere" argument. It is this which has, for a thousand years, made the unmarried woman, the *Old Maid*, the butt of the contemptible jibes of Christian society, whereof you will find no parallel in pagan antiquity. Dramatic writers have held her up to ridicule on the stage on account of the peculiarities of character which are naturally acquired when a person is isolated from participation in the activities of life. It is the doctrine which has made women glad to marry drunkards and rakes, to bring forth children tainted with the sins of their fathers, and to suffer hell on earth rather than incur the ridicule of the Christian gentleman who may, without incurring the protest of society, remain unmarried and sow an unlimited quantity of wild oats. It is this doctrine which was indirectly responsible for the hanging and burning of eccentric old women on the charge that they were witches. As men found a divine sanction for keeping women in subjection, so in those days of superstition did they blaspheme their Creator by digging out of the Old Testament, as a justification for their brutality, the text, "Thou shalt not suffer a witch to live."

"Politics will degrade women"—this naïve confession that politics are rotten is a fairly strong argument that some good influence is needed to make them cleaner. Generally speaking, it is difficult to imagine how politics could be made any worse. If a woman cannot go to the polls or hold office without being insulted by rowdies, her vote will be potent to elect officials who should be able to secure for the community a standard of reasonable civilisation. There is no case in which more sentimentality is wasted. Lovely woman is urged not to allow her beauty, her gentleness, her tender submissiveness to become the butt of the lounger at the street corner; and in most instances lovely woman, like the celebrated Maître Corbeau, is cajoled effectively. Meanwhile the brothel and the sweat-shop continue on their prosperous way. By a curious inconsistency, man will permit woman to help him out of a political dilemma and will then suavely remark that suffrage will degrade her. During the Civil War, Anna Dickinson by her remarkable lecture entitled, "The National Crisis" saved New Hampshire and Connecticut for the Republicans; Anna Carroll not only gave such a crushing rejoinder to Breckinridge's secession speech that the government printed and distributed it, but she also, as is now generally believed, planned the campaign which led to the fall of Forts Henry and Donelson and opened the Mississippi to Vicksburg. How many men realise these facts? . . .

IV. Another argument that is made much of is the intellectual inferiority of woman. For ages women were allowed no higher education than reading, writing, and simple arithmetic, often not even these; yet Elizabeth Barrett Browning, George Sand, George Eliot, Harriet Martineau, Jane Austen, and some scores of others did work which showed them to be the peers of any minds of their day. And if no woman can justly claim to have attained an eminence such as that of Shakespeare in letters or of Darwin in science, we may question whether Shakespeare would have been Shakespeare or Darwin Darwin if the society which surrounded them had insisted that it was a sin for them to use their minds and that they should not presume to meddle with knowledge. When a girl for the first time in America took a public examination in geometry, in 1829, men wagged their heads gravely and prophesied the speedy dissolution of family and state.

To the list of women whose service for their fellows would have been lost if the old-time barriers had been maintained, may be added the name of the late Dr. Mary Putnam Jacobi. . . .

At the time in question, the medical profession took the ground that women might enjoy the benefit of a little medical education but they were denied the facilities for any thorough training or for any research work. Mary Putnam secured her graduate degree from the great medical school of the University of Paris, being the first woman who had been admitted to the school since the fourteenth century. Returning after six years of thorough training, she did much during the remaining years of her life to secure and to maintain for women physicians the highest possible standard of training and of practice. . . .

One needs but recall the admirable intellectual work of women to-day to wonder at the imbecility of those who assert that women are intellectually the inferiors of men. Madame Curie in science, Miss Tarbell in political and economic history, Miss Jane Addams in sociological writings and practice, the Rev. Anna Howard Shaw in the ministry, Mrs. Hetty Green in business, are a few examples of women whose mental ability ought to bring a blush to the Old Guard. . . .

V. The last objection I would call the *moral*. It embraces such arguments as, that woman is too impulsive, too easily swayed by her emotions to hold responsible positions, that the world is very evil and slippery, and that she must therefore constantly have man to protect her—a pious duty, which he avows solemnly it has ever been his special delight to perform. The preceding pages are a commentary on the manner in which man has discharged this duty. In Delaware, for instance, the age of legal consent was until 1889 *seven* years. The institution of Chivalry, to take another example, is usually praised for the high estimation and protection it secured for women; yet any one who has read its literature knows that, in practice, it did nothing of the sort. The noble lord who was so gallant to his lady love—who, by the way, was frequently the wife of another man—had very little scruple about seducing a maid of low degree. The same gallantry is conspicuous in the *Letters* of Lord Chesterfield, beneath whose unctuous courtesy the beast of sensuality is always leering.

In the past the main function of woman outside of the rearing of children has been to satisfy the carnal appetite of man, to prepare his food, to minister to his physical comfort; she was barred from participation in the intellectual. . . .

It is quite possible that many women are swayed too easily by their emotions. We must recollect, however, that for some thousands of years woman has been carefully drilled to believe that she is an emotional creature. If a dozen people conspire to tell a man that he is looking badly, it is not unlikely that he will feel ill. Certainly Florence Nightingale and Clara Barton exhibited no lack of firmness on the shambles of battlefields; and there are few men living who cannot recall instances of women who have, in the face of disaster and evil fortune, shown a steady perseverance and will-power in earning a living for themselves and their children that men have not surpassed. . . .

The old conception of woman's position was subjection, based on mental and physical inferiority and supported by Biblical arguments. The newer conception is that of a complement, in which neither inferiority nor superiority finds place. . . .

. . . It often happens that the history of words will give a hint of the progress of civilisation. Such a story is told by the use of *lady* and *woman*. Not many decades ago the use of the word *woman* in referring to respectable members of the sex was interpreted as a lack of courtesy. To-day, women prefer to be called *women*. . . .

Much more serious is the glaring discrepancy in the wages paid to men and to women. For doing precisely the same work as a man and often doing it better, woman receives a much lower wage. The reasons are several and specious. We are told that men have families to support, that women do not have such expensive tastes as men, that they are incapable of doing as much as men, that by granting them equal wages one of the inducements to marry is removed. . . . If men have families to support, women by the hundreds support brothers and sisters and weak parents. . . . when men argue that women should be forced to marry by giving them smaller wages, they are simply reverting to the time-honoured idea that the goal of every woman's ambition should be fixed as matrimony. . . .

The fact is, the institution of marriage is going through a crisis. The old view that marriage is a complete merging of the wife in the husband and that the latter is absolute monarch of his home is being questioned. When a man with this idea and a woman with a far different one marry, there is likely to be a clash. Marriage as a real partnership based on equality of goods and of interests finds an increasing number of advocates. There is great reason to believe that the issue will be only for the good and that from doubt and revolt a more enduring ideal will arise, based on a sure foundation of perfect understanding.

NOTES

1. Paulus, iii, 4a, I.
2. Ulpian, Tit., xx, 16. Gaius, ii, 112.
3. Male relatives on the father's side—agnati—were guardians in such cases; . . . See Ulpian, Tit., xi, 3, 4, and 24. Gaius, i, 185, and iii, 10. . . .
4. Ulpian, Tit., xi, 27.
5. The power of the father was called *potestas;* that of the husband, *manus.*
6. Aulus Gellius, x, 23. Cf. Suetonius, *Tiberius,* 35.
7. Gaius, i, 144.
8. Ulpian, Tit., xi, 1.
9. Ulpian, Tit., xi, 28a. Gaius, i, 194. Paulus, iv, 9, 1–9.
10. Gaius, i, 145. Ulpian, Tit., x, 5.
11. Gaius, i, 137. . . .
12. Ulpian, Tit., viii, 7a.
13. Paulus, i, 4, 4. . . .
14. Ulpian in Dig., 25, 3, 5.
15. For Livia's great influence over Augustus see Seneca, *de Clementia,* i, 9, 6. Tacitus, *Annals,* i, 3, 4, and 5, and ii, 34. Dio, 55, 14–21, and 56, 47.
16. Tacitus, *Annals,* xv, 63, 64; Pliny, *Letters,* iii, 16; Martial, i, 13. . . .
17. Pliny, *Panegyricus,* 26. . . .
18. Pliny, *Letters,* i, 14. . . .
19. Paulus, ii, 19, 2.
20. Cf. Alexander Severus in Codex, viii, 38, 2. . . .
21. Modestinus in Dig., xxiii, 2, 1.
22. Gaius, ii, 159.
23. Paulus, ii, xx, 1.
24. Note the rescript of Alexander Severus to a certain Aquila (Codex, ii, 18, 13). . . .
25. See, e.g., Dig., 47, 10, and Ulpian, ibid., 48, 14, 27.
26. Cf. Gaius, i, 141. . . .
27. Paulus, i, 21, 13.
28. Paulus in Dig., iii, 2, 9.
29. Aulus Gellius, xvii, 6, speech of Cato. . . .
30. Ulpian in Dig., 24, 1, 1. . . .
31. Ulpian in Dig., 48, 5, 14 (13). . . .
32. Papinian in Dig., 48, 5, 21 (20). . . .
33. Macer in Dig., 48, 5, 25 (24).
34. Paulus, ii, xxvi. Macer in Dig., 48, 5, 25 (24), ibid., Ulpian, 48, 5, 30 (29).
35. Paulus, ii, xxvi.
36. See, e.g., Capitolinus, *Anton. Pius,* 3. . . .
37. Digest, xiv, 1 and 3 and 8. . . .
38. CIL, xiv, 326.
39. Martial, xi, 71. Apuleius, *Metam.,* v. 10. . . .
40. E.g., Suetonius, *Nero,* 27.
41. Carmina Priapea, 18 and 27. Ulpian, xiii, 1. . . .
42. Martial, ii, 17, 1.

43. Petronius, *Sat.*, 45. . . .

44. Paulus, ii, xi; id. in Dig., 16, 1, 1. . . .

45. Juvenal, vi, 242–245.

46. Ulpian in Dig., 38, 16, 1. . . .

47. Callistratus in Dig., 48, 19, 26. . . .

48. Paulus, v, 4, 14. . . .

49. Paulus, v, 23, 14.

50. Martial, x, 35, and x, 38.

51. Sappho, Telesilla, and Corinna belong to an earlier period, when the Oriental idea of seclusion for women had not yet become firmly fixed in Greece. . . .

52. See, e.g., Pliny, *Letters*, v, 16.

53. Juvenal, vi, 434–440.

54. Cf. Martial, ii, 90. . . .

55. Quintilian, vii, 3, 27. . . .

56. Gaius, i, 52 ff.

57. Paulus, iii, v, 5 ff. . . .

58. Valerius Maximus, vi, 8. . . .

59. Plutarch lived in the second century A.D.: but he has inherited the Greek point of view and advises a wife to bear with meekness the infidelities of the husband—see *Praecep. Coniug.*, 16. His words are often curiously similar to those of the Apostles, e.g., *Coniug. Praecep.*, 33: "The husband shall rule the wife not as if master of a chattel, but as the soul does the body." Id. 37: "Wives who are sensible will be silent when their husbands are angry and vent their passion; when their husbands are silent, then let them speak to them and mollify them." However, like the Apostles, he enjoins upon husbands to honour their wives; his essay on the "Virtues of Women"— . . . is an affectionate tribute to their worth.

Some of the respectable Puritan gentlemen at Rome also held that a wife be content to be a humble admirer of her husband (e.g., Pliny, *Paneg.*, 83, . . .). But Roman law insisted that what was morally right for the man was equally so for the woman; just as it compelled a husband himself to observe chastity, if he expected it from his wife.

60. *Ecclesiasticus* 42, 14.

61. *Leviticus* xii, 1–5.

62. *Romans* 7, 2–4.

63. *Corinthians* i, 7, 39.

64. *Corinthians* i, 7, 1 ff.

65. *Corinthians* i, 7, 37.

66. *Ephesians* 5, 22 and 33.

67. *Peter* i, 3, 7.

68. *Corinthians* i, 14, 34.

69. *Timothy* i, 2, 12–15.

70. Abelard, *Ep.*, 9, in vol. 178, p. 325. . . .

71. Adversus Iovianum, i, 48—Migne, v. 23, p. 278.

72. Adversus Iovianum, i, 28—Migne, v. 23, pp. 249–250. . . .

73. S. Maximi Episcopi Taurinensis—Homilia 53, 1—Migne, vol. 57, p. 350.

74. Augustinus: *Quaest. ex vet. Test.*, 21: . . .

75. Migne, vol. 171, pp. 1698–1699.

76. Basilius, *ad Amphil.*, c. 42: . . .

77. Codex, v, 17, 11.

78. Novellae, 140, 1: . . .

79. Codex, v, 4, 20, and 5, 18.

80. Codex, i, 9, 6.

81. Novellae, cix, 1.

82. Codex, v, 35, 2 and 3.

83. Codex, ii, 55, 6.

84. Codex, ix, 8, 5.

85. This law was evidently lasting, for it is quoted with approval by Pope Innocent iii, in the year 1199—see Friedberg, *Corpus Iuris Canonici,* vol. ii, p. 782.

86. Codex, v, 16, 24.

87. For all these enactments see Codex, i, 3, 53 (54), and ix, 13.

88. *de Bell. Gall.,* vi, 19.

89. Id., i, 50.

90. Id., v, 14.

91. *Agricola,* 16. *Germania,* 45: . . .

92. *Agricola,* 16.

93. *Germania,* 8.

94. Procopius, *de bello Vandalico,* ii, 8, . . .

95. Tacitus, *Hist.,* iv, 61, and v, 24.

96. Id., *Germania,* 8.

97. Ibid., 7.

98. Ibid., 18.

99. Ibid., 19.

100. Liutprand, i, 5: . . .

101. Leges Liutprand, vi, 119: . . .

102. By a law of the Alemanni (Tit., 57), if two sisters were heiresses to a father's estate and one married a vassal (colonus) of the King or Church and the other became the wife of a free man equal to her in rank, the latter only was allowed to hold her father's land, although the rest of the goods were divided equally.

103. Lex Wisigothorum, iii, 2, 2.

104. Lex Burgundionum, *Add. primum,* xiii: . . .

105. Einhard, *Vita Kar.* Mag., 17: . . .

106. It was deemed sufficient for a male relative, say, the father, to assert the innocence of the woman under solemn oath; . . . An example of this solemn ceremony is told interestingly by Gregory of Tours, 5, 33. . . .

107. Lex Abgliorum et Werinorum, xiv: . . .

108. Augustine quoted by Gratian, *Causa,* 33, *Quaest.* 5, chapters 12–16— . . .

109. Gratian, *Distinctio,* 30, c. 2— . . .

110. Gratian, *Dist.,* 30, c. 6, . . .

111. Gratian, *Dist.,* 23, c. 29— . . .

112. Id., *Causa,* 15, *Quaest.* 3— . . .

113. Id., *Causa,* 20, Quaest. 1, c. 2— . . .

114. Id., *Causa,* 30, Quaest. 2— . . .

115. Id., *Causa,* 30, Quaest. 5, c. 7—Friedberg, i, p. 1106.

116. For this . . . see Session 24 of the Council of Trent "On the Sacrament of Matrimony" and also the Catholic Encyclopedia under "Divorce."

117. Gratian, *Causa,* 28, Quaest. i, c. 5— . . .

118. See an excellent article on "The American Woman" by Miss Ida M. Tarbell, in the *American Magazine* for April, 1910.

PART 4

Pleas for Equality for Women

PLATO (427–347 B.C.)

Plato hardly needs any introduction. Who can encompass in a short review the encomiums heaped upon him through the ages? Possibly the greatest metaphysical genius of all time, in his work he laid the foundation for the sciences of logic and psychology.

The Republic is probably the foremost early treatise on education known to Western civilization. It presents Plato's conception of the ideal State, whose goal is Justice: philosophers are kings; religion and morality are improved; education is the first concern of the rulers; no man calls anything his own; education continues throughout life; and men and women shall have a common training and education in preparation for the same occupations.

The argument is presented in the form of a discussion carried on by Socrates, the master of dialectic, and a few companions. Socrates is represented as the disinterested seeker after truth. The speculations attributed to him are really Plato's.

I daresay that the one item of information preserved through centuries regarding Socrates and the female sex is the reputation of his wife, Xantippe. Webster's Dictionary says of her: "Socrates's wife, whose peevish scoldings and quarrelsome temper have become proverbial."[1] Yes, we all know that "Xantippe" is practically a synonym for a shrewish wife. Since it is probably common knowledge that Plato often expressed less than admiration for women, and that he was convinced that they were inferior to men, it will surely come as a surprise to many that he advocated a revolutionary theory of equality in opportunities for education and occupations for women. And how ironic that in his dialogues he attributed expression of these ideas to Socrates!

The Republic

[Glaucon speaking to Socrates] We have been long expecting that you would tell us something about the family life of your citizens—how they will bring children into the world, and rear

From *The Dialogues of Plato*, trans. B. Jowett, 3d ed. (Oxford University Press, 1892), vol. III, Book V, pp. 140 ff.

them when they have arrived, and, in general, what is the nature of this community of women and children—for we are of opinion that the right or wrong management of such matters will have a great and paramount influence on the State for good or for evil. . . .

. . . I suppose that I must retrace my steps and say what I perhaps ought to have said before in the proper place. The part of the men has been played out, and now properly enough comes the turn of the women. Of them I will proceed to speak, and the more readily since I am invited by you.

For men born and educated like our citizens, the only way, in my opinion, of arriving at a right conclusion about the possession and use of women and children is to follow the path on which we originally started, when we said that the men were to be the guardians and watchdogs of the herd.

True.

Let us further suppose the birth and education of our women to be subject to similar or nearly similar regulations; then we shall see whether the result accords with our design.

What do you mean?

What I mean may be put into the form of a question, I said: Are dogs divided into hes and shes, or do they both share equally in hunting and in keeping watch and in the other duties of dogs? or do we entrust to the males the entire and exclusive care of the flocks, while we leave the females at home, under the idea that the bearing and suckling their puppies is labour enough for them?

No, he said, they share alike; the only difference between them is that the males are stronger and the females weaker.

But can you use different animals for the same purpose, unless they are bred and fed in the same way?

You cannot.

Then, if women are to have the same duties as men, they must have the same nurture and education?

Yes.

The education which was assigned to the men was music and gymnastic.

Yes.

Then women must be taught music and gymnastic and also the art of war, which they must practise like the men?

That is the inference, I suppose.

I should rather expect, I said, that several of our proposals, if they are carried out, being unusual, may appear ridiculous.

No doubt of it.

Yes, and the most ridiculous thing of all will be the sight of women naked in the palaestra, exercising with the men, especially when they are no longer young; they certainly will not be a vision of beauty, any more than the enthusiatic old men who in spite of wrinkles and ugliness continue to frequent the gymnasia.

Yes, indeed, he said: according to present notions the proposal would be thought ridiculous.

But then, I said, as we have determined to speak our minds, we must not fear the jests of the wits which will be directed against this sort of innovation; how they will talk of women's attainments both in music and gymnastic, and above all about their wearing armour and riding upon horseback!

Very true, he replied.

Yet having begun we must go forward to the rough places of the law; at the same time begging of these gentlemen for once in their life to be serious. Not long ago, as we shall remind them, the Hellenes were of the opinion, which is still generally received among the barbarians, that the sight of a naked man was ridiculous and improper; and when first the Cretans and then the Lacedaemonians introduced the custom, the wits of that day might equally have ridiculed the innovation.

No doubt.

But when experience showed that to let all things be uncovered was far better than to cover them up, and the ludicrous effect to the outward eye vanished before the better principle which reason asserted, then the man was perceived to be a fool who directs the shafts of his ridicule at any other sight but that of folly and vice, or seriously inclines to weigh the beautiful by any other standard but that of the good.

Very true, he replied.

First, then, whether the question is to be put in jest or in earnest, let us come to an understanding about the nature of woman: Is she capable of sharing either wholly or partially in the actions of men, or not at all? And is the art of war one of those arts in which she can or can not share? That will be the best way of commencing the enquiry, and will probably lead to the fairest conclusion.

That will be much the best way.

Shall we take the other side first and begin by arguing against ourselves; in this manner the adversary's position will not be undefended.

Why not? he said.

Then let us put a speech into the mouths of our opponents. They will say: 'Socrates and Glaucon, no adversary need convict you, for you yourselves, at the first foundation of the State, admitted the principle that everybody was to do the one work suited to his own nature.' And certainly, if I am not mistaken, such an admission was made by us. 'And do not the natures of men and women differ very much indeed?' And we shall reply: Of course they do. Then we shall be asked, 'Whether the tasks assigned to men and to women should not be different, and such as are agreeable to their different natures?' Certainly they should. 'But if so, have you not fallen into a serious inconsistency in saying that men and women, whose natures are so entirely different, ought to perform the same actions?'—What defence will you make for us, my good Sir, against any one who offers these objections? . . .

These are the objections, Glaucon, and there are many others of a like kind, which I foresaw long ago; they made me afraid and reluctant to take in hand any law about the possession and nurture of women and children. . . .

Well, then, let us see if any way of escape can be found. We acknowledged—did we not? that different natures ought to have different pursuits, and that men's and women's natures are different. And now what are we saying?—that different natures ought to have the same pursuits,—this is the inconsistency which is charged upon us.

Precisely.

Verily, Glaucon, I said, glorious is the power of the art of contradiction!

Why do you say so?

Because I think that many a man falls into the practice against his will. When he thinks that he is reasoning he is really disputing, just because he cannot define and divide, and so know that of which he is speaking; and he will pursue a merely verbal opposition in the spirit of contention and not of fair discussion.

Yes, he replied, such is very often the case; but what has that to do with us and our argument?

A great deal; for there is certainly a danger of our getting unintentionally into a verbal opposition.

In what way?

Why we valiantly and pugnaciously insist upon the verbal truth, that different natures ought to have different pursuits, but we never considered at all what was the meaning of sameness or difference of nature, or why we distinguished them when we assigned different pursuits to different natures and the same to the same natures.

Why, no, he said, that was never considered by us.

I said: Suppose that by way of illustration we were to ask the question whether there is not an opposition in nature between bald men and hairy men; and if this is admitted by us, then, if bald men are cobblers, we should forbid the hairy men to be cobblers, and conversely?

That would be a jest, he said.

Yes, I said, a jest; and why? because we never meant when we constructed the State, that the opposition of natures should extend to every difference, but only to those differences which affected the pursuit in which the individual is engaged; we should have argued, for example, that a physician and one who is in mind a physician may be said to have the same nature.

True.

Whereas the physician and the carpenter have different natures?

Certainly.

And if, I said, the male and female sex appear to differ in their fitness for any art or pursuit, we should say that such pursuit or art ought to be assigned to one or the other of them; but if the difference consists only in women bearing and men begetting children, this does not amount to a proof that a woman differs from a man in respect of the sort of education she should receive; and we shall therefore continue to maintain that our guardians and their wives ought to have the same pursuits.

Very true, he said.

Next, we shall ask our opponent how, in reference to any of the pursuits or arts of civic life, the nature of a woman differs from that of a man?

That will be quite fair.

And perhaps he, like yourself, will reply that to give a sufficient answer on the instant is not easy; but after a little reflection there is no difficulty.

Yes, perhaps.

Suppose then that we invite him to accompany us in the argument, and then we may hope to show him that there is nothing peculiar in the constitution of women which would affect them in the administration of the State.

By all means.

Let us say to him: Come now, and we will ask you a question:—when you spoke of a nature gifted or not gifted in any respect, did you mean to say that one man will acquire a thing easily, another with difficulty; a little learning will lead the one to discover a great deal; whereas the other, after much study and application, no sooner learns than he forgets; or again, did you mean, that the one has a body which is a good servant to his mind, while the body of the other is a hindrance to him?—would not these be the sort of differences which distinguish the man gifted by nature from the one who is ungifted?

No one will deny that.

And can you mention any pursuit of mankind in which the male sex has not all these gifts and qualities in a higher degree than the female? Need I waste time in speaking of the art of weaving, and the management of pancakes and preserves, in which womankind does really appear to be great, and in which for her to be beaten by a man is of all things the most absurd?

You are quite right, he replied, in maintaining the general inferiority of the female sex: although many women are in many things superior to many men, yet on the whole what you say is true.

And if so, my friend, I said, there is no special faculty of administration in a state which a woman has because she is a woman, or which a man has by virtue of his sex, but the gifts of nature are alike diffused in both; all the pursuits of men are the pursuits of women also, but in all of them a woman is inferior to a man.

Very true.

Then are we to impose all our enactments on men and none of them on women?

That will never do.

One woman has a gift of healing, another not; one is a musician, and another has no music in her nature?

Very true.

And one woman has a turn for gymnastic and military exercises, and another is unwarlike and hates gymnastics?

Certainly.

And one woman is a philosopher, and another is an enemy of philosophy; one has spirit, and another is without spirit?

That is also true.

Then one woman will have the temper of a guardian, and another not. Was not the selection of the male guardians determined by differences of this sort?

Yes.

Men and women alike possess the qualities which make a guardian; they differ only in their comparative strength or weakness.

Obviously.

And those women who have such qualities are to be selected as the companions and colleagues of men who have similar qualities and whom they resemble in capacity and in character?

Very true.

And ought not the same natures to have the same pursuits?

They ought.

Then, as we were saying before, there is nothing unnatural in assigning music and gymnastic to the wives of the guardians—to that point we come round again . . . and the contrary practice, which prevails at present, is in reality a violation of nature. . . .

Then let the wives of our guardians strip, for their virtue will be their robe, and let them share in the toils of war and the defence of their country; only in the distribution of labours the lighter are to be assigned to the women, who are the weaker natures, but in other respects their duties are to be the same. And as for the man who laughs at naked women exercising their bodies from the best of motives, in his laughter he is plucking

'A fruit of unripe wisdom,'

and he himself is ignorant of what he is laughing at, or what he is about;—for that is, and ever will be, the best of sayings, *That the useful is the noble and the hurtful is the base.*

MARIE-JEAN-ANTOINE-NICOLAS-CARITAT, MARQUIS DE CONDORCET (1743–1794)

In the preparation of this book I have had the sensation of unearthing buried treasure. This reaction was particularly true in regard to the essay of Condorcet. Most of us who have studied the French Revolution have heard the name, but little more, of this extraordinary man, who was both philosopher and active participant in the battle for human rights in the eighteenth century. An aristocrat and a man of science, Condorcet was convinced of the infinite perfectibility of human nature through the spread of knowledge and the grant of liberty and equality to all. Among the evils of the past he included the social inequality of women compared with men. It was his contention that equality between the sexes would remove repression, fear, and shame from sexual relationships, and would lead to a higher morality. He had the idea, revolutionary for his time, that women's disabilities were attributable to poor education rather than to native inferiority. His feminism encompasses coeducation, eligibility of women for public office, advocacy of birth control, and leniency toward prostitution. However, in contrast to other libertarians, he did not interpret sexual freedom as meaning license for the man to indulge in sexual looseness. He stands in marked distinction from other revolutionary philosophers of his time like Rousseau and Diderot, who saw woman as an inferior sex and restricted her to the traditional role of wife and mother.

In reading Condorcet it is well to remember that, while his liberal feminist views may seem old-hat today, they were unique in his time and were regarded with bewilderment by contemporary revolutionists. His thinking anticipated by many decades John Stuart Mill, himself considered a pioneer feminist for his essay "The Subjection of Women." Recognizing the originality and courage of Condorcet's perception of women, J. Salwyn Schapiro writes, "It is no small tribute to Condorcet that he regarded woman as a free human personality at a time, like the eighteenth century, which was saturated with sentiment toward the 'fair sex,' and in a country, like France, where cynicism was so frequently the overtone of gallantry.">[1] In contrast to members of fashionable society and to most of the revolutionary *philosophes,* who generally adopted mistresses and led a loose sexual life, Condorcet was a man of austere morals. He was devoted to his wife, the brilliant Sophie de Grouchy, who shared his intellectual interests and who aided him in his writings.

During the Reign of Terror, when Condorcet's moderate Girondist views were rejected in favor of the radical Jacobin concepts, he was proscribed and went into hiding. After nine months he was apprehended and lodged in the prison of Bourg-la-Reine. The next morning he was found dead in his cell.

The reader who will be inspired by the essay included here to pursue the study of Condorcet will be rewarded by the discovery of the ultimate humanist. In developing his philosophy of equal rights for all, Condorcet explored the fields of mathematics, political economy, political science, and education. His proposal for universal education, original and forward-looking as it was, should have been recognized as a landmark in educational history. Yet here, as in other respects, he failed to receive the acclaim accorded to others. This reserved and diffident man, this loving husband of an accomplished woman, devoted to humanity, lived for the ideals of the French Revolution and died a martyr to its excesses.

On the Admission of Women to the Rights of Citizenship

Custom may familiarise mankind with the violation of their natural rights to such an extent, that even among those who have lost or been deprived of these rights, no one thinks of reclaiming them, or is even conscious that they have suffered any injustice.

Certain of these violations (of natural right) have escaped the notice of philosophers and legislators, even while concerning themselves zealously to establish the common rights of individuals of the human race, and in this way to lay the foundation of political

From *The First Essay on the Political Rights of Women: A Translation of Condorcet's Essay "Sur l'admission des femmes au droit de Cité"* [On the admission of women to the rights of citizenship], *Collected Writings,* trans. Dr. Alice Drysdale Vickery (1790; Letchworth: Garden City Press Limited, 1893).

institutions. For example, have they not all violated the principle of the equality of rights in tranquilly depriving one-half of the human race of the right of taking part in the formation of laws by the exclusion of women from the rights of citizenship? Could there be a stronger proof of the power of habit, even among enlightened men, than to hear invoked the principle of equal rights in favour of perhaps some 300 or 400 men, who had been deprived of it by an absurd prejudice, and forget it when it concerns some 12,000,000 women?

To show that this exclusion is not an act of tyranny, it must be proved either that the natural rights of women are not absolutely the same as those of men, or that women are not capable of exercising these rights.

But the rights of men result simply from the fact that they are rational, sentient beings, susceptible of acquiring ideas of morality, and of reasoning concerning those ideas. Women having, then, the same qualities, have necessarily the same rights. Either no individual of the human species has any true rights, or all have the same; and he or she who votes against the rights of another, whatever may be his or her religion, colour, or sex, has by that fact abjured his own.

It would be difficult to prove that women are incapable of exercising the rights of citizenship. Although liable to become mothers of families, and exposed to other passing indispositions, why may they not exercise rights of which it has never been proposed to deprive those persons who periodically suffer from gout, bronchitis, etc? Admitting for the moment that there exists in men a superiority of mind, which is not the necessary result of a difference of education (which is by no means proved, but which should be, to permit of women being deprived of a natural right without injustice), this inferiority can only consist in two points. It is said that no woman has made any important discovery in science, or has given any proofs of the possession of genius in arts, literature, etc.; but, on the other hand, it is not pretended that the rights of citizenship should be accorded only to men of genius. It is added that no woman has the same extent of knowledge, the same power of reasoning, as certain men; but what results from that? Only this, that with the exception of a limited number of exceptionally enlightened men, equality is absolute between women and the remainder of the men; that this small class apart, inferiority and superiority are equally divided between the two sexes. But since it would be completely absurd to restrict to this superior class the rights of citizenship and the power of being entrusted with public functions, why should women be excluded any more that those men who are inferior to a great number of women? Lastly, shall it be said that there exists in the minds and hearts of women certain qualities which ought to exclude them from the enjoyment of their natural rights? Let us interrogate the facts. Elizabeth of England, Maria Theresa, the two Catherines of Russia—have they not shown that neither in courage nor in strength of mind are women wanting?

Elizabeth possessed all the failings of women. Did these failings work more harm during her reign than resulted from the failings of men during the reign of her father, Henry VIII, or her successor, James I? Have the lovers of certain empresses exercised a more dangerous influence than the mistresses of Louis XIV, of Louis XV, or even Henry IV?

Will it be maintained that Mistress Macaulay would not have expressed her opinions in the House of Commons better than many representatives of the British nation? In dealing with the question of liberty of conscience, would she not have expressed more elevated principles than those of Pitt, as well as more powerful reasoning? Although as great an enthusiast on behalf of liberty as Mr. Burke could be on behalf of its opposite, would she, while defending the French Constitution, have made use of such absurd and offensive nonsense as that which this celebrated rhetorician made use of in attacking it? Would not the adopted daughter of Montaigne have better defended the rights of citizens in France, in 1614, than the Councillor Courtin, who was a believer in magic and occult powers? Was not the Princesse des Ursins superior to Chamillard? Could not the Marquise de Chatelet have written equally as well as M. Rouillé? Would Mme. de Lambert have made laws as absurd and as barbarous as those of the "garde des Sceaux," of Armenouville, against Protestants, invaders of domestic privacy, robbers and negroes? In looking back over the list of those who have governed the world, men have scarcely the right to be so very uplifted.

Women are superior to men in the gentle and domestic virtues; they, as well as men, know how to love liberty, although they do not participate in all its advantages; and in republics they have been known to sacrifice themselves for it. They have shown that they possess the virtues of citizens whenever chance or civil disasters have brought them upon a scene from which they have been shut out by the pride and the tyranny of men in all nations.

It has been said that women, in spite of much ability, of much sagacity, and of a power of reasoning carried to a degree equalling that of subtle dialecticians, yet are never governed by what is called "reason."

This observation is not correct. Women are not governed, it is true, by the reason (and experience) of men; they are governed by their own reason (and experience).

Their interests not being the same (as those of men) by the fault of the law, the same things not having the same importance for them as for men, they may, without failing in rational conduct, govern themselves by different principles, and tend towards a different result. It is as reasonable for a woman to concern herself respecting her personal attractions as it was for Demosthenes to cultivate his voice and his gestures.

It is said that women, although superior in some respects to man—more gentle, more sensitive, less subject to those vices which proceed from egotism and hardness of heart—yet do not really possess the sentiment of justice; that they obey rather their feelings than their conscience. This observation is more correct, but it proves nothing; it is not nature, it is education, it is social existence which produces this difference.

Neither the one nor the other has habituated women to the idea of what is just, but only to the idea of what is "honnête," or respectable. Excluded from public affairs, from all those things which are judged of according to rigorous ideas of justice, or according to positive laws, the things with which they are occupied and which are affected by them are precisely those which are regulated by natural feelings of honesty (or, rather, propriety) and of sentiment. It is, then, unjust to allege as an excuse for continuing to refuse to women the enjoyment of all their natural rights motives which have only a kind of reality because women lack the experience which comes from the exercise of these rights.

If reasons such as these are to be admitted against women, it will become necessary to deprive of the rights of citizenship that portion of the people who, devoted to constant labour, can neither acquire knowledge nor exercise their reason; and thus, little by little, only those persons would be permitted to be citizens who had completed a course of legal study. If such principles are admitted, we must, as a natural consequence, renounce the idea of a liberal constitution. The various aristocracies have only had such principles as these for foundation or excuse. The etymology of the word is a sufficient proof of this.

Neither can the subjection of wives to their husbands be alleged against their claims, since it would be possible in the same statute to destroy this tyranny of the civil law. The existence of one injustice can never be accepted as a reason for committing another.

There remain, then, only two objections to discuss. And, in truth, these can only oppose motives of expediency against the admission of women to the right of voting; which motives can never be upheld as a bar to the exercise of true justice. The contrary maxim has only too often served as the pretext and excuse of tyrants; it is in the name of expediency that commerce and industry groan in chains; and that Africa remains afflicted with slavery; it was in the name of public expediency that the Bastille was crowded; that the censorship of the press was instituted; that accused persons were not allowed to communicate with their advisers; that torture was resorted to. Nevertheless, we will discuss these objections, so as to leave nothing without reply.

It is necessary, we are warned, to be on guard against the influence exercised by women over men. We reply at once that this, like any other influence, is much more to be feared when not exercised openly; and that, whatever influence may be peculiar to women, if exercised upon more than one individual at a time, will in so far become proportionately lessened. That since, up to this time, women have not been admitted in any country to absolute equality; since their empire has none the less existed everywhere; and since the more women have been degraded by the laws, the more dangerous has their influence been; it does not appear that this remedy of subjection ought to inspire us with much confidence. Is it not probable, on the contrary, that their special empire would diminish if women had less interest in its preservation; if it ceased to be for them their sole means of defence, and of escape from persecution?

If politeness does not permit to men to maintain their opinions against women in society, this politeness, it may be said, is near akin to pride; we yield a victory of no importance; defeat does not humiliate when it is regarded as voluntary. Is it seriously believed that it would be the same in a public discussion on an important topic? Does politeness forbid the bringing of an action at law against a woman?

But, it will be said, this change will be contrary to general expediency, because it will take women away from those duties which nature has reserved for them. This objection scarcely appears to me well founded. Whatever form of constitution may be established, it is certain that in the present state of civilisation among European nations there will never be more than a limited number of citizens required to occupy themselves with public affairs. Women will no more be torn from their homes than agricultural labourers from their ploughs, or artisans from their workshops. And, among the richer classes, we nowhere see women giving themselves up so persistently to domestic affairs that we should fear to distract their attention; and a really serious occupation or interest would take them less away than the frivolous pleasures to which idleness, a want of object in life, and an inferior education have condemned them.

The principal source of this fear is the idea that every person admitted to exercise the rights of citizenship immediately aspires to govern others. This may be true to a certain extent, at a time when the constitution is being established, but the feeling can scarcely prove durable. And so it is scarcely necessary to believe that because women may become members of national assemblies, they would immediately abandon their children, their homes, and their needles. They would only be the better fitted to educate their children and to rear men. It is natural that a woman should suckle her infant; that she should watch over its early childhood. Detained in her home by these cares, and less muscular than the man, it is also natural that she should lead a more retired, a more domestic life. The woman, therefore, as well as the man in a corresponding class of life, would be under the necessity of performing certain duties at certain times according to circumstances. This may be a motive for not giving her the preference in an election, but it cannot be a reason for legal exclusion. Gallantry would doubtless lose by the change, but domestic customs would be improved by equality in this as in other things.

Up to this time the manners of all nations have been more or less brutal and corrupt. I only know of one exception, and that is in favour of the Americans of the United States, who are spread, few in number, over a wide territory. Up to this time, among all nations, legal inequality has existed between men and women; and it would not be difficult to show that, in these two phenomena, the second is one of the causes of the first, because inequality necessarily introduces corruption, and is the most common cause of it, if even it be not the sole cause.

I now demand that opponents should condescend to refute these propositions by other methods than by pleasantries and declamations; above all, that they should show me any natural difference between men and women which may legitimately serve as foundation for the deprivation of a right.

The equality of rights established between men by our new constitution has brought down upon us eloquent declamations and never-ending pleasantries; but up till now no one has been able to oppose to it one single reason, and this is certainly neither from lack of talent nor lack of zeal. I venture to believe that it will be the same with regard to equality of rights between the two sexes. It is sufficiently curious that, in a great number of countries, women have been judged incapable of all public functions yet worthy of royalty; that in France a woman has been able to be regent, and yet that up to 1776 she could not be a milliner or dressmaker in Paris, except under cover of her husband's name;[1] and that, lastly, in our elective assemblies they have accorded to rights of property what they have refused to natural right. Many of our noble deputies owe to ladies the honour of sitting among the representatives of the nation. Why, instead of depriving of this right women who were owners of landed estates, was it not extended to all those who possessed property or were heads of households? Why, if it be found absurd to exercise the right of citizenship by proxy, deprive women of this right, rather than leave them the liberty of exercising it in person?

NOTE

1. Before the suppression of "jurandes," in 1776, women could neither carry on a business of a "marchande des modes" (milliner and dressmaker) nor of any other profession exercised by them, unless they were married, or unless some man lent or sold them his name for that purpose.—See preamble of the Edict of 1776.—Trans.

HERBERT SPENCER (1820–1903)

One of the foremost thinkers of his day, Herbert Spencer developed in his *Synthetic Philosophy* a system which purported to synthesize the fundamental principles of the social sciences. He advocated that social phenomena be subjected to scientific analysis so that the future society could be planned for social betterment. He was a vigorous exponent of "laissez-faire," asserting the preeminence of the individual over society and of science over religion. As a champion of individualism he espoused the rights of various underprivileged groups, such as children and women.

His conviction that the individual, whether male or female, is an independent member of society and should have no restraints put in the way of opportunity led him to the conclusion, radical for his day, that all careers should be open to women. Quite radical too is the statement that "the discharge of domestic and maternal duties by the wife may ordinarily be held a fair equivalent of the earning of an income by the husband."

When he ranged into the maze of complexities involving the choice of male or female dominance in conflictful family situations, he wrestled bravely with the problem only to resort finally to the parochial patriarchal assumption that "since, speaking generally, man is more judicially-minded than woman, the balance of authority should incline to the side of the husband, especially as he usually provides the means which make possible the fulfillment of the will of either or the wills of both." Thus the scientific mind falls victim to the existing cultural bias.

His line of ethical reasoning seems to undergo some bending and twisting when he enters the arena of "political rights." He argues that "political rights" should not be granted women until they assume the same liabilities as men for defending the country, but he sees no objection to women enjoying equal participation in local governments.

Principles of Ethics

When in certain preceding chapters the fundamental principle of justice was discussed, a relevant question which might have been raised, I decided to postpone, because I thought discussion of it would appropriately introduce the subject-matter of this chapter.

"Why," it might have been asked, "should not men have rights proportionate to their faculties? Why should not the sphere of action of the superior individual be greater than that of the inferior individual? Surely, as a big man occupies more space than a little man, so too does he need larger supplies of the necessaries of life; and so, too, does he need greater scope for the use of his powers. Hence it is unreasonable that the activities of great and small, strong and weak, high and low, should be severally restrained within limits too narrow for these and too wide for those."

The first reply is that the metaphors which we are obliged to use are misleading if interpreted literally. Though, as above, and as in previous chapters, men's equal liberties are figured as spaces surrounding each, which mutually limit one another, yet they cannot be truly represented in so simple a manner. The inferior man, who claims as great a right to bodily integrity as the superior man, does not by doing this trespass on the bodily integrity of the superior man. If he asserts like freedom with him to move about and to work, he does not thereby prevent him from moving about and working. And if he retains as his own whatever his activities have gained for him, he in no degree prevents the superior man from retaining the produce of his activities, which, by implication, are greater in amount.

The second reply is that denying to inferior faculty a sphere of action equal to that which superior faculty has, is to add an artificial hardship to a natural hardship. To be born with a dwarfed or deformed body, or imperfect senses, or a feeble constitution, or a low intelligence, or ill-balanced emotions, is in itself a pitiable fate. Could we charge Nature with injustice, we might fitly say it is unjust that some should have natural endowments so much lower than others have, and that they should thus be in large measure incapacitated for the battle of life. And if so, what shall we say to the proposal that, being already disadvantaged by having smaller

From Herbert Spencer, *Principles of Ethics*, Chap. XX, "The Rights of Women" (New York: Appleton & Co., 1893).

powers, they should be further disadvantaged by having narrower spheres for the exercise of those powers? Sympathy might contrariwise urge that, by way of compensation for inherited disabilities, they should have extended opportunities. But, evidently, the least that can be done is to allow them as much freedom as others to make the best of themselves.

A third reply is that, were it equitable to make men's liberties proportionate to their abilities, it would be impracticable; since we have no means by which either the one or the other can be measured. In the great mass of cases there is no difficulty in carrying out the principle of equality. If, (previous aggression being supposed absent,) A kills B, or knocks him down, or locks him up, it is clear that the liberties of action assumed by the two are unlike; or if C, having bought goods of D, does not pay the price agreed upon, it is clear that the contract having been fulfilled on one side and not on the other, the degrees of freedom used are not the same. But if liberties are to be proportioned to abilities, then the implication is that the relative amounts of each faculty, bodily and mental, must be ascertained; and the further implication is that the several kinds of freedom needed must be meted out. Neither of these things can be done; and therefore, apart from other reasons, the regard for practicability would require us to treat men's freedom as equal, irrespective of their endowments.

With change of terms these arguments are applicable to the relation between the rights of men and the rights of women. This is not the place for comparing in detail the capacities of men and women. It suffices for present purposes to recognize the unquestionable fact that some women are physically stronger than some men, and that some women have higher mental endowments than some men—higher, indeed, than the great majority of men. Hence it results, as above, that were liberties to be adjusted to abilities, the adjustment, even could we make it, would have to be made irrespective of sex.

The difficulty reappears under another form, if we set out with the proposition that just as, disregarding exceptions, the average physical powers of women are less than the average physical powers of men, so too are their average mental powers. For we could not conform our plans to this truth: it would be impossible to ascertain the ratio between the two averages; and it would be impossible rightly to proportion the spheres of activity to them.

But, as above argued, generosity prompting equalization would direct that were any difference to be made it ought to be that, by way of compensation, smaller faculties should have greater facilities. Generosity aside however, justice demands the women, if they are not artifically advantaged, must not, at any rate, be artificially disadvantaged.

Hence, if men and women are severally regarded as independent members of a society, each one of whom has to do the best for himself or herself, it results that no restraints can equitably be placed upon women in respect of the occupations, professions, or other careers which they may wish to adopt. They must have like freedom to prepare themselves, and like freedom to profit by such information and skill as they acquire.

But more involved questions arise when we take into account the relations of women to men in marriage, and the relations of women to men in the State.

Of those equal liberties with men which women should have before marriage, we must say that in equity they retain after marriage all those which are not necessarily interfered with by the marital relation—the rights to physical integrity, the rights to ownership of property earned and property given or bequeathed, the rights to free belief and free speech, etc. Their claims can properly be qualified only in so far as they are traversed by the understood or expressed terms of the contract voluntarily entered into; and as these terms vary in different places and times, the resulting qualifications must vary. Here, in default of definite measures, we must be content with approximations.

In respect of property, for instance, it may be reasonably held that where the husband is exclusively responsible for maintenance of the family, property which would otherwise belong to the wife may equitably be assigned to him—the use, at least, if not the possession; since, if not, it becomes possible for the wife to use her property or its proceeds for her personal benefit only, and refuse to contribute towards the expenses of the joint household. Only if she is equally responsible with him for family maintenance, does it seem right that she should have equally unqualified ownership of property. Yet, on the other hand, we cannot say that the responsibilities must be entirely reciprocal. For though, rights of ownership being supposed equal, it would at first sight appear that the one is as much bound as the other to maintain the two and their children; yet this is negatived by the existence on the one side of onerous functions which do not exist on the other, and which largely incapacitate for active life. Nothing more than a compromise, varying according to the circumstances, seems here possible. The discharge of domestic and maternal duties by the wife may ordinarily be held a fair equivalent for the earning of an income by the husband.

Respecting powers of control over one another's actions and over the household, the conclusions to be drawn are still more indefinite. The relative positions of the two as contributors of monies and services have to be taken into account, as well as their respective natures; and these factors in the problem are variable. When there arise conflicting wills of which both cannot be fulfilled, but one of which must issue in action, the law of equal freedom cannot, in each particular case, be conformed to; but can be conformed to only in the average of cases. Whether it should be conformed to in the average of cases must depend on circumstances. We may, however, say that since, speaking generally, man is more judicially-minded than woman, the balance of authority should incline to the side of the husband; especially as he usually provides the means which make possible the fulfilment of the will of either or the wills of both. But in respect of this relation reasoning goes for little: the characters of those concerned determine the form it takes. The only effect which ethical considerations are likely to have is that of moderating the use of such supremacy as eventually arises.

The remaining question, equally involved or more involved, concerns the possession and management of children. Decisions about management have to be made daily; and decisions about possessions must be made in all cases of separation. What are the relative claims of husband and wife in such cases? On the one hand, it may be said of the direct physical claims, otherwise equal, that that of the mother is rendered far greater by the continued nutrition before and after birth, than that of the father. On the other hand, it may be urged on the part of the father, that in the normal order the food by which the mother has been supported and the nutrition of the infant made possible, has been provided by his labour. Whether this counter-claim be or be not equivalent, it must be admitted that the claim of the mother cannot well be less than that of the father. Of the compromise respecting management which justice thus appears to dictate, we may perhaps reasonably say that the power of the mother may fitly predominate during the earlier part of a child's life, and that of the father during the later part. The maternal nature is better adjusted to the needs of infancy and early childhood than the paternal nature; while for fitting children, and especially boys, for the battle of life, the father, who has had most experience of it, may be considered the best guide. But it seems alike inequitable and inexpedient that the power of either should at any time be exercised to the exclusion of the power of the other. Of the respective claims to possession where separation takes place, some guidance is again furnished by consideration of children's welfare; an equal division, where it is possible, being so made that the younger remain with the mother and the elder go with the father. Evidently, however nothing is here possible but compromise based on consideration of the special circumstances.

Concerning the claims of women, as domestically associated with men, I may add that here in England, and still more in America, the need for urging them is not pressing. In some cases, indeed, there is a converse need. But there are other civilized societies in which their claims are very inadequately recognized: instance Germany.[1]

As in other cases, let us look now at the stages through which usage and law have grown into conformity with ethics.

Save among the few primitive peoples who do not preach the virtues called Christian but merely praise them—save among those absolutely peaceful tribes here and there found who, while admirable in their general conduct, treat their women with equity as well as kindness, uncivilized tribes at large have no more conception of the rights of women than of the rights of brutes. Such regard for women's claims as enables mothers to survive and rear offspring, of course exists; since tribes in which it is less than this disappear. But, frequently, the regard is not greater than is needful to prevent extinction.

When we read of a Fijian that he might kill and eat his wife if he pleased; of the Fuegians and wilder Australians that they sacrificed their old women for food; and of the many peoples among whom women are killed to accompany their dead husbands to the other world; we see that they are commonly denied even the first of all rights. The facts that in these low stages women, leading the lives of slaves, are also sold as slaves, and, when married, are either stolen or bought, prove that no liberties are recognized as belonging to them. And on remembering that where wives are habitually considered as property, the implication is that independent ownership of property by them can scarcely exist, we are shown that this further fundamental right is at the outset but very vaguely recognized. Though the matter is in many cases complicated and qualified by the system of descent in the female line, it is certain that, speaking generally, in rude societies where among men aggression is restrained only by fear of vengeance, the claims of women are habitually disregarded.

To trace up in this place the rising status of women is out of the question. Passing over those ancient societies in which descent in the female line gave to women a relatively high position, as it did among the Egyptians, it will suffice to note that in societies which have arisen by aggregation of patriarchal groups, the rights of women, at first scarcely more recognized than among savages, have, during these two thousand years, gradually established themselves. Limiting our attention to the Aryans who overspread Europe, we see that save where, as indicated by Tacitus, women, by sharing in the dangers of war, gained a better position (a connexion of facts which we find among various peoples), they were absolutely subordinated. The primitive Germans bought their wives; and husbands might sell and even kill them. In the early Teutonic society, as in the early Roman society, there was perpetual tutelage of women, and consequent incapacity for independent ownership of property. A like state of things existed here in the old English period. Brides were purchased: their wills counting for nothing in the bargains. Mitigations gradually came. Among the Romans the requirement that a bride should be transferred to the bridegroom by legal conveyance, ceased to be observed. The life and death power came to an end: though sometimes reappearing, as when the early Angevin ruler, Fulc the Black, burnt his wife. Generalizing the facts we see that as life became less exclusively militant, the subjection of women to men became less extreme. How that decline of the system of *status* and rise of the system of contract, which characterizes industrialism, ameliorated, in early days, the position of women, is curiously shown by the occurrence of their signatures in the documents of guilds, while yet their position outside of the guilds remained much as before. This connexion has continued to be a general one. Both in England and in America, where the industrial type of organization is most developed, the legal *status* of women is higher than on the continent, where militancy is more pronounced. Add to which that among ourselves, along with the modern growth of free institutions characterizing predominant industrialism, the positions of women have been with increasing rapidity approximated to those of men.

Here again, then, ethical deductions harmonize with historical inductions. As in preceding chapters we saw that each of those corollaries from the law of equal freedom which we call a right, has been better established as fast as a higher social life has been reached; so here, we see that the general body of such rights, originally denied entirely to women, has, in the course of this same progress, been acquired by them.

There has still to be considered from the ethical point of view, the political position of women as compared with the political position of men; but until the last of these has been dealt with, we cannot in a complete way deal with the first. When presently, we enter on the consideration of what are commonly called "political rights," we shall find need for changing, in essential ways, the current conceptions of them; and until this has been done the political rights of women cannot be adequately treated of. There is, however, one aspect of the matter which we may deal with now no less conveniently than hereafter.

Are the political rights of women the same as those of men? The assumption that they are the same is now widely made. Along with that identity of rights above set forth as arising from the human nature common to the two sexes, there is supposed to go an identity of rights in respect to the direction of public affairs. At first sight it seems that the two properly go together; but consideration shows that this is not so. Citizenship does not include only the giving of votes, joined now and again with the fulfilment of representative functions. It includes also certain serious responsibilities. But if so, there cannot be equality of citizenship unless along with the share of good there goes the share of evil. To call that equality of citizenship under which some have their powers *gratis*, while others pay for their powers by undertaking risks, is absurd. Now men, whatever political powers they may in any case possess, are at the same time severally liable to the loss of liberty, to the privation, and occasionally to the death, consequent on having to defend the country; and if women, along with the same political powers, have not the same liabilities, their position is not one of equality but one of supremacy.

Unless, therefore, women furnish contingents to the army and navy such as men furnish, it is manifest that, ethically considered, the question of the equal "political rights," so-called, of women, cannot be entertained until there is reached a state of permanent peace. Then only will it be possible (whether desirable or not) to make the political positions of men and women the same.

It should be added that of course this reason does not negative the claims of women to equal shares in local governments and administrations. If it is contended that these should be withheld, it must be for reasons of other kinds.

NOTE

1. With other reasons prompting this remark, is joined the remembrance of a conversation between two Germans residing in England, in which, with contemptuous laughter, they were describing how they had often seen, on a Sunday or other holiday, an English artizan relieving his wife by carrying the child they had with them. Their sneers produced in me a feeling of shame—but not for the artizan.

PART 5

Voices of Protest

FRANK MOND, Editor of
The Burden of Woman (1908)

In *The Burden of Woman* Frank Mond wished to present the views of different schools of thought on the condition of woman and the relations of the sexes. At the time he was writing there was a vigorous reform movement in England concerned with the education of women for employment, the maintenance of health among girls and women, legislation to protect women, infant mortality owing to ignorance and neglect on the part of mothers, the dangers of venereal disease, and women's rights, and these topics are the subject matter of his collection.

The title page attributes compilation of this book to Frank Mond, but each of the five chapters is ascribed to a woman, and only one chapter carries a full name. Chapter I, incorporated here in abridged form, is called "The Tyranny of Man" and is attributed only to "Stella." It is written with passionate intensity, with no holds barred. The author tears away the privileged curtain of sacrosanctness from the Bible and traces the evidence of its persistent debasement of women. She dares to assert the imperative for women to play a prominent role in the Church, for example, as female confessors. She espouses the cause of equality for women in politics, in employment, and in the law, and she deplores the manner in which men have depicted women in literature and in art. Finally, she recommends female vigilance in exposing men's transgressions, hoping thereby to make men's consciences more tender and sensitive. The somewhat inflated rhetoric has a turn-of-the-century flavor, yet the content conveys with uncanny similitude the ideas of our present-day women's liberationists.

"The Tyranny of Man"
by Stella

The question is—What is the Burden of Woman? My answer is, The Tyranny of Man.

I shall endeavour to sum up as fully and concisely as possible . . . the views of the noble band of lady workers who have devoted their talents and their energies to the stupendous task of rescuing woman from her degraded position of inferiority and servitude, and of securing for her the freedom and equality without which the progress of humanity to the glorious triumphs of the future is impossible. The beautiful vision of the perfect woman, still hid by destiny, inspires us with merciless hands to rend asunder the shackles of conventionalism so artfully concealed by gilded compliments; and we insist upon the plain and full discussion of the relation of the sexes, until all the clouds which impede her progress disappear in noon-day light, and Woman stands erect and unabashed in all the pride of conscious worth.

I am called upon to prove that we are not already in the enjoyment of all our rights, and to state the grievances of which we complain. Men ask, Where is the inequality? Where is there any injustice to woman? Where is there any evidence of a desire to treat her as an inferior, or to tyrannise over her? The evidence is so overwhelming that I am almost lost in the superabundance of it, and scarce know where to begin.

The most natural starting-point seems to be the religious teaching which girls are compelled to accept, and which men point to as the unalterable and infallible statement of the principles upon which society depends. We cannot help feeling peculiarly influenced by the principles which have been instilled into us from our earliest childhood, and which our parents have impressed upon our minds with all the awful solemnity of those convinced that infinite happiness or misery depends upon the acceptance or rejection of their dogmas. It is extremely difficult to emancipate ourselves from the influence of our early training, so as to criticise with impartial mind the doctrines once regarded as infallible truth the doubting of which would entail everlasting punishment. Yet I see clearly that

From Frank Mond, ed., *The Burden of Woman*, Chap. I, "The Tyranny of Man," by Stella (London: The New Age Press, 1908).

the religious idea is the central fortress we have to storm, since upon it are built all our customs, and regulations, and laws, and beliefs.

Beneath all the beautiful poetry and elevating sentiment of Christianity is concealed the idea of the inferiority of woman; and the girl of independent spirit never knows the moment her self-respect will be wounded, and her thoughts embittered, by some reference to the evil influence of her sex upon men, and the dangerous consequences they have to fear if they neglect to guard against her deceitful nature.

We are told that man was created first, and that woman was only created as an afterthought; not because she was worth creating for herself, but because man was lonely and needed a companion. Thus man maintains that he has the sanction of the Creator for regarding woman as inferior to himself.

The writer of Genesis is apparently not very certain of the real facts of the case. First he says that God created man male and female, without any mention of priority; and if a woman had been the writer she would have been satisfied to let the account stand so. If they were created male and female separately, and at the same time, they were equal from the first. The male writer is not satisfied with this state of the case, since it gives him no excuse for telling the woman that it is her duty to obey him; so in the next chapter we find it stated that she was not created independently at all, but was only formed from a part of the man, and because he could not be happy without her. What girl can help feeling annoyed and mortified when she hears such a statement read in public? . . .

Now comes the great historical humiliation of woman, upon which the whole superstructure of Christianity is built. Adam is perfect, so that his Creator can find no fault in him, until Eve causes him to sin. Thus woman is the cause of all sin and disease, and all our hereditary woe.

Preachers now quibble, and shuffle, and prevaricate about the account given of Adam and Eve. . . . The vital question to put to every preacher is, Do you believe the account which says that Adam and Eve were created perfect, and that she caused him to fall? . . .

The modern girl is too well educated to be deceived by unmeaning phrases, and knows that if she accepts Christianity she must accept the statements made in the Bible about the first man and woman. We have to meekly admit that sin and sorrow would never have been the lot of mankind but for the transgression of Eve; and no woman who desires to preserve her complete independence can help feeling insulted by the references to this ancient tradition which are continually being made by men, and even by those who profess to believe in evolution. Instead of being the cause of human degradation we see woman in every-day life acting as the reformer and the purifier of society.

Supposing that the story of the Fall is true, does it prove the natural inferiority of woman? Eve displayed greater enterprise and curiosity than Adam; and curiosity is an essential element in the progress of science. The child without curiosity is an imbecile. What produces a Newton but curiosity? The superior being is the one that has the greater strength of will; and we find that a mysterious supernatural power was needed to overcome the will of Eve, while the man surrendered all his principles at her request.

Why should a girl cast down her eyes and look like a criminal in the presence of a man? Her education is designed to destroy her self-confidence. If she looks at him with straight, honest eyes as an equal, or a superior, she is described as a bold, immodest woman, disgracing her sex; and girls are taught that they must be meek, and modest, and gentle, and submissive, and never say plainly what they think of social questions. They must listen with docility to sermons which describe such men as Isaac and Jacob as saints of olden time, whose history is recorded for our edification. The story of Isaac and his wife is to be read with delight; and Rebecca is to be looked up to as a model dutiful girl. Abraham sent a servant to look for a wife for his son; and Isaac did not even take the trouble of going to see the woman who was to be the object of his affections; while Rebecca left her home in the company of a strange servant to marry a man she had never seen. The courtship consisted in presenting her with a gold ring for her nose and bracelets for her arms; but the presents were given by Abraham's servant, who might have given them to any other girl who had happened to be servile enough to carry water for his camels. Some precious things had also to be given to her mother and brother in payment for her. What independence of spirit can be expected in girls who are taught to think with respect and admiration of a woman who accepted presents as equivalent to courtship, and was ready to go at once with a man who said he was looking for a wife for his master? . . .

The notion that woman is the property of man, to be disposed of at his pleasure, seems to have taken possession of man's mind as soon as his muscles were strong enough to secure her as his slave; and, since laws were merely devised for the advantage of the dominating party, all legislation was framed in the interests of the property owners. Among tribes accustomed to acquire property by robbing their neighbours, the women were classed with the cattle; and when there were no hostile tribes to make war against, it was only natural that an imitation of real capture should become the fashionable mode of obtaining a wife. The girl was taught to run as if a hunted animal, and the noble sportsman then pursued and secured the prey; just as a tame deer is taught to run in order that men pursuing it may imagine themselves brave. . . .

Abraham, who became the "father of the faithful," turned Hagar and Ishmael out to gain their own living, though he was a rich man. It is true he waited till the boy was old enough to herd sheep; whereas in modern England the father of an illegitimate child is apt to leave his offspring to be murdered by a baby-farmer. . . . The Bible informs us that "David did that which was right in the eyes of the Lord, and turned not aside from anything that He commanded him all the days of his life, save only in the matter of Uriah the Hittite"—that is save only when he interfered with the right of another man to tyrannise over a woman and to keep her in slavery.

It may be said that I am writing of savage ages, and that Christian nations have learned to look upon the ancient theories of woman's inferiority as the errors of ignorance and barbarism. What is Christianity without its Adam and Eve? What is the Church without the Prophets? The highest claim that a Christian can make is that he is an enlightened Jew.

What do we find in the New Testament? There was not a single woman among the apostles—not one in twelve—and there is no report of the speech of any female disciple. Male supremacy is everywhere asserting itself, and strenuous efforts are being made to crush female emancipation. Paul writes to Timothy,—"Let a woman learn in quietness with all subjection. For I permit not a woman to teach, nor to have dominion over a man, but to be in quietness. For Adam was first formed, then Eve: and Adam was not beguiled, but the woman being beguiled hath fallen into transgression." We never get away from the old story of Adam and Eve. One cannot but pity this unfortunate old bachelor who warns Timothy to keep the tongues of women silent, while he at the same time has the candour to confess that Timothy owes his superior religious knowledge and estimable qualities to the training received from his mother and grandmother. . . .

No one suffered more than Paul himself from the absence of female guidance and assistance; for he confesses that he had little ability as an orator, and that he had often to suffer great discomfort, so that it is very evident that he was badly fitted to wander about alone. . . .

It is strange how prejudice and selfishness can make men forget all they owe to their mothers and sisters, and apparently to forget that ever they had mothers. We find Paul writing to the Corinthians, "It is good for a man not to touch a woman." . . . He could not get rid of the notion of the woman's inferiority; and he could not be blind to the fact that women who are physically strong are often both graceful in form and clever in oratory, while it had been said of him "his bodily presence is weak, and his speech contemptible." . . .

The only way of discovering our weaknesses is by open competition; and now that man is compelled to compete on equal terms with woman for public appointments the tendency to sneer at her inferiority is beginning to be replaced by dread of her ability. When Paul found himself dependent on woman's forethought and self-denial for food and shelter, he spoke quite respectfully of her ability and devotion; but when he got to the seclusion of his solitary chamber, and had his imagination no longer restrained by the facts of every-day life, he saw himself in fancy exercising authority and dominating over her; and in his longing to have someone looking up to him as a superior he thought he recognised a natural instinct, and not the outcome of mere selfishness and pride. Hence, in writing to the Ephesians, he gets to the climax of his greatness, and says,—"Wives, be in subjection unto your own husbands, as unto the Lord. For the husband is the head of the wife, as Christ also is the Head of the Church, being Himself the Saviour of the body. But as the Church is subject to Christ so let the wives also be to their husbands in everything."

. . . Was there ever a woman who practised such obedience, or who regarded a man as infallible? Was there ever a man who deserved to have his commands so implicitly obeyed, and his judgment treated with such awe?

The rules of the Latin Church push beyond its legitimate consequences the teaching of Paul with regard to the relation of the sexes. Marriage is supposed to render a man unfit to be a priest; and women are treated as inferior beings whose influence must always be guarded against as morally polluting, and who must regularly confess their faults to men in order to obtain forgiveness and absolution, without which they are utterly unfit for society. In order to be holy, men must live in monasteries, and even avoid looking at a woman; or if they are permitted to have female housekeepers or servants the corrupt nature of the female must ever be kept in mind.

The attempts made by earnest theologians to reconcile this treatment of women with Christianity and common sense are amazingly ridiculous and absurd. The most extravagant terms of praise and adoration are lavished upon the "Mother of God"; and the most prominent painting or figure in almost every church is that of a woman. A stranger would almost fancy that she had at last found a society of Woman-worshippers, who not merely recognised the perfect equality of the sexes, but positively asserted the superiority of woman. What a contrast the reality is to the deceptive mockery! Instead of the priests respecting women as children ought to respect their mothers, a female voice is not permitted to be heard in the choir except upon rare occasions. Women crawl about the church with the downcast eyes and cowed mien of criminals awaiting sentence. Even in our prisons the female thief is provided with a female searcher; but in the Church where the "Mother of God" has hymns sung to her praise there is no female trusted to search another's mind, and no toleration of the voice of a woman except in tones of humble penitence confessing her sins to a man and imploring absolution from him. One might expect that a man would confess his sins to his mother if he were not a hopelessly abandoned wretch, but the male despots do not even allow a woman to have a female confessor. No woman can ever give a woman absolution in the Church of the Immaculate Conception of the "Mother of God."

. . . Every celibate priest and layman ought to be compelled to marry, if only for the sake of his own mental sanity. . . . I can excuse and even admire a man who remains unmarried because he has been disappointed in love, or because he is in bad health; but I cannot understand how any woman with self-respect can tolerate men who openly profess to regard marriage as a disqualification for the office of a clergyman.

Not long ago I went to hear a preacher of the Church of England who has gained some notoriety by his outspoken language on social questions. To my surprise and indignation he took for a text the words in the 14th chapter of Revelation, "These are they which were not defiled with women." There was a stillness as of death over the audience as the words were coolly repeated again and again. People seemed almost afraid to breathe. The vast majority of the congregation were women, and many were apparently working girls; yet there was no protection from this insult. Many must have felt inclined to rush out of the building, but the conventions of modern society chained us down to listen in silence while it was plainly stated that those who wished for the best places in heaven must avoid contamination by women. I need hardly say that the preacher was unmarried. The text that he needs to meditate on is the saying of the Jewish Rabbi that to live in celibacy is to live in sin. . . .

There is no need of a long historical dissertation to prove the tyranny of man in the past. The facts are no longer denied. All history is a record of man's domination and woman's suffering. Every nation has kept woman in ignorance, and has used its religion as a means of securing her subjection. Is it any wonder then that the world has always been a scene of bloodshed and cruelty? Men are not able to govern themselves; and it is only when women are consulted and honoured that civilization can exist. . . .

The present relation of the sexes cannot be adequately discussed or understood without reference to the past. The ideal plan would be to establish definite scientific principles, and to found all our laws and customs upon them; but our morality is not established upon a definite scientific basis, unless we suppose the statements regarding Adam and Eve to furnish such a basis. All the laws of England are professedly founded upon the Bible; and the Bible is always the supreme authority appealed to in all doubtful questions of morality. The modern woman refuses to accept any longer the appeals to ancient tradition, and insists on a rational explanation of the conduct of man when he refuses to grant her the same freedom as himself.

The advance made within late years by women in the political world has been so great and continuous that it seems like striking the fallen to point out the evidences that remain of men's selfishness and injustice. . . .

In the political world woman is almost triumphant, and every year witnesses an advance. Women are appointed to posts which they were formerly supposed to be utterly incapable of filling; and their success takes away all excuse for refusing to grant them further opportunities of exercising their talents. . . .

For many years the portals of the medical profession were closed to woman, but that is now a thing of the past, and the medical student has learned to respect his female competitor. Every argument the selfish dominating male mind could invent was employed to prevent women from studying medicine. They were declared to be incapable of enduring the severe study, as if the hypocritical men cared for their health; they were warned that the atmosphere of the dissecting-room was bad, and its moral tone low; and they were told that even if they did get qualified nobody would have confidence in them. They simply asked for a chance of trying, and the result caused the brutal element among medical students to shrink into its proper darkness. The refining influence of woman's presence now makes itself felt by silencing the coarse jest and "smutty" anecdote; while the impudent and worthless chronic loafers, who bring disgrace on the name of medical student, are quite unable to convince their friends that they are martyrs to unfair examiners and terribly high standards when those friends see that a quiet graceful girl comes out at the head of the list.

The Law seems to be the last stronghold of the opponents of woman's freedom; but solicitors will soon learn the superiority of female clerks, and the anxiety of politicians to secure the services of eloquent lady orators at their meetings will soon make it impossible to keep such ladies shut out from the ranks of the advocates in the law courts. . . . Eminent lawyers admit that there are cases which would be best referred to a jury of matrons, . . . so that we might at first have juries composed of equal numbers of men and women, and then we might easily advance to the appointment of tribunals composed of an equal number of male and female judges. . . .

. . . Whatever is right for man is right for woman. Whatever is too foul for woman is too foul for man. There must be no compromise. We insist on all things being freely discussed by both sexes, for in no other way can we live openly and truthfully. Wherever a man can go a woman must go with him. Is there any reason why men should say that some books are not fit for their womankind to read? The attempt to restrict our reading is an insult. . . . In the courts of law there must be no shrinking from any discussion, however odious, and no exclusion of women from any trial, however disgusting. How can women hope to be judges if they are afraid to insist on their right to hear all the evidence? . . .

The literature of the past is naturally impregnated with the old false ideas of woman's inherent stupidity and inferiority, so that the modern school-girl finds her sex insulted and held up to contempt in works which she is compelled to read as classical. "Paradise Lost" is founded on the old story of Adam and Eve; and Shakespeare is often disgusting from his habit of making his female characters speak of their husbands as lords and masters. Sometimes he rises above his prejudices, and his description of the success of Portia as an advocate seems a prophetic vision of the future, when the most distinguished lawyers shall be ladies. In the case of Lady Macbeth we have a woman superior to her husband in energy and courage, though superior also in ambition; and another instance in which Shakespeare tries to do justice to woman is in his portrayal of Queen Katharine, for anyone who has seen the play well acted must have felt that the Queen was a far nobler character than the King or the Cardinal. Nevertheless the low degrading notion of woman's essential inferiority pervades all Shakespeare's work, and must necessarily do so in so far as it is a true holding of the mirror up to nature, since centuries of ignorance and dependence had crushed the spirit of woman until she readily assumed the servile aspect as her natural one. She was taught to pretend to feel delighted with the grossest flattery, though she knew that it was only the repetition of empty phrases by debauched braggarts, who wished to humiliate her in order to boast of their triumph; and who would vilify and despise the very women they had flattered most as soon as those women had been deceived by them.

Even yet the new spirit of justice has not pervaded all womankind, for I have seen many women apparently satisfied and delighted at a performance of the "Taming of the Shrew"; a play at which it is interesting to watch the manifestations of pleasure displayed by a weakly, shrivelled, blear-eyed creature in male attire who fancies for the moment that some woman may acknowledge his right to be her tyrant. Unfortunately such female slaves still exist; and I have noted the tall and handsome female beside such a male, pretending that she quite approved of all the references to man's supremacy and woman's subjection. It makes one's blood boil with indignation to see the clever, virtuous Katharina promising to give up her reason and yield the most abject submission to the vulgar bully who treats her as his property; and every girl ought to be warned to give no countenance to sentiments so destructive of all self-respect and of all feeling of responsibility.

Girls are still taught to read such works as those of Goldsmith without any explanation from their teachers that the sentiments expressed belong to a barbarous and brutal age, and must be regarded with disgust by every true woman. The truth regarding authors and their lives must be taught, and then there will be less risk of their base principles being accepted as trustworthy by the innocent. No child ought to be permitted to read "She Stoops to Conquer" without sufficient comment to excite a feeling of contempt for Miss Hardcastle, who, as a virtuous, intelligent girl, is described as eagerly demeaning herself to find favour with a low blackguard possessed of a title. The "Vicar of Wakefield" is no better in its degrading tendency, for in it we have a clergyman's daughter held up for admiration, though she is delighted to marry a dissipated liar whom she knows to have been guilty of the basest villainy; and the old vicar is supposed to be a godly man, though he gives his innocent daughter to be the wife of a most contemptible wretch who happens to have money. . . .

In Art as in Literature we are daily compelled to witness mortifying evidences of the degrading position assigned to woman by man; and so completely has the dominating party succeeded in impressing upon history his one-sided and unfair misrepresentation of woman, that we feel ourselves almost powerless to struggle against the calumny in marble which has been accepted for thousands of years as true to nature. The tyrant has embodied his ideal woman in statues and paintings, and his vilified victim has not been allowed to utter a word of explanation or protest.

The nude figure of the normal man is always made boldly erect without sense of shame. How is the normal woman depicted? Although she is formed by nature to stand erect without any exposure which a moralist could consider indecent, she is always represented as cowering in dread of exposure, or as if ashamed of herself and longing for clothing. The modern woman is determined to put an end to this notion that she is ashamed of herself. If there is any clothing needed it is the man that needs it; and the woman has no need either of the fig-leaves or the skin of beasts.

Girls can swim, and ride, and perform gymnastic exercises with so much ease and grace that men cannot help applauding: poets exhaust their adjectives in attempting to express their admiration for the beauty of the female form; artists can think of no more perfect model than a nude female; and yet, when the figure of a woman is to be represented free from the encumbrances of dress which conceal her natural symmetry and beauty, she is made to appear as if ashamed of herself. Why is this? Must we for ever hang our heads and avert our eyes as slaves in dread of punishment? Have we done anything to take away our right to look a man boldly in the face when we meet him? The story of Eve pervades all history.

Artists simply represent the ideal in their own minds; . . . and they were unchecked by the opposition of a school of female artists. There was no competition with the opposite sex; and we all know how the conceit and impudence of men have been modified since girls have got an opportunity of proving their ability and worth. We do not hear so much about woman's natural inferiority, and her inability to comprehend scientific discussions or to manage her own affairs. Instead of fondling their plaything with patronising delight and confident zest, men have now been taught to shiver with fear of our hidden power to undermine their tower of pride. . . .

Girls have been taught to regard courtship as very flattering to them, but the woman accustomed to weigh evidence and to criticise dogma is able to see through the imposture. One of the emancipators of her sex informs us that during her life she has met many men who have asked to be allowed to love her and to marry her, but not one who has invited her to be his comrade, so she prefers to remain independent. . . .

Men did not know themselves so long as women were without education and freedom; but now the little male tyrant is in daily dread of finding all his petty meanness held up to public contempt by a lady novelist. . . . How many callous men have shuddered at the thought of marriage after reading the works of modern female reformers? Men dread publicity because their deeds are evil, and our effort must be to keep the electric light turned on day and night; . . .

The time has now come when Man must submit to be judged by Woman. He may seem to have no conscience, but those who can see beneath the surface know that his conscience is becoming as tender as an inflamed eye, and is as sensitive to the Light. All that is needed is to compel him to look straight at the image of himself held up constantly before him by the clever female critic. . . .

ELIZABETH ROBINS (1862–1943)

I first discovered *Ancilla's Share* in a section of the Yale Sterling Library stacks, in a collection of antiquated, yellowing volumes on the subject of women. To my chagrin this feisty challenge to male domination was attributed to an anonymous author. I could only speculate as to the identity of the writer, assuming that it was an Englishwoman, probably fearful of some kind of reprisal were her radical views made public. How wide of the mark I was! For quite fortuitously I recently learned the authorship of *Ancilla's Share* and at the same time discovered an extraordinary woman. Elizabeth Robins was born in Louisville, Kentucky, in 1862, but spent a large part of her life in England. She was a woman of many parts, probably most renowned as an interpreter of Ibsen. On this score Leonard Woolf wrote of her: "She was a great actress, the first and, almost certainly, the best actress of Ibsen in English."[1] In *International Who's Who*[2] her first designation is as a novelist, for she did indeed publish no less than fourteen novels. In addition, she wrote two autobiographical books, a play, and two books on women's rights and edited a volume of letters that Henry James wrote to her. Her writings suggest close friendship not only with James but also with George Bernard Shaw and Leonard and Virginia Woolf. In crises she was from time to time called upon by the Women's Movement for speeches or lectures. Some of these were published in American journals of the period, such as *Collier's Weekly, Metropolitan Magazine,* and *Everybody's Magazine.*

The subject of *Ancilla's Share* is, as the title suggests, the ancillary role assigned to women. What is most remarkable about this book is that it addresses numerous issues which in the past few years have appeared to us as startlingly new and iconoclastic. The book could almost be a sex-consciousness-raising manual. With cogent illustrations the author pinpoints "sexist" patterns such as: women's acceptance of the masculinist view of themselves, women's unprotesting submission to male disparagement and insult; women's antagonism toward accomplished women; men's denial of women's contributions to civilization; the etymological evidence of society's contempt for women through the systematic debasement of female appellations; the exploitation of women as fund collectors for public charities, while excluding them from administration; designation of mental vigor in woman as "masculine"; parents' preference for a male child; the assumption that woman derives her worth from association with a successful man; and the insensitivity of men in confronting women with humiliating symbols of male power over women.

The foregoing does not exhaust the points made with candor and vehemence in this short extract from a large text. A modern reader feels somewhat like Sleeping Beauty, awakening after a fifty-year sleep to find the status quo in the position of women.

Ancilla's Share

Chapter VIII.   Origin and Effect of Sex Antagonism

. . . Women, like those men who labour under inherited disadvantage, have not for exactly the same reason found it possible to rise from the depths of traditional submission and protest against the conditions imposed on them. They have sought to persuade themselves the conditions were fair. . . .

The demand for freedom has never come from slaves. You must have tasted freedom in order to thirst for more. . . .

As woman has accustomed herself to accept the focussed intensity of man's preoccupation about her physical beauty—or that which could do beauty's work on man—so she has accustomed herself to accept his view of woman's moral character and intellectual attainments, and even her future possibilities in that direction.

Not, then, alone her physique and her occupation; her mind has been subdued to man's requirement of what a woman's mind should be. This should not strike us as strange.

There are still vast numbers of women (especially among the middle-aged and the old) in whom the power to take the woman's view has been done to death. Some in whom this power from time to time stirs uneasily are among those most determined to cudgel it

From [Elizabeth Robins], *Ancilla's Share*, 2d ed. (London: Hutchinson & Co., 1924).

to unconsciousness. Such minds are either so timid, or long so poignantly to soothe and reassure the men who stand nearest to them, that women of this temper will be found proclaiming, with a greater emphasis than the most primitive-minded man, that view of the feminine half of humanity which has been imposed by the masculine half.

Such women are much quoted by men. They may as cogently quote the Kaffir woman's pride in the fetters on her ankles, and the fact that the heavier her fetters the greater her sense of worth. . . .

Many a woman has learned so well the lesson of the past—the lesson that livelihood, security, ease, honour could come to her only through her sex-relationship to man—that she is unable to conceive herself making any effectual appeal on the score of being of real account except as being mother of a son, or a wife, or at least a widow.

By no one is this appeal made with such insistence as by the widow. To emphasize the dead man's sex-superiority over woman is her favourite way of burning incense to his memory.

Among the innumerable witnesses of this commonplace in current speech and record, the casual eye falls newly on a passage in the life of Jack London by his wife:

> I do not think any woman ever made him miss an engagement with a man. In short, passionate lover though he might be, he was no follower of petticoats to the extent of clouding his manly attitude towards his own sex.

Thus the man's sex-pride is adopted by the woman, with no consciousness of failure in loyalty to, or even recognition of, the sex-dignity of woman.

Jack London is entirely frank about his own attitude:

> . . . Along with a prestige that obtained from holding my own woman against all comers, I knew the handicap of being considered tied by apron-strings, and there were times when the Queen knew better than to show her head above the deck. . . .

The temptation to adopt man's assumption of his own sex-superiority appears to be irresistible to three types:

1st.—The woman who undervalues her own capacities, and therefore undervalues those of other women.

2nd.—The woman who knows she has capacity and shrinks from the discipline of using it—and therefore does not wish to see other, perhaps lesser, women proving publicly a power which the onlooking woman wishes to hide and deny.

3rd.—The woman who pursues with success some path not hitherto trodden by woman, and who likes to think of herself as exceptional. Exceptional not only in opportunity, *in herself.* Even if she remembers, and can estimate, the exceptional circumstances which enabled her to reach the particular place which she alone of women has yet attained, she will seldom feel sure that any average man similarly circumstanced could not have made as good use of the opportunity. She will be quite sure no other woman could.

The readiness of this type of woman to think meanly of her sex as a whole, is so reassuring to man, that he is known to forgive the exception to the rule on this express ground of her exceptionalness. . . .

. . . If in the past the woman, she who has both gifts and so-called education, is found to be nevertheless so consistently "Ancilla" still, why is it not reasonable to suppose that woman's essential quality and natural contribution is ancillary? Before there were schools there were poets and philosophers. They were all men, or are supposed so to have been.

We will take it they were all men. If, then, women are not essentially inferior to men in intellectual genius, why has the mind of her sex never yet flowered in terms of a Homer, a Shakespeare, a Leonardo, a Beethoven, an Edison?

Our spur-of-the-moment answer would be to present a stranger fact than the absence of feminine counterparts of these great names. The stranger fact is that faces such as those of Joan of Arc, Saint Teresa, Catherine of Siena, Sonia Kovalefsky, Mary Somerville, Caroline Herschell, Christina Rossetti, Jane Austen, the Brontës, George Eliot, Florence Nightingale, Susan Anthony and Mary Wolstonecroft, look out upon us from the shades.

But women, we find, are not primarily concerned about the

genius of the exceptional woman. Woman's primary and more active concern is for two factors which, if they are a part of environment, do indeed foster genius, and if lacking, do indeed leave an impoverished air in which genius dies. Our concern about these two factors is not on behalf of genius, but is rooted in our consciousness that these factors can be applied with advantage to the many among women, as with advantage they are applied to the many among men. The factors are training and opportunity. These in their relation to women will be examined presently. To the immediate question: What have women done with their untrained gifts?—the answer is: They have done in the main what love prompted. For the rest, what maimed opportunity offered.

They have poured their gifts into the hands of men.

Caroline Herschell ground lenses with hers, as well as helped her brother to discover stars. Harriet Beecher Stowe baked bread and nursed an ailing husband and delicate children with hers, as well as wrote a book whose circulation had, in her time, been outstripped by no other in English except the Bible. Of *Uncle Tom's Cabin*, by the way, it cannot in justice be said that men failed to recognise its merit. Lord Cockburn declared it "had done more for humanity than was ever before accomplished by any single book of fiction." Lord Palmerston said he had read it "three times not only for the story but for the statesmanship. . . ." Were not these praises high enough? So high, in sooth, they all but left the little household drudge behind. For she had a brother, brilliant beyond common. A writer, too, and a reformer. Beyond shadow of doubt he had written the astonishing book and generously allowed his sister the credit. But Henry Ward Beecher was himself not only richly endowed, but was a person of humour. He said in public, at least once, that for years people would insist on making him the author of *Uncle Tom's Cabin*. "So," said he, "I wrote *Norwood* and that settled it."

But suppose *Norwood* instead of being an indifferent performance had been a great book? Whatever Mr. Beecher might say, would there not have lingered in most minds the conviction that anything good in the sister's book was the work of the brother, and anything feeble or bad was all her own? . . .

Other brothers of useful sisters were probably as ready to correct the public misapprehension as was the brother of Mrs. Harriet Beecher Stowe. But the masculine recorder has seldom been interested in these corrections.

Any contravention of this habit wears for us an air of painstaking research. We are moved to pass on our own sentiment of grateful astonishment at Mr. Russell H. Conwell's testimony:

> When you say a woman doesn't invent anything, I ask, Who invented the Jacquard loom that wove every stitch you wear? Mrs. Jacquard. The printer's roller, the printing-press, were invented by farmers' wives. Who invented the cotton-gin of the South that enriched our country so amazingly? Mrs. General Greene invented the cotton-gin and showed the idea to Mr. Whitney, and he, like a man, seized it. Who was it that invented the sewing-machine? If I would go to school to-morrow and ask your children they would say, "Elias Howe."
>
> He was in the Civil War with me, and often in my tent, and I often heard him say that he worked fourteen years to get up that sewing-machine. But his wife made up her mind one day that they would starve to death if there wasn't something or other invented pretty soon, and so in two hours she invented the sewing-machine. Of course he took out the patent in his name. Men always do that. Who was it that invented the mower and the reaper? According to Mr. McCormick's confidential communication, so recently published, it was a West Virginia woman, who, after his father and he had failed altogether in making a reaper and gave it up, took a lot of shears and nailed them together on the edge of a board, with one shaft of each pair loose, and then wired them so that when she pulled the wire one way it closed them, and when she pulled the wire the other way, it opened them, and there she had the principle of the mowing-machine. If you look at a mowing-machine, you will see that it is nothing but a lot of shears. If a woman can invent a mowing-machine, if a woman can invent a Jacquard loom, if a woman can invent a cotton-gin, if a woman can invent a trolley-switch—as she did and made the trolleys possible; if a woman can invent, as Mr. Carnegie said, the great iron squeezers that laid the foundation of all the steel millions of the United States, "we" men can invent anything under the stars. I say that for the encouragement of the men.[1]

It may be that even for women a little encouragement accrues.

Enough to enable us when challenged: "Where is woman's inventiveness, her humour, her intellectual passion, her vision, her poetry?" to answer: Dorothy Wordsworth's is in her brother William's. Mary Lamb's is in her brother's. Henrietta Renan's is in her brother's. Mary Shelley's in her husband's. Louise Colet's in Madame Bovary. Is not this the history of woman's genius? . . .

It is the commonplace of current life and of biography that the greater spirits among women, like the lesser, have thus supplemented and enriched the minds of men, whether by direct illumination and inspiration, or by ministering to that material welfare by which, in the more intimate essentials (those of home life), no man has ever yet served the creative spirit of woman. Conceive a man so sensitively, generously understanding of the value of a woman's intellectual contribution, as to play the part in her life which woman has by custom played in the intellectual life of man.[2] . . .

While we recognise these things, we are not concerned to make out a case for the possible women-Socrates or Homer. It was not Miss Jane Harrison nor any classicist of her sex, who claimed the Odyssey as a woman's work. We did not hear of women being much beholden to Mr. Samuel Butler for his theory. The gentleman would prove too little. If he, or another, were to establish the given instance, it would but prove again what we already knew—that genius in a woman availed her little, unless, in one form or another, she made a present of it to a man.

To speak so is to forget that by custom what a man had was his own; what a woman had was her husband's. Therefore, was no question of gift from her to him.

This reflection excuses much and explains more, though what the word family has meant to women is yet to be explored. As this is not our task, we content ourselves with a hasty glance in the direction of that national authority which admits guardedly, that "family" comes from *familia*, which the Romans derived from a word signifying "the servile property, the thralls of a master," and also other domestic property as well as persons. If this was the status of girls and women who had acquired merit in the only way open to them, through the closest association with man by blood or marriage, what of the others?

While the unlearned must be wary of accepting scraps of uncorrelated fact for history, let women-philologists and women-historians interpret for us man's witness to woman's place in the scheme of things.

Let qualified women tell us whether these vestiges of the past, lodged fossil-like in the bed-rock of language, do not show an insistence upon women's inferiority deeper than the roots of her father-tongue; whether our inheritance reached us through operation of a law by which meanness or dishonour tends to be associated with the feminine term. Or how else it so often comes about that even where the word was framed deliberately to impute honour, it was presently degraded in the "shaping" mouth, hardly hers, since even the beast will not befoul itself.

Does the influence at work stand forth clear in the fact that the complementary form of the word—that which man allows to be applied to himself—most frequently retains its noble connotation? The new philologists must tell us why, if the courtesan was once a lady of the Court, as the gentleman was the courtier, he is still to be found at Court, while the courtesan has so long been relegated to another region?

If there is no word for shrew, or slut in male form, is it because there were no bad-tempered, no slovenly men? Or is it because only the male tongue might safely point out defects? If a female did so, was the scold's bridle and the ducking stool the proper repartee?

Where the feminine form of a word has not suffered gross degradation as "mistress" has, in contradistinction to "master," the feminine counterpart has been at least belittled. "Lord." What a word! Fit for the majesty of Heaven. "Lady." The governess is not quite a lady. Who would say: The tutor is not quite a lord.

So dwindled, so redolent of petty gentility and inhibitions is "lady," that though with a grand gesture we still say of a poet, "Lord of language!" to say "Lady of language" conjures an impression of the loose tongue blaspheming in a back alley.

For the greatest of her sex, in whatever art or high estate, is any term left but would belittle her, save that of woman? Then motherhood be praised for permitting that plain word to emerge with an inextinguishable dignity from the rubbish and the foulness men have heaped on her throughout the ages.

Not nouns only have had to suffer for her poor sake. The most innocuous-seeming adjective will execute a somersault in hasty obedience to the rule that, by alliance with man, it acquires merit, allied with woman it falls on ridicule, if not on shame. "I am a plain man," is said with the squared shoulder of one proud to walk without disguise. He would not take it kindly did you say: "A plain woman, his wife!"

"Harlot" we are told is of uncertain origin. It may come from "hirlawd"—a stripling, a male servant, a fellow. Chaucer uses it in this sense. "He was a gentle harlot and a kind."

> A sturdy harlot went them aye behind
> That was her hostes man.

Foxe uses it so, but by Shakespeare's time the word had fallen yet lower, so low it could refer only to women. "Whore" was originally a word applied to either sex. It is so used in the Bible: "Oh, Ephraim, thou committest whoredom. . . ."

Two types of women we might think man had been able to keep unsmirched by his sex-contempt. The women of his own family and the women of patience, strength, skill, who served his house for hire. As to these last, we shall be told the work of Ancilla is noble and beautiful, that we are mean-minded to read meanness into it.

Is it, indeed, women who do this? Is not literature studded with contempt of servants, and more especially of women servants?

As man's contempt for her is a part of etymology, so is it a part of his rhetoric. The handmaid's quality of being subordinate to, of not being essential, has crystallised in adjective form. Ancillary industries are still the inferior industries. The young girl who must work in what man insists is "her sphere"—the home—might count herself fortunate were her master content with imputation of inferiority. But he must not only associate humbleness and helplessness with the maid who serves. He does not expect her to have a moral sense. . . .

We may think ourselves safe from the British domestic problem when we take up a work dealing with the politics of the Far East.

> If Justice (says the author of *The Government of India*) gave eye or ear to the Executive she could be impartial no longer, but would become a serving maid. No one who entered a Court would be sure of finding uprightness there.

Ancilla, then, is the contemptible handmaid, by origin a slave, and hardly less a slave when she works for hire. Man in his dealings with her need as little pick his words as mind his manners.

That old immunity of his still presses hard not only upon Ancilla.

Man's age-long immunity from necessity to look at things from any woman's point of view left him, as we have seen, with but one sure perception about her. Not her likeness to himself, but her most obvious unlikeness. . . .

Her lack of frankness still plays a large part in life. Obstructive as it has become to the ultimate higher interests of man as well as to the ultimate higher interests of woman, her deceptive asquies-cence in man's report of her served for uncounted ages as her protective colouring. For however much more on an equality with man in physical strength was the primitive woman, there were times when physically, she, or something dearer to her than herself, was at the mercy of man. . . . For the infant's sake much, practically anything, would be endured by the mother. . . .

It were too much to expect of primitive man that he should not mistake the attitude which was one of instinctive self-subjugation of the woman to the child for an instinctive subjugation to the man. Nor could he foresee that her terribly intimate knowledge alike of his power and his weakness—knowledge acquired in its final poignancy by her "mothering"—would still be there when the child's need of it was ended.

Man's fierce need of the woman could be satisfied by fierceness or by wooing. No end visible to the primitive intelligence made it necessary for him to "learn" woman.

Thus in his uncorrected vision she was not only much obscured. She was, aside from her twofold use to him, non-existent.

It was so, that the old convention by which the pronoun "he" was supposed to include "her," turned out misleading in practice. "He" was found not to indicate inclusion but rather that exclusion which expressed the true inclination of the predominant partner.

The ground of the modern woman's protest has been precisely the fact that "he" meant in man's mind what the plain word said, and not what he assured her that it meant.

Chapter IX.   The Passing of Contempt

. . . It will be to many something in the nature of a discovery that the duration in social life of the chief enemy of woman, and of the world, lies in the hands of the "ordinary" women. . . .

The worser effect on both man and woman is found where woman's acceptance of insult, having grown mechanical, is eventually unconscious.

This is not only the worser but the more common effect. Her unconsciousnesss becomes the foster-mother of his unconsciousness. Thus it is that her share in the continuance of his unconsciousness has laid on those women who are conscious responsibility for the first step in the immediate task: which is to make more women "conscious."

That done, no woman, however weak, uneducated, lowly-placed, will bear the deeper insult, which is unconscious insult.

For though she will not for a while yet be able to prevent the ordinary man from cherishing contempt, she can begin at once the process of waking him from his long dream that she accepts contempt as her fair desert.

To nerve her for refusal, let her remember: everytime she insists that, if insult is to be, it shall at least be conscious, she has at the lowest estimate taken away one man's power to inflict the deeper wound.

Her opportunities will be fewer as she uses them. At present they are sown thick along the common way. . . .

For man's unconsciousness that he is still in the first, the contempt stage, of primitive sex antagonism is nowhere more complete than in those cases where he is appealing to so-called "educated" woman for her indispensable support. He comes to her unblushing for aid to maintain a social order, and in particular those masculine monopolies, which were established in contempt of her. He is not ashamed, not yet, to entreat women by their personal self-denial and by every conceivable form of organised effort to constitute themselves the financial backbone as well as the pack-horse of the vast system of public charities, many of which are necessitated largely by the exclusion of woman's view from public affairs.[3] She is asked to support by money, or menial service, institutions from whose administration she is expressly excluded. She is called on to do the nursing, cooking, washing and *subscribing* for the very hospitals which debar women from practising medicine there, or so much as studying.

Women who give their support under these conditions are strictly responsible for continuance of that contempt which offers insult while it asks favours—while it asks, indeed, the very means of continuance.

The case of woman and the newspaper Press is much the same. The most enterprising of the editors are aware that the measure of their financial success is the degree to which they can successfully appeal to that immense section of the reading public—women. Unenlightened, on the one hand, by the numbers of men in trains or waiting in public places, who will be found reading sensation, or looking at picture papers; unenlightened, on the other hand, by the recognised fact that a daily paper devoted to what are called "women's interests" could not live a week, your editor does not realise that, for the vast body of women subscribers what constitutes good journalism for men constitutes good journalism for women. In the very act of his appeal your editor sets forth his conviction that the ordinary news of the world is above the heads even of those women of the educated class to whom he addresses himself.

In the twilight of his contempt, he will invent his "special attractions for women." Only when he goes so far as to offer a woman's supplement at an extra cost is he able to gauge the degree to which his special attraction has failed to attract. Yet he clings with touching faith to that column which vast numbers of women know need not detain them. It is called "The Woman's View," and is easily recognised as man's view of woman's view. . . .

The enterprising editor will expend postage upon women with a lavish hand, he will incur heavy advertising charges, and daily will pass copy which is an offence against the very *clientèle* he has been at expensive pains to enlist. He is wholly unaware that what with his ignorance, both of woman and the uses of the blue pencil, the woman subscriber can hardly read an issue without stumbling upon insult.

She might think a sympathetic article of to-day dealing with Nelson as the "great lover" would be guiltless of such blemish. But your man writer is not content with calling any mental vigour or firmness of character in woman "masculine." When vile temper or hysteria appears in a man—Listen: "Arthur Wellesley was proud and manly, Horatio Nelson was vain, and, *tranchons le mot*—at least sometimes womanish, capable of hysterical vixenish rancour and fits of the nerves. When he suddenly burst out with his untimely 'mainsail haul' and threw the ship into irons, to the dumb bewilderment of the officers of the watch, and then flounced off the quarterdeck banging the cabin door behind him, he was making an exhibition of the everlasting feminine—tantrum."[4]

Any woman who thinks these manifestations are exceptional should, for a month, keep a notebook tally of general Press comment. In the reading-room of her club she would probably find, any week in the year, enough to instruct her. Even the blind may find enlightenment in ordinary social intercourse, since masculine unconsciousness permits a man to perform this office by way of being bright and agreeable. In almost any woman's memory countless instances out of the past rise up to keep company with the newest.

Only yesterday an ornament of one of the great professions, entertaining visitors before his wife "comes down," shows himself hospitable and gracious.

By way of reciprocity: "Your little girl," inquires the man visitor, "how is she?"

"Little *girl!* I'd like my wife to hear you call her boy a little girl!"

Hurried apologies from the man. The women visitors smile indulgently. . . .

So little does it bite on the woman's mind, this unconscious contempt has to be forced home upon the calloused victim.

What else but the numbing effect both on her and on him of the old pretence, that she shares man's optical illusion, could lead him to invite women of high place—women to whom he desires to show civility—to rejoice with him over evidences of his own domination and her subservience, even her degradation?

One such scene comes back. A chamber in a town hall. City fathers showing to a company of visiting aldermen and officials a collection of municipal plate.

After an outside function, the mayor has brought in a yet greater, a county dignitary, and has explicitly included the ladies of his party.

They find the Master of Ceremonies standing at the head of a long table spread with antique treasures. He is obligingly ready to explain the baldric, heavy with silver shields, the mace, the Saxon horn, Jacobean tankards, Charles snuff-boxes, loving-cups, punch-ladles, mayoral chains and badges of office descended through the centuries. He descants with a natural enthusiasm upon these relics of jovial sovereignty. He looks to the ladies for their admiration and their praise.

These, indeed, require no prompting, even if one feminine mind is lightly brushed by the thought: All these beautiful and treasured symbols—memorials of men; of their pleasure, honour, power. No smallest trace of woman.

Yes, one. A chain for the lady mayoress. This the women present duly admire, if with an enthusiasm somewhat perfunctory, and with no comment on its chief title to interest.

This lay, undoubtedly, in the circumstance that, among all those ancient symbols, the one purporting to lend honour to a woman was the only new object there. The honour is indeed one "lent." For should a woman be elected to the mayoral chair this is not the chain she will wear. The new chain is for the woman whose service to the city is that she is wife to the mayor. Newer than the chain, still too new in 1922 to be so much as a subject of facetiousness among the City fathers, was the idea of a woman occupying in her own right the mayoral seat.

A seat, however, was presently discovered to be among the treasures—a seat, moreover, specially reserved for woman.

An armchair. A little austere, but of some dignity in aspect, being ancient oak, fashioned solidly, and having for sole ornament an iron upright at the back ratcheted as though for some such purpose of comfort as adjusting the height of the seat, an adjustment promised further aid by dangling loops of leather.

It was the scold's chair, with the bridle agape, rigged and ready.

This relic was pointed out with pride to the county lady, wife of a high official of the King, and herself a person of greater gift and more renown than any man there save one.

The truly "great" lady smiles at the ancient "reserved seat" for her sex, and turns to greet the entrance of the City horn-blower, specially summoned, to do honour to the occasion by waking yet other echoes of old days.

To her shame, the unknown woman of the party did not, till the small hours of the morning, wake to the significance of that scene. A company of "elect" men occupied in celebrating the memory of their fathers, of their civic state, their snuffing and drinking, their free speech, their mighty blowing on the horn. Women invited to admire what had survived of woman's share in the most precious of all those things—free speech. Women of to-day standing before the symbol of man's determination to teach her silence—smiling in a room full of smiling men.

On reflection, woman's smiling will have less taint of the obsequious when the symbol of her coerced silence shall have an interest purely antiquarian.

The facetious alderman had offered to show the ladies how the crank and bridle worked. Without his help, a dozen hours after in the dark, one of the ladies "saw." The chair no longer empty. It was filled with the humiliation suffered there. The silence caught the accent of voices long stilled. It rang with the old courage that so perilously insisted on giving discontent a tongue. The phantom sat there, grotesque, half-throttled, dishevelled, wild, being wrenched and choked into submission. Then the release in a rabble of triumphant men and boys, not voiceless they, nor voiceless those of her own sex needing to win immunity from man's reprisals by joining in the hue and cry.

And so home—the celebrant of wrong, whether wrong real or wrong imagined. Back to a more wounding displeasure at her own fireside, an intenser obloquy, branded for ever now with that name which before it fell from its old high state the immortals among men had been proud to bear.

For "scold" was "skald" [poet] before it was woman.

What if your discontent, oh skald of the market-place, *was* blind, ignorant, perverse? Was man's none of these?

Did he give you any other vent for your sense of wrong? Did he try whether you, too, like him, could suffer from mere suppressed lung power? Did he ever once invite you to cleanse your bosom of perilous stuff by so much as blowing a blast on his blessed horn?

If your women-descendants are ready to excuse him for that particular omission, it is because they know that the rough schooling given left you little spirit for the toys of men—left you only with spirit here and there for protest in the teeth of penalty.

Perhaps not all in vain. The long-stilled voice is heard and understood by more to-day than ever before since speech was shaped.

It may be, oh woman who sat in the chair of humiliation, that because you dared cry out, and cry again and yet again your discontents—it may be that, counting over the cost to you, we shall reach a surer estimate of the reason why the woman witness is still so little heard in Councils and in Parliaments. Certain it is that, so long as there stands yet in the way any wrong so cankerous as reprisal for free speech, so long must the woman-skald of the future cry unwelcome truth in the market-place, or be ranked with those who walk there selling smiles and acquiescence.

NOTES

1. In [Russell H. Conwell], *Acres of Diamonds,* published by Messrs. Harper Bros.

2. An instance of this being done with gain to personal relationship and gain to the world, seems to be offered by the very noble example of M. Curie—an exception to the immemorial rule which deserves to be recorded with respect and gratitude. [Some might also cite Henry Lewes' support and encouragement of George Eliot as another "noble example."]

3. *The New Humanism,* by Laurence Housman.

4. *Times Literary Supplement,* Oct. 19th, 1922.

CONCLUSION

This collection of writings has attempted to bring to light a small portion of a larger body of our cultural inheritance concerned with women that has been obscured and overlooked. It must surely give us pause to discover that most of us, even highly educated persons, had not learned in the course of our education that equal rights for women had been espoused by Plato, Condorcet, Spencer, and Mill.

Read any book being published now with a title like *The Ascent of Man* or *The History of Civilization* and it will betray the underlying assumption that all that is valued was done by men.

The nineteenth century witnessed a veritable ferment of new and unconventional ideas about women, which continued through the early decades of our own century. During this period many scholars were intrigued by information flowing from varied fields suggesting the possibility that woman had not been predestined to be an underling, both mentally and physically inferior to man, Evidence from newly deciphered ancient writings, from recently unearthed archeological finds of neolithic periods, from studies of primitive peoples, from intelligence testing, from statistics of morbidity and mortality, and from studies of the sex life of plants and animals other than humans gave rise to speculation that woman's potential might well be comparable to man's and that in the far distant past she may have played a powerful, possibly dominant role.

The reader will have noted a thread that runs with melancholy monotony through the introductory comments to the selections —that is, that the writings here included, though brilliant, provocative, and innovative, have been dismissed or ignored. Can we be confident that the present women's movement will change this pattern? We may be congratulating ourselves too soon. My own complacence in this respect was recently shaken when I came across a little volume written in 1914, *Feminist Writers of the Seventeenth Century* by S. A. Richards. The author begins his preface with words very much like those I have used in the introduction to this book: "The emancipation of women and the agitation in favour of female suffrage, which are commonly regarded as the latest social developments, and as especially associated with this country, are not new, nor did they originate in England." He proceeds to reveal a serious movement in seventeenth-century France advocating equality of the sexes. Paralleling my own statements, he continues: ". . . we find in the feminist writers of the day views as advanced as any put forward at the present time."[1] How disconcerting! *Plus ça change, plus c'est la même chose.* In 1914 Richards must surely have been convinced that woman's cause was approaching fruition. Yet a period followed in which its aims were belittled and well-nigh forgotten. Will the swings of the pendulum continue, and will a writer some fifty years hence be making the same analogy between that period and the present day?

If the masculine academic mind, clinging tenaciously to traditional bias, continues to give limited attention to the concerns of women, perhaps a change can come only if women in large numbers enter all the fields of knowledge and pursue the truth themselves. It may be the task of women to unearth the literary treasures of the past in order to help shape a more accurate concept of woman in relation to the world. With the recent upsurge of interest in feminism we are suddenly seeing a proliferation of books bringing to light information about the accomplishments and the potential of women, information which for ages has been hidden, soft-pedaled, distorted, denied, or ignored. It is not surprising that there is such a rush into print; there is so much to be corrected.

The effect of my exposure to the writers in this book and to others like them has been to create for me a new image of woman, one no longer abject, no longer in a subordinate role, but rather a primary force in human advancement. Only those who have spent a lifetime plagued by that irrational feeling of automatic inferiority because of skin color or ethnic origin or sex know the burden that women are finally beginning to shed. Much of the feeling came from incessant indoctrination in all branches of learning of male primacy in every phase of human endeavor. The determination and vigilance of the present and coming generations of women, with the support of many sympathetic men, can insure that henceforth woman's role, past, present, and future, will receive its just due in the story of humanity.

NOTES

Introduction

1. Simone de Beauvoir, *The Second Sex* (1949; New York: Alfred A. Knopf, 1952).
2. Betty Friedan, *The Feminine Mystique* (New York: Dell, 1963).
3. John Stuart Mill, *On The Subjection of Women* (London: Oxford University Press, 1912).
4. Johann Jakob Bachofen, *Das Mutterrecht: Eine Untersuchung über die Gynaikokratie der alten Welt nach ihrer religiösen und rechtlichen Natur* (Stuttgart, 1861).
5. John Bartlett, *Familiar Quotations*, 13th ed. (Boston: Little, Brown and Company, 1955), p. 340, quoting from Boswell's *Life of Johnson*.
6. Friedrich Nietzsche, *Beyond Good and Evil*, trans. Helen Zimmern (New York: Boni. & Liveright), pp. 161–69.
7. Jean Jacques Rousseau, *Emile or Education*, trans. Barbara Foxley (New York: E. P. Dutton & Co.), pp. 349, 442, 443.
8. Arthur Schopenhauer, "Studies in Pessimism: Of Women," in *Essays of Arthur Schopenhauer*, trans. T. Bailey Saunders (New York: Willey Book Company), pp. 72–89.
9. Lewis Henry Morgan, *Ancient Society* (1877; Cambridge: Harvard University Press, 1965).
10. John F. MacLennan, *Primitive Marriage* (Edinburgh: Adam and Charles Black, 1865).
11. Edward Carpenter, *Love's Coming of Age* (1896; New York: Vanguard Press, 1927).
12. Robert Briffault, *The Mothers* (New York: Macmillan Co., 1927).
13. James G. Frazer, *The Golden Bough* (London: Macmillan & Co., 1890).
14. Havelock Ellis, *Man and Woman* (1894; Boston: Houghton Mifflin Co., 1929).
15. Robert Ardrey, *The Territorial Imperative* (New York: Atheneum, 1966).
16. Lionel Tiger, *Men in Groups* (New York: Random House, 1969).
17. George F. Gilder, *Sexual Suicide* (Quadrangle, 1973).
18. Steven Goldberg, *The Inevitability of Patriarchy* (New York: Morrow, 1973).
19. Carl N. Degler, "Woman as Force in History," *Daedalus*, Winter 1974, p. 67.
20. James Mellaart, *Çatal Hüyük* (New York: McGraw-Hill, 1967), p. 207.
21. Jacques Heurgon, *Daily Life of the Etruscans*, trans. James Kirkup (New York: Macmillan Co., 1964), pp. 94–95.

Eliza Burt Gamble: The Evolution of Woman

1. *The National Cyclopaedia of American Biography* (New York: James T. White & Company, 1922), vol. 18, pp. 220–21.
2. Eliza Burt Gamble, *The Evolution of Woman* (New York: G. P. Putnam's Sons, 1894), p. 171.

Lester Frank Ward: The Gynaecocentric Theory

1. John C. Burnham, "Lester Frank Ward in American Thought," *Annals of American Sociology* (Washington, D.C.: Public Affairs Press, 1956), p. 1.
2. Ibid.

3. Charlotte Perkins Gilman, *The Man-Made World* (New York: Charlton Co., 1911), p. 3.
4. Samuel Chugerman, *Lester F. Ward, The American Aristotle* (Durham, North Carolina: Duke University Press, 1939).

Johann Jakob Bachofen: Mother Right

1. Lionel Tiger, *Men in Groups* (New York: Random House, 1969).
2. James G. Frazer, "The Succession to the Kingdom in Ancient Latium," in *The Golden Bough* (New York: Macmillan Co., 1930), pp. 152–58.
3. Jane Ellen Harrison, *Prolegomena to the Study of Greek Religion* (Cambridge: At the University Press, 1932); also, *Epilegomena to the Study of Greek Religion and Themis* (New Hyde Park, New York, 1962).
4. Sir Arthur Evans, *The Palace of Minos at Knossos* (London: Macmillan & Co., 1921).
5. Michael Ventris and John Chadwick, *Documents in Mycenean Greek* (Cambridge: At the University Press, 1956).
6. James Mellaart, *Çatal Hüyük* (New York: McGraw-Hill, 1967), Chaps. VI, IX–XI.

Eliza Burt Gamble: The God-Idea of the Ancients

1. Robert Briffault, *The Mothers* (New York: Macmillan Co., 1927).
2. Erich Neumann, *The Great Mother*, trans. Ralph Manheim (Princeton, N.J.: Princeton University Press, 1955).
3. Raphael Patai, *The Hebrew Goddess* (Ktav Publishing House, 1967).

Mathilde and Mathias Vaerting: The Dominant Sex

1. Mathilde and Mathias Vaerting, *The Dominant Sex* (London: George Allen & Unwin, Ltd., 1923), p. 70.

Lydia Maria Child: Brief History of the Condition of Women

1. John G. Whittier, biographical introduction to *Letters of Lydia Maria Child* (Boston and New York: Houghton Mifflin Co., 1883).
2. Ibid.
3. Lydia Maria Child, *Brief History of the Condition of Women* (New York: C. S. Francis & Co., 1845), vol. 1, p. 117.
4. Ibid., vol. 1, p. 143.
5. Helene G. Baer, *The Heart is Like Heaven: The Life of Lydia Maria Child* (Philadelphia: University of Pennsylvania Press, 1964), p. 292.

Lady Sydney Morgan: Woman and Her Master

1. William John Fitzpatrick, J.P., *Lady Morgan: Her Career, Literary and Personal* (London: Charles J. Skeet, 1869), p. 266.
2. Ibid., p. 306.
3. Ibid., pp. 298–99.

Otis Tufton Mason: Woman's Share in Primitive Culture

1. Otis Tufton Mason, *Woman's Share in Primitive Culture* (New York: D. Appleton & Co., 1894), p. 240.

Plato: Dialogues

1. Webster's *New International Dictionary*, 2d ed. (Springfield: G. & C. Merriam Co., 1960), p. 2962.

Condorcet: The Political Rights of Women

1. J. Salwyn Schapiro, *Condorcet and the Rise of Liberalism* (New York: Harcourt, Brace & Co., 1934), p. 195.

Elizabeth Robins: Ancilla's Share

1. Foreword by Leonard Woolf to Elizabeth Robins, *Raymond and I* (New York: Macmillan Co., 1956).
2. *International Who's Who* (London: Europa Publications Ltd., 1935), p. 885.

Conclusion

1. S. A. Richards, *Feminist Writers of the Seventeenth Century* (London: David Nutt, 1914), p. viii.